Human–Computer Interaction Series

Editors-in-Chief

Desney Tan, Microsoft Research, USA
Jean Vanderdonckt, Université catholique de Louvain, Belgium

HCI is a multidisciplinary field focused on human aspects of the development of computer technology. As computer-based technology becomes increasingly pervasive—not just in developed countries, but worldwide—the need to take a human-centered approach in the design and development of this technology becomes ever more important. For roughly 30 years now, researchers and practitioners in computational and behavioral sciences have worked to identify theory and practice that influences the direction of these technologies, and this diverse work makes up the field of human-computer interaction. Broadly speaking it includes the study of what technology might be able to do for people and how people might interact with the technology. The HCI series publishes books that advance the science and technology of developing systems which are both effective and satisfying for people in a wide variety of contexts. Titles focus on theoretical perspectives (such as formal approaches drawn from a variety of behavioral sciences), practical approaches (such as the techniques for effectively integrating user needs in system development), and social issues (such as the determinants of utility, usability and acceptability).

Titles published within the Human–Computer Interaction Series are included in Thomson Reuters' Book Citation Index, The DBLP Computer Science Bibliography and The HCI Bibliography.

For further volumes:
http://www.springer.com/series/6033

Ahmed Seffah

Patterns of HCI Design and HCI Design of Patterns

Bridging HCI Design and Model-Driven Software Engineering

With Contributions by:
Peter Forbrig, Jean Vanderdonckt, Mohamed Taleb, Homa Javahery,
Daniel Sinnig, Daniel Engelberg, Christophe Kolski, Michel Labour,
Ashraf Gaffar and Thanh Diane Nguyen

 Springer

Ahmed Seffah
Department of Information Management
and Software Engineering
Lappeenranta University of Technology
Lappeenranta
Finland

ISSN 1571-5035
Human–Computer Interaction Series
ISBN 978-3-319-36402-5   ISBN 978-3-319-15687-3 (eBook)
DOI 10.1007/978-3-319-15687-3

Printed on acid-free paper

For Honey Mjaltë...

Executive Summary

The success of a whole interactive software system, a mobile service, a Web site, or any new emerging tangible or ambient system can be attributed to many software engineering (SE) technical quality concerns and human–computer interaction (HCI)/human factors working in harmony. Because this harmony between HCI and SE is hard to predict before a fully functional system is actually put to work, extensive design experience and collaboration are crucial. Interaction design patterns—also called user experience design patters, HCI or user interface (UI) design patterns, or usability engineering patterns have been proposed as a means to discover, encapsulate, and disseminate the best HCI design experiences, hence improving the chances of success of new systems.

Despite the obvious and acclaimed potential to support the use of patterns within the whole user experience-centric design process, and the rich variety of design pattern collections we have today, the reuse of HCI patterns among human factors, interaction designers, and software developers has not achieved the acceptance and widespread applicability foreseen by design pattern pioneers in SE. It has been recently found in the research community that patterns are greatly underused by mainstream user interface and human factors designers/engineers.

The architect Christopher Alexander introduced design patterns in early 1970. He defines a pattern as follows, "Each pattern is a three-part rule, which expresses a relation between a certain context, a problem, and a solution." He goes on to explain the nature of a pattern, "Each pattern describes a problem which occurs over and over again in our environment, and then describes the core of the solution to that problem, in such a way that you can use this solution a million times over." The concept of patterns became very popular in the software engineering community with the wide acceptance of the book *"Design Patterns: Elements of Reusable Object-Oriented Software."*

Since then, the software engineering community has generalized this concept by using it in different areas including software architecture, requirements, analysis, and more recently in software process reengineering and improvement. During the last decade, the HCI community has also adopted patterns as a user interface design tool. Researchers describe a user interface pattern as a possible good solution to a common design problem within a certain context, by describing the invariant qualities of all those solutions. Using patterns should be like asking your experienced colleague in the next room for advice.

The concept of usability patterns has been introduced and discussed in different workshops. In this tutorial, we define a pattern as a proven design solution or the best human–computer interface design (HCID) practice for a user problem that occurs in several contexts. The primary goal of an HCID pattern in general is to create an inventory of solutions to help user interface designers resolve UI development problems that are common, difficult, and frequently encountered.

The material of this book is organized around the following idea. There are not many specialists in user interface development, so most software user interfaces are designed and built by software engineers. These engineers need training in effective design and how to build usable and useful user interfaces, but the scarcity of user interface specialists is correlated with the lack of ready-to-use design tools for user interface developers unfamiliar with usability engineering. The content focuses on an iterative development lifecycle of practical cost-effective patterns for the analysis, design, implementation, and evaluation of user interfaces. There will be discussion of lecture material, motivating demonstrations, and reinforcing exercises. Widely available HCI patterns will be discussed also, with references to the best practices in usability engineering.

The book provides background and hands-on experience on patterns for the user interface world, explaining how to discover, describe, and apply patterns. It gives the necessary theory, but goes beyond explaining, providing hands-on experiences of the patterns-assisted design approach. The readers will be exposed to an innovative and comprehensive framework for:

- Gathering the best practices in user-centered design and compiling them in the format of patterns
- Transferring the knowledge of human factors experts to software engineers unfamiliar with usability principles by means of software tools
- Facilitating the human-to-human communication between usability experts and software engineers
- Using XML-compliant descriptions as a high-level notation for describing, documenting, and disseminating patterns
- Translating XML descriptions of a pattern into reusable software components such as Java beans
- Creating a sound set of principles and techniques for both software and usability engineering. The pattern-based framework that we suggest is an example
- Guiding the evolution of software and usability engineering to assist with their convergence and cross-pollination

Via different industry case studies and research investigations presented by different academic researchers and industry practitioners, this book explores two different avenues to enhance the discovery, dissemination, and effective application of HCI design patterns, pattern languages, and the associated pattern-oriented design toolbox.

On the pattern user's side (the patterns of HCI design), the book investigates the applicability of various HCI patterns and pattern languages in enhancing user interface usability and supporting the user-centric design approach. We provide several examples that demonstrate how patterns can support, among others, the integration of HCI design practices and tools into HCI design artifacts (prototypes, task models, etc.). We look also at current software engineering methods (model driven, agile, and service oriented) and the commonly used HCI modeling and engineering techniques. We suggest several major improvements in terms of usable systems through informed application of HCI design patterns within these HCI modeling techniques and software engineering methods.

On the HCI pattern authors' side (the HCI design of patterns), the book discusses the current pattern lifecycle and the format of documenting and representing HCI patterns. The book proposes a new integrative schema to document patterns and to facilitate their discovery and dissemination. The authors show how this format can be embedded in supporting software tools as well as how it can be grounded in HCI design theories. A research roadmap is also drawn by collecting and gluing together interrelated patterns and HCI models within a comprehensive and structured step-by-step pattern-oriented design approach. We finally explore games as a way of facilitating the sharing of patterns between HCI design pattern users and authors.

Audience

This book is best viewed as an intermediate level reading because it assumes some general knowledge in software engineering and a basic expertise in human–computer interaction design. There are no other prerequisites, other than an interest in the topic of user interface design and usability using patterns.

For industry practitioners, the book provides pointers to HCI pattern languages for user interface design, most of which are freely available on the Web. The book covers how to use these catalogs of patterns for the design and evaluation of a large variety of user interfaces including traditional graphical user interfaces (GUIs), Web applications, personal digital assistants (PDAs), and mobiles. Also covered are the uses of the tools and notations that can support the development and dissemination of HCI patterns within the model-driven engineering approaches.

For academic researchers and graduate students, the book investigates the relevant pattern-assisted design theory and methodologies while exploring avenues for integrating HCI design patterns into the software development lifecycle and practices. The book exposes the HCI design fundamentals of patterns, and the practices of discovery, description, and delivery of patterns through hands-on experiences and real world examples. The book demonstrates how we can apply the ideas of HCI design to the design of HCI design patterns themselves.

Book Structure and Contributions

The book consists of 12 chapters. Except Chaps. 5, 7, and 12, all the other chapters are the results of 10 years of research conducted by Ph.D. and Master's students under the supervision of Dr. Seffah at Concordia University, Montreal Canada.

In Chap. 1, the concept of software design pattern and HCI design pattern are investigated from the HCI and software engineering perspectives, contrasting two opposite visions.

In Chap. 2, mainly based on the Ph.D. dissertation of Homa Javahery and Mohamed Taleb, HCI patterns as a design tool are first reviewed from an historical perspective. Then, the different design approaches based on HCI patterns are surveyed, ranging from HCI pattern languages to pattern-oriented design.

Within the view to fostering reuse in the instantiation and transformation of user interface models, Chaps. 3, 4, and 5 investigate how patterns can supplement the model-driven user interface engineering approaches.

In Chap. 3, HCI patterns are viewed as building blocks. They can be first used to construct different models. Then, these models are transformed into concrete user interface artifacts. In particular, the chapter describes how different kinds of HCI design patterns can be used for building task, dialog, presentation, and layout models as well as concrete user interface artifacts.

In Chap. 4, we first highlight the fact that traditional interactive system architectures did not provide sufficient support to usability aspects. HCI design patterns are proposed as a tool to model the relationships between internal software attributes and externally visible usability measures. We demonstrate how enhanced HCI patterns with usability measures can lead to a development approach for improving interactive system architectures, and how these patterns can support the integration of usability in the software development process. This chapter includes contributions from Daniel Engelberg and Ashraf Gaffar.

Authored by Peter Forbrig and some of his students, Chap. 5 supplements the two previous ones. It proposes a tool for combining pattern-driven and task-based development. Additionally, the role of task models for smart environments is discussed. Specific task patterns for task-driven development in this domain are described. The chapter builds on a long collaboration between Prof. Seffah and Prof. Forbrig in which several graduate students from Concordia and Rostock Universities have been involved.

More and more HCI designers are asked to reengineer user interfaces for accommodating a diversity of users while taking into account variations in geographical regions, population, languages, and cultures. Chapter 6 demonstrates how patterns can drive the whole reengineering design process when dealing with the constraints of each computing platform. To illustrate this idea, several examples are described including how to adapt a Web navigation system to different sizes and models of abstract information structure (architecture) and to different contexts of use. Without the help of Daniel Engelberg and Homa Javahery, this chapter would not look the same. This chapter paved the road for the next one.

Chapter 7, authored by Thanh Diane Nguyen, Jean Vanderdonckt, and Ahmed Seffah, highlighted the fact that a good documentation of patterns is not sufficient for the effective use of patterns in cross-platform user interface design. Supplementing pattern description with an implementation is required. The chapter introduces the concept generative pattern which defines the rules for implementing a UI design considered as a generic solution to a problem at different levels of abstraction (in the way that a UI could be modeled). Generative patterns also describe how to transform these expressions into programmable code for diverse computing platforms, while being compliant with the style guide rules that may prevail for these platforms.

Chapter 8 is mainly based on the Ph.D. work of Mohamed Taleb under the supervision of Ahmed Seffah and Alain Abran from ETS Montreal, Canada. The chapter details an integrative pattern-oriented and model-driven architecture (POMA). It integrates in a single framework all the previous research work presented in Chaps. 2–7. Chapter 9 illustrates how POMA can be used in the context of Web information systems.

The remaining chapters, Chaps. 10–12, address the design concerns of HCI patterns themselves, or what we called the HCI design of patterns. Day-to-day field observations show that pattern users—the developers and novice designers using patterns to develop software products—may spend a huge amount of time just to find the right pattern for their use from the very large and heterogeneous collection of patterns that are available via different websites and databases. One key reason for this problem is the way patterns are documented.

Chapter 10 discusses pattern documentation concerns from the perspective of pattern authors and pattern users. It suggests a generalized format of pattern representation, originally proposed by Ashraf Gaffar and Anwar Faraz in their thesis. The chapter shows how this format can be embedded in a database-based environment for facilitating pattern dissemination as well as for supporting the pattern-oriented design approach presented in other chapters. The underlying pattern lifecycle is also discussed.

Chapter 11 introduces an innovative tool, PatternCity, a serious game in which HCI design patterns are represented as buildings in a virtual city, and where the players—designers and developers—can collaboratively build and improve these buildings. In doing so, designers and developers are engaged in the capture and dissemination of patterns while having fun as game players. The game acts as a communication platform between designers and developers in the stages of the patterns capture and dissemination lifecycle.

Michel Labour, Christophe Kolski, and Ahmed Seffah proposed a pedagogical pattern in Chap. 12 that aims to facilitate the learning and the effective use of HCI design practices captured as HCI design patterns. The proposed pedagogic pattern model is based on learning theories from pedagogy and the original work of Christopher Alexander, the father of design patterns.

Contents

Chapter 1
The Patterns of HCI Design: Origin, Perceptions, and Misconceptions

Abstract This chapter introduces the concept of human–computer interaction (HCI) design pattern—also called UI design pattern, interaction design patterns, HCI patterns, user experience pattern and usability engineering pattern. In this book, we mainly use the term *HCI Design pattern*, but we also use all these terms interchangeably to refer to HCI design pattern. HCI design patterns—have been introduced as a medium to capture and represent users' experiences as well as to disseminate it as design knowledge. Patterns have the potential of transferring the design expertise of HCI designers to software engineers, who are usually unfamiliar with UI design and usability principles. What is the difference between design patterns and HCI design patterns? Why are they important among HCI designers and SE practitioners? Why design patterns have been considered as a HCI design tool? Why and how HCI design patterns can make a difference? This chapter provides a first answer to these questions that are the key objectives of this book.

1.1 Original Ideas About Design Pattern

Among the early attempts to capture and use design knowledge in the format of design patterns, the first major milestone is often attributed to the architect *Christopher Alexander,* in the late 1970s. In his two books, *A Pattern Language* (Alexander 1977) and *A Timeless Way of Building* (Alexander 1979), Alexander, the father of patterns, discusses the avenues to capture and use design knowledge, and presents a large collection of pattern examples to help architects and engineers with the design of buildings, towns, and other urban entities. To illustrate the concept of pattern, Alexander proposes an architectural pattern called *Wings of Light* (Alexander 1977), where the problem is:

> Modern buildings are often shaped with no concern for natural light—they depend almost entirely on artificial light. But, buildings which displace natural light as the major source of illumination are not fit places to spend the day.

Amongst other information such as design rationale, examples, and links to related patterns, the solution statement to this problem is:

© Springer International Publishing Switzerland 2015
A. Seffah, *Patterns of HCI Design and HCI Design of Patterns,*
Human-Computer Interaction Series, DOI 10.1007/978-3-319-15687-3_1

Arrange each building so that it breaks down into wings which correspond, approximately, to the most important natural social groups within the building. Make each wing long and as narrow as you can—never more than 25 ft wide.

According to Alexander, every pattern has three essential elements illustrated in Fig. 1.1, which are: a context, a problem, and a solution. The context describes a recurring set of situations in which the pattern can be applied. The problem refers to a set of forces, i.e., goals and constraints, which occur in the context. Generally, the problem describes when to apply the pattern. The solution refers to a design form or a design rule that can be applied to resolve the forces. It also describes the elements that constitute a pattern, relationships among these elements, as well as responsibilities and collaboration.

All of Alexander's patterns address recurrent problems that designers face by providing a possible solution within a specific context. They follow a similar structure, and the presented information is organized into pattern attributes, such as *Problem* and *Design Rationale*. Most noteworthy, the presented solution statement is abstract enough to capture only the invariant properties of good design. The specific pattern implementation is dependent on the design details and the designer's creativity (Dix et al. 2003). In the example above, there is no mention of specific details such as the corresponding positions of wings to one another, or even the number of wings. These implementation details are left to the designer, allowing different instances of the same pattern solution.

In addition, Alexander (1977) recognized that the design and construction of buildings required all stakeholders to make use of a common language for facilitating the implementation of the project from its very beginnings to its completion. If organized properly, patterns could achieve this for all the participants of a design project, acting as a communication tool for design.

The pattern concept was not well known until 1987 when patterns appeared again at Object-Oriented Programming, Systems, Languages & Applications (OOPSLA), the object orientation conference in Orlando. There Kent Beck and Ward Cunningham (1987) introduced pattern languages for object-oriented program construction in a seminal paper. Since then many papers and presentations have appeared, authored by renowned software design practitioners such as Grady Booch, Richard Helm, Erich Gamma, and Kent Beck. In 1993, the formation of Hildside Group (1993) by Beck, Cunningham, Coplien, Booch, Johnson and others was the first step forward to forming a design patterns community in the field of software engineering.

Fig. 1.1 Elements of design pattern

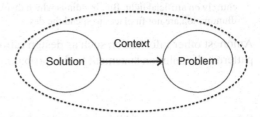

In 1995, Erich Gamma, Richard Helm, Ralph Johnson, and John Vlissides (the Gang-of-Four, GoF) published *"Design Patterns: Elements of Reusable Object-Oriented Software* (Gamma et al. 1995). Gamma et al. (1995) documented 23 design patterns in their book, one example being the "Observer Pattern". Like all other patterns, the observer pattern is described in a specific format, with consistent attributes. A short description of this pattern is given in Table 2.1. For comparative purposes, Table 1.1 also illustrates an organizational pattern called *Review the Architecture*, by (Coplien and Schmidt 1995). Organizational patterns are also documented in a specific format, with consistent attributes. Although these attributes may differ from those used to describe software design patterns, the principle is similar. Indeed, Van Duyne et al. (2006) use the term <Background> to refer to the context and Coplien and Schmidt (1995) prefer to use the <Context>.

Alexander argues that traditional architectural design practices fail to create products that meet the real needs of the user, and are ultimately inadequate in improving the human condition. His patterns were introduced in a hierarchical collection with the purpose of making buildings and urban entities more usable and pleasing for their inhabitants. Interestingly enough, this very same idea can be extrapolated to human–computer interaction (HCI) design, where the primary goal is to make interactive systems that are usable and pleasing to users. This will be discussed further in the next section.

Table 1.1 Examples of design and organizational patterns

Design Pattern (Gamma et al. 1995)	Organizational Pattern (Coplien and Schmidt 1995)
Name: Observer	*Name*: Review The architecture
Intent: Define a one-to-many dependency between objects. When one object changes state, all its dependents are notified	*Problem*: Blind spots occur in the architecture and design
	Context: A software artifact whose quality is to be assessed for improvement
	Forces: (1) A shared architectural vision is important, (2) Even low-level design and implementation decisions matter, (3) Individual architects and designers can develop tunnel vision
Applicability: (1) A change to one object requires changing other unknown objects, (2) Object should be able to notify other objects, but you don't want them to be tightly coupled	*Solution*: All architects should review all architectural decisions. Architects should review each other's code. The reviews should be frequent and informal early in the project
Participants: Classes are subject, observer, concrete_subject, and concrete_observer	*Resulting Context*: The intent of this pattern is to increase coupling between those with a stake in the architecture and implementation, which solves the stated problem indirectly
Consequences: (1) Abstract for broadcast communication, (2) Support for broadcast communication, (3) Unexpected updates	*Related Patterns*: Mercenary analyst, Code ownership
Related Patterns: Mediator, Singleton	

1.2 HCI Design Patterns—A Working Definition

In the last few years, the HCI community has tried to address the quality of HCI design by promoting patterns. An HCI pattern, also called a User Interface (UI) patterns, have been defined as a proven solution for a common user problem that occurs in a specific context of work. Many HCI experts devoted themselves to the development of HCI pattern languages, encapsulating their knowledge in a reusable format for designers. Among the heterogeneous collections of patterns, "Common Ground" (Tidwell 1997); "Amsterdam" (Welie 1999) and "Experience" (Coram and Lee 1998) play a major role in this field and wield significant influence It has often been reported that all HCI patterns and pattern languages are useful design tool (Erickson 2000; Granlund et al. 2000; Sinnig 2004)

One important remark that needs to be made at the forefront of this book is that HCI design patterns are a great source of interest, not necessarily because they provide novel ideas to the software engineering community, but because of the way that they package already-available design knowledge. This way of presenting information to software designers and developers allows the reuse of best practices, and avoids reinventing the wheel each time. In addition, HCI patterns are a great way of incorporating usability of best practices into software development. In light of this, pattern use has not just gained popularity amongst software engineers, but is of great interest to usability engineers and specialists who are concerned with the construction of usable systems.

HCI design pattern has different definitions sometimes contradictory. From the most generic to more HCI domain dependant, a pattern is:

- A form, template, or model or, more abstractly, a set of rules which can be used to make or to generate things or parts of a thing;
- A general repeatable solution to a commonly occurring problem;
- "A three-part rule that expresses a relation between a certain context, a problem, and a solution" (Alexander 1979);
- "An invariant solution to address a recurrent design problem within a specific context" (Dix 1998);
- A general repeatable solution to a commonly-occurring usability problem in interface design or interaction design;
- A solution to a usability problem that occurs in different contexts of use;
- "A successful HCI design solution among HCI professionals that provides best practices for HCI design to anyone involved in the design, development, evaluation, or use of interactive systems" (Borchers 2001).

In essence, patterns give an invariant solution to a problem and are abstract enough to draw on the common elements that hold between all instances of the resulting solution. What is notable about design patterns is that they are both concrete and abstract at the same time. They are concrete enough to provide sound solutions to design problems, which can be put immediately into practice. On the other hand, they are abstract enough to be applied to different situations.

HCI focuses on the design of *usable* systems, and HCI patterns are one of a handful of design tools that provide a means to abstract and reuse the essential details of successful and usable design solutions. Prior to discussing patterns in detail, it is important to review guidelines and claims, two other tools that have influenced and promoted the reuse of design knowledge in HCI.

Within the scope of this book, we define an HCI design pattern as:

A proven HCI design solution among interaction/usability/user experience professionals that provides best practices for HCI design to anyone involved in the design, engineering, evaluation, or usage of interactive system, generally characterized by its user interface.

Beyond this working definition, HCI design patterns should have the following properties:

- Are problem-oriented, yet not toolkit-specific meaning they are specific to a computing platform
- Are more concrete and easier to use for novice designers, context-oriented, and promote reusability
- Are a relatively intuitive means to document design knowledge and best practices;
- Are straightforward and readable for designers, developers and other stakeholders, and can therefore be used for communication purposes;
- Come from experiments on good know-how and were not created artificially;
- Represent design knowledge from different views, including social and organizational aspects, conceptual and detailed design;
- Capture essential principles of good design by telling the designer what to do and why, but are generic enough to allow for different implementations.

1.3 Examples of Patterns in HCI

These properties are an especially discriminating characteristic of patterns, meaning a pattern is a good one if and only if it respects these properties. They allow patterns to give rise to different implementations of the same design solution for different work environments, projects, computing platforms, and type of interactive systems. In other words, patterns are an opportunity to bring together a UI design solution and a software implementation solution in the same place.

For example, different implementations are necessary to support variations in design look and feel, platform preference and usage context. Figure 1.2 illustrates how the *Quick Access* pattern, used to logically group the most frequently used pages on a website, can be implemented on three different platforms. For a web browser on a desktop, the Quick Access pattern is implemented as an *Index Browsing Toolbar*; for a PDA, as a *Combo Box*; and for a mobile phone, as a *Selection* (Javahery and Seffah 2002).

Another example is *Overview and Detail* (Table 1.2), a pattern for visualization environments. This pattern can be implemented differently by the designer,

Fig. 1.2 *Quick Access* pattern

Table 1.2 HCI Pattern for visualization environments

Title	Overview and detail
Context	The dataset is large, too large for all the details to fit in a single view, and there is a need to view details about subsets of data items. The data can be viewed at one or more levels of abstraction e.g. directories and files within a directory, aggregated document content and detailed document content, etc. Alternatively the dataset may be large and continuous but only a subset can be viewed at any one time, e.g., Map data
Problem	How to display the entire contents of a large dataset at once, allow users to explore the dataset, and at the same time show details about subsets of items
Solution	Show an overview of the entire dataset together with some visual indication as to which part of the dataset is currently being viewed. Show details about subsets of items in a separate view The overview can be a scaled version of the main view, i.e., a spatial zoom, or some other representation, i.e., a semantic zoom. Since the overview tends to display a higher number of data items than any more detailed view it is necessary to use simple glyphs that minimize clutter, maximize use of screen space and portrait the data attributes most relevant to the task
Examples	Windows explorer Google maps
Other attributes	Forces, related patterns, design rationale

depending on variations in data and usage context. To illustrate, *Windows Explorer* and *Google Maps* demonstrate two different implementations. In Windows Explorer, the user is provided with two views—one which presents a hierarchical overview of folders, and the other, the contents of the selected folder. In Google Maps, the

Fig. 1.3 Pattern's ingredients

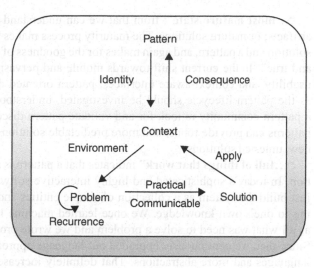

user is also provided with two views of the data—an orienting view of the selected area presented as a corner map, and a detailed view of the same geographic location.

Two cardinal properties of patterns have made their use increasingly valuable for designers. First, patterns include user-centered values within their rationale. Second, the concept of patterns and their associated pattern languages are generative, and can therefore support the development of complete designs. The remainder of this chapter will look at how these two properties have allowed patterns to evolve from a simple compilation of "best practices" to a powerful tool for designers, to be used as building blocks in a user-centered design process.

Some important defining characteristics and basic terminologies that are relevant to patterns include: **identification** of the problem in context and with imposed constraints, **existence** of the solution, **recurrence** of the problem, **invariance** abstraction of aspects of the solution, **practicality** of the solution, which needs to strike a balance between **optimality** and **objectivity**, and **communicability** of the problem and the process of arriving at the solution to the user. The relationship between some of these characteristics is illustrated in Figs. 1.2 and 1.3.

1.4   Pattern Benefits

Out of huge literature about pattern benefits, we will briefly explore one as cited by Grady Booch:

> *...at its most mature state, a pattern is full of things that work, absent of things that don't work, and revealing of the wisdom and rationale of its designers.*

Being carefully stated to summarize several aspects of patterns, this statement is acceptable on its own merits. The statement focuses on the benefits that stem from the basic nature of pattern concept. We briefly provide some insight into this statement.

"**...most mature state**": from that we can understand that patterns are mature artifacts; or mature solutions. The maturity process makes the difference between a solution and a pattern, and again makes for the goodness of patterns as "tried, tested, and true". In the current shift towards mobile and pervasive computing, universal usability, and context-aware interfaces, pattern oriented design processes as well as the pattern lifecycle should be investigated, understood, and promoted within a pattern community to look for and validate pattern discovery and reuse. Mature patterns can provide robust and more predictable solutions in new paradigms than new, untested solutions.

"**...full of things that work**" indicates that a pattern is more than a simple solution. In today's sophisticated and highly interactive software, it is not effective to just build the system as a collection of simple entities and assemble them according to one's own knowledge. We once learned machine language instruction sets as all what was need to solve a problem and we wrote programs that worked well. Since then we continuously upgraded our language approach towards higher level languages and more abstractions. That definitely increased our ability to address and solve more complex problems with relatively less effort. As the complexity increased, we tended to reuse existing composite structures instead of building new ones every time, and we are constantly looking for better aggregation and abstraction techniques, both in languages as well as in running software. Patterns enhance this trend—in a context sensitive paradigm—as a collection of usable solutions that happen to appear repeatedly together in successful applications. Being known—or proven—to work better than other combinations, we need to discover and collect them, understand why they work well as a group, and in which context, then put them in a suitable format that insures their effective reuse with a complete understanding description.

"**Absent of things that don't work**" reveals another advantage of patterns, namely the reduction of failure by warning us of concealed traps. It is human nature that we prefer to focus on things that we have seen before, and ignore things that are unfamiliar to us. In other words, the ability to analytically observe things is biased towards their familiarity to the observer, and not towards their actual importance. Consequently, we could underestimate things that are important just because we don't understand them or because we never saw them before or, even worse, because they are accompanied by other things that are more familiar to us. That might explain why experts do better jobs in recognizing more important things faster.

In the huge stream of knowledge that is passing by software designers, they tend to only catch those things that they know, and anchor them to their memory, and to their design. This can have a negative effect as designers may see the system from a programmer's point of view or point of understanding and not from the users. That said, an interface designer might be tempted to think that a certain combination of objects will definitely work in the envisioned interface, and indeed they will work, only not for the end user's satisfaction, but rather for the designer's.

Realizing this fact has promoted the rise of usability patterns, user centered design, and quality-in-use concepts. While it is hard to explain why certain things that had great design were less successful than anticipated, they help guide interaction designers into seeing things from the user's perspective and hence avoid things that "don't work".

"...revealing the wisdom and rationale of its designers" indicates an important facet of patterns. Many of us have had the opportunity to work with mentors that left great impression on us about their professional "wisdom". We then learned how to follow the same approach or a similar one in other situations. While often implicit and hard to quantify, we use our intelligence and reasoning to acquire, adapt, and reuse this wisdom to new situations, or contexts. Besides giving a solution to a problem, patterns often provide other information that reveals the wisdom of the designer or of the solution. The other end of the spectrum would be the famous expression of "reinventing the wheel".

1.5   Misconceptions About Design Patterns

One possible reason that justifies why these benefits have not yet been reached is due to the common misconceptions about patterns in the software engineering community. These misconceptions have been promoted by HCI practitioners (Beck et al. 1996).

These misconceptions can be summarized as follows:

- Patterns are only object-oriented
- Patterns provide only one solution
- Patterns are implementations
- Every solution is a pattern

Although most of the patterns are object-oriented, patterns can also be found in a variety of software systems, independent of the methods used in developing those systems (Beck et al. 1996). Patterns are widely applicable to every software system, since they describe software abstractions (Beck et al. 1996).

Patterns Provide More Than One Solution Patterns describe solutions to the recurring problems, but do not provide an exact solution, rather they capture more than one solution. This implies that a pattern is not an implementation, although it may provide hints about potential implementation issues. The pattern only describes when, why, and how one could create an implementation.

Every Solution Is Not Necessary a Pattern Not every solution, algorithm, or heuristic can be viewed as a pattern. In order to be considered as a pattern, the solution must be verified as a recurring solution to a recurring problem. The verification of the recurring phenomenon is usually done by identifying the solution and the problem (the solution solves the problem) in at least three different existing systems. This method of verification is often referred to as the *rule of three*.

The following example of (Alexander 1979) illustrates this misconception:

Window place: Consider one simple problem that can appear in the architecture. Let us assume that a person wants be comfortable in a room, implying that the person needs to sit down to really feel comfortable. Additionally, the sunlight is an issue, since the person is most likely to prefer sitting near the light. Thus, the forces of pattern in this example are:

(i)   The desire to sit down, and
(ii) The desire to be near light. The *solution* to this *problem* could be that in every room the architect should make one window into a *window place*.

Not every pattern can be considered to be a good pattern. There is a set of criteria that a pattern must fulfill in order to be a good one. A pattern encapsulating these criteria is considered to be a good pattern (Gamma et al. 1995; Alexander 1977; Coplien and Zhao 2001):

- A solution (but not obvious);
- A proven concept;
- Relationships;
- Human component.

Thus, Gamma et al. (1995), Alexander (1977), and Coplien (2001) claim, according to the criteria quoted above, that a good pattern should solve a problem, i.e., patterns should capture solutions, not just abstract principles or strategies. A good pattern should be a proven concept, i.e., patterns should capture solutions with a track record, not theories or speculation. A good pattern should not provide an obvious solution, i.e., many problem-solving techniques (such as software design paradigms or methods) try to derive solutions from first principles. The best patterns generate a solution to a problem indirectly, which is a necessary approach for the most difficult problems of design. A good pattern also describes a relationship, i.e., it does not just describe modules, but describes deeper system structures and mechanisms. Additionally, a good pattern should contain a significant human component (minimize human intervention). All software serves human comfort or quality of life; the best patterns explicitly appeal to aesthetic and utility.

1.6   Why and How Design Patterns Can Make a Difference?

As already mentioned, a wide set of HCI patterns have been suggested. For example, Van Duyne's *The Design of Sites* (Van Duyne et al. 2003), Welie's *Interaction Design Patterns* (Welie 1999), and Tidwell's *UI Patterns and Techniques* (Tidwell 1997) play an important role. In addition, specific languages such as Laakso's *User Interface Design Patterns and the UPADE Web Language* (Engelberg and Seffah 2002; Laakso 2003) have been proposed as well. Different pattern collections have been published including patterns for Web page layout design (Tidwell 1997; Coram and Lee 1998) for navigation in large information architectures, as well as for visualizing and presenting information.

Similar to the Software Engineering, the HCI design community has also created online forums for sharing and discussing this large diversity of patterns among professionals. These forums provide a common ground for anyone involved in the design, development, and the usability testing of highly interactive systems including Web sites and mobile applications. As it will be demonstrated in this book, these HCI pattern catalogs make a difference. Furthermore, the Pattern-Oriented Design (POD) proposed in this book in various chapters takes HCI patterns to the next level of the effective and efficient use of HCI patterns.

Whether you are a software architect, HCI designer, developer, or manager, (Yacoub and Ammar 2003) claim that pattern-oriented design and analysis will help you build better software systems faster. POD is a methodology of gluing patterns together and deriving a design seen as a combination of HCI patterns. It is based on various models that detail the structure, behavior, and implementation of HCI design patterns. Examples of models include model as business, task, dialog, presentation, and layout models. All these types of models are necessary for the success of the development of any application with HCI patterns.

Up to this point, the only positive feedback is from interaction designers presented with the POD approach. People appreciate the strength of the format, and believe it would really support them in their work (Granlund et al. 2001). However, POD approach has started building a language of patterns, and many questions remain unsolved.

Originally, the POD approach offered conceptual design patterns, but as these turned out to be too abstract to be useful, and turned to the more practical subtask patterns. However, POD approach is striving to capture the more complex aspects of modeling. POD is also concerned with the robustness of the chain of patterns that are offered. What happens if some but not all forces of patterns apply? Can the link to the next level of patterns be trusted? Having a "template" component for which pointers are always valid. But at the same time, such approach and related patterns will become too unwieldy. The goal is that the user of the patterns should never be concerned with the construction of the patterns just to choose and to compose them to get a structured representation of patterns for his application—they must be easy and intuitive.

But above all, the POD architecture and the patterns need to be adapted through practical usage. Today, the patterns do not fully supply a lingua franca, but are more or less targeting interaction designers. The descriptions, structure, and level of detail must be adapted to fit actual design projects. This can only be done through iteration based, practical use. In addition, whether or not the patterns can hold their promise of facilitating communication must be evaluated.

Unequivocally, people are and will remain the "original ingredient" necessary for success. However, with the unified modeling language's (UML's) modeling techniques and the model-driven architecture's (MDA's) architectural framework, individuals and teams are further empowered not only to simply address change and complexity, but also leverage change and complexity for a competitive advantage by capturing and leveraging knowledge encoded in models. Furthermore, it is experience, experimentation, and application of the UML, MDA, and other associated standards and technologies that will enable us to realize their benefits. The UML is a good modeling language (Meservy and Fensternacher 2005). While it does not support complete code generation, UML does lessen the burden on programmers which may be used to facilitate the construction routine code, which allows programmers to concentrate their efforts on modeling the system's more difficult aspects.

Among others, a new architecture of interactive system development called pattern-oriented and model-driven architecture (POMA) proposed in this book. It bridges the POD and the model-driven architecture while defining:

- HCI patterns and their relationships;
- Models and the underlying MDA architecture;
- Categories and composition rules of HCI patterns

One last comment and not the less important, as it will be discussed in the next chapter, certain issues remain to be addressed in patterns and current HCI patterns languages. To begin with, there are no standards for the documentation of patterns. The HCI community has no uniformly accepted pattern form. Furthermore, when patterns are documented (usually in narrative text), there are no tools to formally validate them. There should be formal reasoning and methodology behind the creation of patterns, and in turn, pattern languages. A language in computer science has syntax and semantics. None of the current pattern languages follow this principle; rather they tend to resort to narrative text formats as illustrated in the Experiences example. Finally, the interrelationships described in the patterns are static and not context-oriented. This is a major drawback since the conditions underlying the use of a pattern are related to its context of use (platforms, environment, and users).

References

Alexander C (1979) The timeless way of building. Oxford University Press, New York

Alexander C, Ishikawa S, Silverstein M, Jacobson M, Fiskdahl-King I, Angel S (1977) A pattern language. Oxford University Press, New York

Beck K, Cunningham W (1987) Using pattern languages for object-oriented programs. The 3nd Conference on Object-Oriented Programming System, Languages and Applications, Orlando

Beck K, Coplien JO, Crocker R, Dominick L, Meszaros G, Paulisch F, Vlissides J (1996) Industrial experience with design patterns. In Proceedings of the 18th International Conference on Software Engineering. pp. 103–114. IEEE Computer Society Press

Borchers JO (2001) A pattern approach to interaction design. Wiley, New York

Coplien JO, Schmidt DC (1995) Pattern language of program design. Addison Wesley, Reading

Coplien J, Zhao L (2001) Symmetry breaking in software patterns. In: Butler G, Jarzabek S (eds) Springer lecture notes in computer science series, LNCS 2177

Coram T, Lee J (1998) A pattern language for user interface design. http://www.maplefish.com/todd/papers/experiences. Accessed 14 April 2014

Dix A, Finlay J, Abowd and G, Beale R (1998) Human-computer interaction, 2nd edn. Prentice Hall, London. (ISBN 0-13-239864-8)

Dix A, Finlay JE, Abowd GD, Beale R (2003) Human-computer interaction, 3rd edn. Pearson, London

Engelberg D, Seffah A (2002) A design patterns for the navigation of large information architectures. 11th Annual Usability Professional Association Conference. Orlando (Florida).USA

Erickson T (2000) Lingua Franca for design: sacred places and pattern language. In *Proceedings of Designing Interactive Systems*. ACM Press, New York

Gamma E, Helm R, Johnson R, Vlissides J (1995) Design patterns: elements of reusable object-oriented software. Addison Wesley, Reading

Granlund Åsa Lafrenière D Carr DA (2001) A pattern-supported approach to the user interface design process. Proceedings of HCI International 2001 9th International Conference on human-computer interaction. August 5–10, 2001. New Orleans. USA

Hillside Group (1993) Online available at http://hillside.net/home/history. Accessed 14 April 2014

Javahery H, Seffah A (2002) A model for usability pattern-oriented design. In *Proceedings of TAMODIA 2002*. Bucharest. Romania. pp. 104–110

Laakso SA (2003) Collection of user interface design patterns. University of Helsinki, Dept. of Computer Science

Meservy TO, Fensternacher KD (2005) Transforming software development: an MDA Road Map. Computer 38(8):52–58

Sinnig D (2004) The complicity of patterns and model-based UI development. Master of Computer Science, Montreal, Concordia University, 148 p

Tidwell J (1997). Common Ground: a pattern language for human-computer interface design. Online. http://www.mit.edu/~jtidwell/common_ground.html. Accessed 14 April 2014

van Duyne DK Landay JA Hong JI (2003) The design of sites: patterns, principles and processes for crafting a customer-centered web experience. Addison Wesley, Boston

van Duyne DK Landay JA Hong JI (2006) The design of sites: patterns, patterns for creating winning web sites. Pearson, Upper Saddle River

Welie MV (1999) The Amsterdam collection of patterns in user interface design. Online http://www.welie.com/patterns/. Accessed 14 April 2014

Yacoub S, Ammar H (2003) Pattern-oriented analysis and design: composing patterns to design software systems (1st edn; p. 416). Addison Wesley Professional, Germany, ISBN 0-201-77640-5

Chapter 2
From HCI Patterns Languages to Pattern-Oriented Design

Abstract During last decade, several human–computer interaction (HCI) researchers and practitioners introduced their own pattern languages with specific terminology and classification. Pattern languages have been considered as a lingua franca for crossing cultural and professional barriers between different stakeholders. Pattern languages have also been presented as building blocks at different levels of granularity, which can be combined to compose new interactive systems. Despite the obvious and acclaimed potential for supporting design, patterns languages has not achieved the acceptance and widespread applicability envisaged by their authors. This chapter provides an analysis of the facts about pattern languages and pattern-based design approaches. Some shortcomings in the presentation and application of HCI patterns languages are identified and discussed under the prevailing fallacies. Based on the analysis of how pattern languages have been used so far, we draw some recommendations and future perspectives on what can be done to address the existing shortcomings. Making pattern languages more accessible, easily understandable, comparable and integratable in software, and usability in engineering tools can promote HCI patterns to claim the usability, usefulness, and importance originally envisaged for the pattern-oriented design approach.

2.1 Patterns as Tool to Capture Design Knowledge and Best Practices

Historically, best practices reusability in human–computer interaction (HCI) has attracted far less attention in comparison with other disciplines like software engineering, but this trend has been changing. The user interface (UI) occupies a large share of the total size of a typical system (Myers et al. 1993), and the design of interactive systems can be facilitated by applying best design practices. In current practice, tools for capturing and disseminating design knowledge include guidelines, claims and patterns (Macintosh 1992; Microsoft 1995), and within organizations (Billingsley 1995; Rosenzweig 1996; Weinschenk and Yeo 1995). Guidelines concentrate most often on the physical design attributes of the user interface, and examples are the *Macintosh Human Interface* Guidelines (Macintosh 1992) and the *Java Look and Feel* Design Guidelines (Sun Microsystems 2001). Claims (Sutcliffe 2000) are

© Springer International Publishing Switzerland 2015   15
A. Seffah, *Patterns of HCI Design and HCI Design of Patterns*,
Human-Computer Interaction Series, DOI 10.1007/978-3-319-15687-3_2

Table 2.1 Reused claim for a safety-critical application

Reused claim: safety-critical application
Claim ID: rare event monitor
Target artifact: user interface for a chemical analysis instrument control system
Description: infrequent, dangerous events are detected by the system and a warning is issued to the user; in this case operational failures in a laser gas chromatograph control system
Upside: automatic detection of dangerous events relieves the user of constant monitoring; automatic detection and warning gives the user time to analyze the problem
Downside: issuing too many warnings may lead the user to ignore critical events; automated monitoring may lead to user's overconfidence in the automated system and decrease their situation awareness
Scenario: no events are detected in the laser emission controller or power supply, so the system gives an audio warning to the user and visually signals the location of the problem on a diagram of the instrument

a means to capture HCI knowledge in association with a specific artefact and usage context. They provide design advice based on theoretical foundations, cognitive design rationale, and possible trade-offs.

In the 1990s, design guidelines became an increasingly popular way to disseminate usability knowledge and ensure a degree of consistency across applications (Macintosh 1992; Microsoft 1995) and within organizations (Billingsley 1995; Rosenzweig 1996; Weinschenk and Yeo 1995). These guidelines often took the form of style guides and were usually platform-specific, prescribing how different kinds of windows should look and interact with the user for tasks such as choosing from lists or menu controls. An example of a *Java Look and Feel* guideline for a toolbar is described in Table 2.1. To date, guidelines have yet to realize their full potential and have had little impact on the design of user interface software (Gould et al. 1991; De Souza and Bevan 1990). Apart from not adequately addressing concerns facing designers such as which guidelines should be used under what circumstances (Henninger et al. 1995), studies have shown that interface guidelines suffer from being too abstract to be applied directly (Tetzlaff and Schwartz 1991; Thovtrup and Nielsen 1991). Most guidelines fall short of the goal of putting the accumulated knowledge of user-centered design at the fingertips of everyday designers, often becoming a static document read only by human factors specialists.

Introduced in the last decade, Claims (Sutcliffe 2000) are another means to capture and disseminate HCI design knowledge. They are associated with a specific artefact and usage context, providing design advice and possible trade-offs. Claims are powerful tools because, in addition to providing negative and positive design implications, they contain both theoretical and cognitive rationales. They also contain associated scenarios that provide designers with a concrete idea of the context of use. When first introduced, claims were limited in their generality as they were too narrowly defined with specific scenarios and examples. Subsequently, the paradigm of reuse was applied to claims in order to make them more generic and applicable to a wider range of application contexts. An example of such a *reused claim* for a safety-critical application is given in Table 2.1.

Although both guidelines and claims promote reuse, they have yet to be adopted by the mainstream designer. Studies have shown that interface guidelines suffer from being too abstract to directly apply (Tetzlaff and Schwartz 1991; Thovtrup and Nielsen 1991), while claims are too grounded in specific scenarios and examples, limiting their generality (Sutcliffe 2000).

HCI design patterns only capture essential details of design knowledge, and abstract away from superfluous, toolkit-dependent, and platform-specific design information. In addition, the presented information is organized intuitively within a set of predefined attributes, allowing designers, for example, to search rapidly and effectively through different design solutions while assessing the relevance of each pattern to their design. Every pattern has three necessary elements, usually presented as separate attributes, which are: a context, a problem, and a solution. The context describes a recurring set of situations in which the pattern can be applied. The problem refers to a set of forces, i.e., goals and constraints, which occur in the context. The solution refers to a design form or a design rule that can be applied to resolve the problem. The solution describes the elements that constitute a pattern, the relationships between these elements, as well as their responsibilities and collaboration. Other attributes that may be included are additional design rationale, specific examples, and related patterns.

Patterns alleviate many of the shortcomings associated with guidelines. Above all, they are a good alternative to guidelines as they are problem-oriented, but not platform-specific. Their descriptive format, with the use of defined attributes, is more concrete and easier to apply for novice designers. Guidelines can be quite abstract and intangible when it comes to practical application, whereas patterns are more structured and the knowledge is placed in a context. The designer is told when, how, and why the solution can be applied. Since patterns are context-oriented, the solution is related to a specific user activity. Table 2.2 compares a guideline and a pattern that addresses the same problem: helping the user to find frequently used commands or pages. The pattern version of the description gives detailed information about the context in which the solution can be applied.

Patterns have a more complementary association with claims; this in contrast to their somewhat antagonistic relationship with guidelines. Claims are tightly bound to specific domains of use, but contain valuable information including design tradeoffs, and a possibility is to use them to complement patterns creating a "package of reusable knowledge" (Sutcliffe 2000). Such detailed information can be incorporated when the pattern is instantiated to a specific context of use. Furthermore, details from claims about design and cognitive rationale, including scenario descriptions, can provide additional information to designers when combining patterns to create comprehensive designs.

Table 2.2 Guideline versus pattern for the toolbar

Guideline	Pattern
A **toolbar** is a collection of frequently used commands or options that appear as a row of toolbar buttons.	**Pattern Name:** Convenient Toolbar **Type:** Navigation Support
Toolbars normally appear horizontally beneath a primary window's menu bar, but they can be dragged anywhere in the window or into their own window.	**Context** – Task: Assist the user to reach convenient and key web pages at any time – User: Novice or expert – Environment: Website
Toolbars typically contain buttons, but you can provide other components (such as text fields and combo boxes) as well.	**Problem** – Help the user find useful and "safe" pages that need to be accessed from any location on the site, regardless of the current state of the
Toolbar buttons can contain menu indicators, which denote the presence of a menu. Toolbars are provided as shortcuts to features available elsewhere in the application, often in the menus. [toolbar icons] Toolbar Source: Java Look and Feel Design Guidelines (Sun Microsystems, 2001).	artefact. – The user should reach these pages promptly. **Solution** – Group the most convenient action links such as home, site map, and help – Use meaningful metaphors and accurate phrases as labels. – Place them consistently throughout the website
	Other attributes – Specific Forces, Related Patterns, Design Rationale
	Specific example [toolbar: OCLC Home, Search, Site Map, What's New, Feedback, Site Help]

2.2   HCI Design Pattern Languages

Patterns have been organized into pattern languages. Just as words must have grammatical and semantic relationships with each other in order to create sentences with meaning, design patterns must be related to each other in order to form meaningful design constructs. Pattern languages are a structured method of describing good design practices, containing a collection of interrelated patterns that aim to disseminate the body of contained knowledge. For designers, pattern languages are a means to traverse common HCI problems in a logical way, describing the key characteristics of effective solutions for meeting various design goals. Furthermore, they act as a communicative design tool and give rise to many different paths through the design activity.

A number of pattern languages have been suggested in HCI. For example, (Duyne 2003) "The Design of Sites," (Welie 1999) Interaction Design Patterns, and (Tidwell 1997) UI Patterns and Techniques play an important role. In addition, specific languages such as (Laakso 2003) User Interface Design Patterns and the UPADE Language (Engelberg and Seffah 2002) have been proposed as well. Different pattern collections have been published including patterns for web page layout design (Tidwell 1997) and (Coram and Lee 1998) for navigation in large information architectures, as well as for visualizing and presenting information.

Pattern languages have three essential elements. First, the language has to contain a standard pattern definition. One format for defining patterns was presented in the previous section (Table 2.1 and 2.2)—with the common attributes context, problem, solution, forces, related patterns, and examples. Second, the language must logically group patterns. Tidwell (1997) organizes her patterns according to different facets of UI design; categories include content organization, navigation, page layout, and actions/commands. Another example is the experiences pattern language (Fig. 2.1) developed by (Coram and Lee 1998), which concentrates on the user's experience within software systems. The main focus is on the interactions between the user and the interfaces of software applications. Patterns are grouped according to different focus areas and user interface paths such as interaction style, explorable interface, and symbols. Third, pattern interrelationships should be described. In experiences,

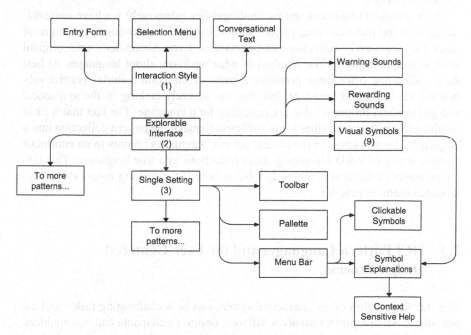

Fig. 2.1 The experiences pattern language

the relationships between the patterns are mapped and indicated by arrows, creating a sort of "flow" within the language. This is illustrated in Fig. 2.1.

Distinguishing between different types of relationships reinforces the generative nature of pattern languages, and supports the idea of using patterns to develop complete designs. However, for designers to be able to use patterns effectively and with efficacy to solve problems in HCI and interactive system design, patterns need to be intimately related to a design process. Based on the design problem, pattern languages should provide starting points for the designer, and a means to systematically walk the designer from pattern to pattern.

For example, in experiences, the metapattern *Interaction style* (denoted with "(1)" in Fig. 2.1) is the first pattern that leads the designer along the major paths through the language. The design advice (Coram and Lee 1998) for this pattern includes studying the user and environment, working with the user to determine what interaction style is best, and keeping the interface simple and consistent. This pattern is connected to four other patterns as indicated by arrows in Fig. 2.1 (entry form, selection menu, conversational text, and *explorable interface*). Based on the context of use, the designer is free to choose any of these patterns to incorporate into the design. This is a repetitive process as some patterns, such as *Explorable Interface*, are subsequently connected to even more suggested patterns.

Although the experiences language showed the beginnings of associating its patterns to a design process, it was regrettably not developed in its entirety. In the next section, we will present some attempts at further linking pattern languages to the UI design process.

Having studied linguistics and psycholinguistics extensively, we have some difficulty with the fact that some pattern authors call their works languages. In most cases they are merely collections or taxonomies. Even Alexander's own original work is disappointing by the standard of what we know about languages. At best these collections offer some primitive aspects of the combinatorial generatively that we see in natural language, but they are severely lacking in the syntactical and grammatical properties that are necessary for a language. The fact that we can combine two patterns together is not sufficient to make the pattern collection into a language. This weakness in the current pattern "languages" points to an enormous uncharted area of R&D for turning these collections into true languages. This language aspect of patterns is precisely what is needed for making model-driven approaches useful in practice.

2.3   HCI Pattern Languages and the User-Centered Design Process

The interface design of an interactive system can be a challenging task—and especially so when a project involves different design participants and stakeholders. Successful designs require individuals to communicate their concepts and ideas, building a common forum for the discussion of already available design practices.

As in any culture or society, the HCI community needs a common ground for such communication and dissemination of knowledge. Designers focus on the creation of an artifact that integrates various behavioral theories and technologies. This is done without regard to the evaluation of individual variables that may affect the design (Zimmerman et al. 2004). Usability experts take a more scientific approach, looking at specific behavioral and design elements that best satisfy the requirements. Software developers are interested in finding an applicable design and implementing it correctly in the most efficient manner, and are often not familiar with usability engineering techniques and human interaction theories (Myers and Rosson 1992).

This is a proving ground for patterns as they provide a mechanism to successfully integrate and satisfy the different goals of all individuals involved in the design process, crossing cultural and professional barriers, and overcoming limitations in communication. Patterns are presented consistently, are easy to read, and provide background reasoning. They act as a lingua franca (Erickson 2000) for design, which can be read and understood by all. (Erickson 2000) discusses the potential of this as a way of making communication in design a more "egalitarian process," with the focus relying less on technical design issues, and more upon broader design problems and solutions. A lingua franca facilitates discussion, presentation, and negotiation for the many different individuals who play a role in designing interactive systems.

Acting as a communicative vehicle, pattern languages are interesting tools that can guide software designers through the design process. However, there exists no commonly agreed upon UI design process that employs pattern languages as first class tools. Several people have tried to link patterns to a process or framework, bringing some order to pattern languages, and suggesting that potentially applicable patterns be identified early on based on user, task, and context requirements. A pattern-driven design process should lead designers to relevant patterns based on the problem at hand, demonstrate how they can be used, as well as illustrate combinations with related patterns. In the following section, we describe three design approaches driven by patterns.

In the pattern-supported approach (PSA) framework (Fig. 3.2), HCI patterns are used at various levels to solve problems related to business domains and processes, tasks, structure and navigation, and graphical user interface (GUI) design (Granlund and Lafrenière 1999). The main idea that can be drawn from PSA is that HCI patterns can be documented identified and instantiated according to different parts of the design process—giving us knowledge as early on as during system definition. For example, during system definition or task and user analysis, depending on the context of use, we can decide which HCI patterns are appropriate for the design phase. Although PSA shows the beginnings of associating patterns to the design process, pattern interrelationships and their possible impact on the final design are not tackled in detail.

Duyne et al. (2003) describe a second approach, where patterns are arranged into 12 groups that are available at different levels of web design. Their pattern language has 90 patterns that address various aspects of web design, ranging from creating a navigation structure to designing effective page layouts. The order of their pattern

Table 2.3 Pattern groups ordered according to a web design process

Step	Pattern groups	Description	Pattern examples
A	Site genres	Construct particular site type	Personal e-commerce Nonprofits as networks of help
B	Creating a navigation framework	Choose patterns to navigate, browse and search on the site	Multiple ways to navigate Task-based organization
C	Creating a powerful homepage	Design the homepage based on user needs	Homepage portal Up-front value proposition
D	Writing and managing content	Manage content and address user accessibility	Page templates Internationalized and local content
E	Building trust and credibility	Address issues dealing with trust and credibility	Site branding Fair information practices
F	Basic e-commerce	Create a good customer experience for e-commerce	Quick-flow checkout Clean product details
G	Advanced e-commerce	Incorporate advanced e-commerce features	Featured products Cross-selling and up-selling
H	Helping customers complete tasks	Structure your site to improve task completion	Process funnel Persistent customer sessions
I	Designing effective page layouts	Create clear, predictable and understandable layouts	Grid layout Expanding width screen size
J	Making site search fast and relevant	Design interaction so that user searches are effective	Search action module Straightforward search forms
K	Making navigation easy	Display helpful navigation elements	Unified browsing hierarchy Action buttons
L	Speeding up your site	Incorporate patterns to make your site look and feel fast	Low number of files Fast downloading images

groups generally indicates the order in which they should be used in the design process (Table 2.3). In addition, patterns chosen from the various groups have links to related patterns in the language. The highest level pattern group in their scheme is *Site Genres*, which provides a convenient starting point into the language, allowing the designer to choose the type of site to be created. Starting from a particular Site Genre pattern, various lower level patterns are subsequently referenced. In this way, the approach succeeds not only in providing a starting point into the language, but also demonstrates how patterns of different levels may interact with one another.

2.4   Pattern Supported Approach (PSA)

The "Pattern Supported Approach" (PSA) addresses patterns not only during the design phase, but also during the entire software development process. PSA (Granlund et al. 2001) aims to support early system definition and conceptual design through the use of HCI patterns. In particular, patterns have been used to describe business domains, processes, and tasks to aid early system definition and conceptual design.

The main idea of PSA is that HCI patterns can be documented according to the development lifecycle. In other words, during system definition and task analysis, depending on the context of use, it can be decided which HCI patterns are appropriate for the design phase. In contrast to POD, the concept of linking patterns together to result in a design is not tackled in this approach.

The PSA to the user interface design process suggests a wider scope for the use of patterns by looking at the overall design process. Based on the fact that the usability of a system emerges as the product of the user, the task and the context of use, PSA integrates this knowledge in most of its patterns, dividing the forces in the pattern description correspondingly (i.e., describing task, user, and context forces). PSA provides a double-linked chain of patterns (parts of an emerging pattern language) that *support* each step of the design process (Granlund et al. 2001).

Building on PSA, PSA-proposed approach highlights another important aspect of pattern-oriented design: *pattern combination*. By combining different patterns, developers can use pattern relationships and combine them in order to produce an effective design solution. As a result, patterns become a more effective vehicle that supports design reuse.

Up to this point, most of the work on patterns in HCI has focused on screen design issues. PSA addresses patterns not only at the design phase, but also *before* design (Fig. 2.2).

For example, *task* patterns point to *Structure and Navigation Patterns*, which in turn point to *GUI Design Patterns*, and vice-versa. These patterns offer a way to capture and communicate knowledge from previous designs (including the knowledge from system definition, task/user analysis and structure and navigation design). Given a mature language of patterns belonging to the described classes, the PSA approach provides an entry point to this pattern language, and suggests (without restricting the pattern usage) a chain of appropriate patterns at different levels of analysis and design (Granlund et al. 2001).

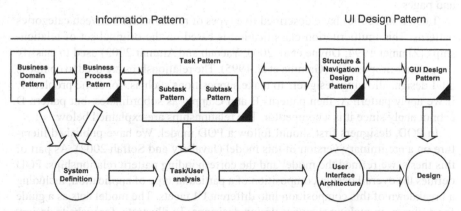

Fig. 2.2 The PSA framework with the relationships between PSA patterns

2.5   Pattern-Oriented Design

Javahery and Seffah (2002) proposed first the design approach called Pattern-Oriented Design (POD). The initial motivation for POD arose from interviews carried out with software developers using our patterns from the UPADE web language. These interviews revealed that in order for patterns to be useful, developers need to know how to combine them to create complete or partial designs. Providing a list of patterns and loosely defined relationships, as is the case for most HCI pattern languages, is insufficient to effectively drive design solutions. Understanding when a pattern is applicable during the design process, how it can be used, as well as how and why it can or cannot be combined with other related patterns, are key notions in the application of patterns.

First, POD provides a framework for guiding designers through stepwise design suggestions. At each predefined design step, designers are given a set of patterns that are applicable. This is in stark contrast to the current use of pattern languages, where there is no defined link to any sort of systematic process. Pattern relationships are explicitly described, allowing designers to compose patterns based on an understanding of these relationships.

As a practical illustration, we have applied POD within the context of the UPADE pattern language for web design. Each pattern in UPADE provides a proven solution for a common usability and HCI-related problem occurring in a specific context of use for web applications. Patterns are grouped into three categories, corresponding closely to the various steps and decisions during the process of web design: architectural, structural, and navigation support. Structural patterns are further subcategorized into page manager and information container patterns (Fig. 2.3 for pattern examples). During each design step, designers choose from a variety of applicable patterns: (1) architectural, relating to the architecture of the entire website; (2) page manager, establishing the physical and logical screen layout; (3) information container, providing ways to organize and structure information; and (4) navigation support, suggesting different models for navigating between information segments and pages.

Taleb et al. (2006) have described five types of relationships between categories patterns. This multicriterion classification is based on the original set of relationships (Zimmer 1994; Duyne et al. 2003; Yacoub and Ammar 2003) used to classify the patterns proposed in (Gamma et al. 1995). The relationships are used to compose a UI design, allowing designers to make suppositions such as: for some problem P, if we apply pattern A, then patterns B and C apply as subordinates, but pattern D cannot apply since it is a competitor. The relationships are explained below:

In POD, designers first should follow a POD model. We have published literature on a preliminary version of this model (Javahery and Seffah 2002). As part of this thesis, we refined the model and the corresponding pattern relationships. POD defines the overall design composition of a particular type of application, including a breakdown of this composition into different UI facets. The model acts as a guide for designers in making stepwise design decisions. To illustrate, for website design,

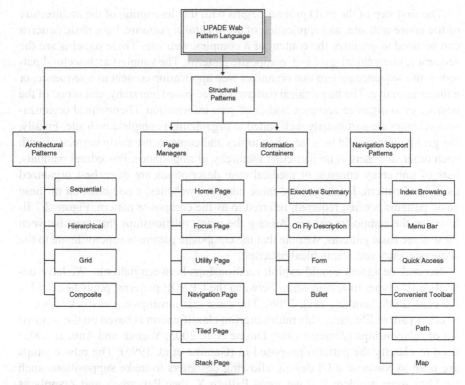

Fig. 2.3 An overview of the UPADE pattern language

we define four steps that designers should follow: (1) defining the architecture of the site with architectural patterns, (2) establishing the overall structure of each page with page manager patterns, (3) identifying content-related elements for each page with information container patterns, and (4) organizing the interaction with navigation support patterns. Landay and Myers (2001) and Welie and Van Der Veer (2003) also propose to organize their web pattern languages according to both the design process and UI structuring elements (such as navigation, page layout, and basic dialog style).

Second, designers should exploit relationships between patterns. We have described five types of relationships between the UPADE patterns, published in (Taleb et al. 2006; Javahery et al. 2006). The same relationships can easily be applied to other pattern libraries. This multicriterion classification is based on the original set of relationships (Zimmer 1994; Duyne et al. 2003; Yacoub and Ammar 2003) used to classify the patterns proposed in (Gamma et al. 1995). The relationships are used to compose a UI design, allowing designers to make suppositions such as: "For some problem P, if we apply Pattern X, then Patterns Y and Z apply as subordinates, but Pattern S cannot apply since it is a competitor." The relationships are:

The first step of the POD process begins with the description of the architecture of the entire web site, and application of *architectural patterns*. Four basic patterns can be used to organize the content of a complex web site. These patterns are the sequence, hierarchical, grid and, composite patterns. The simplest architectural pattern is the sequence pattern that organizes web application content as a sequence, or a linear narrative. The hierarchical pattern is a tree-based hierarchy, and is one of the best ways to organize complex bodies of web information. Hierarchical organization schemes are particularly well suited to organizing a complete web site. Finally, the grid pattern should be used when topics and contents are fairly correlated with each other, and there is no particular hierarchy of importance. Procedural manuals, lists of university courses, or medical case descriptions are often best organized using grid pattern. For larger and more complex websites, a combination of these basic patterns is often required, referred to as the composite pattern. Figure 2.7 illustrates the composite pattern. Among the many relationships that exist between these three basic patterns, we note that the composite pattern is superordinate to the sequence, grid, and hierarchical patterns.

Second, designers should exploit relationships between patterns. We have described five types of relationships between the UPADE patterns, published in (Taleb et al. 2006; Javahery et al. 2006). The same relationships can easily be applied to other pattern libraries. This multicriterion classification is based on the original set of relationships (Zimmer 1994; Duyne et al. 2003; Yacoub and Ammar 2003) used to classify the patterns proposed in (Gamma et al. 1995). The relationships are used to compose a UI design, allowing designers to make suppositions such as: "For some problem P, if we apply Pattern X, then Patterns Y and Z apply as sub-ordinates, but pattern S cannot apply since it is a competitor." The relationships are:

1. **Similar** (X, Y) if X and Y address the same problem within a similar context, by providing different solutions. As a result, X and Y can be replaced by each other in a certain composition. For example, index browsing and menu bar patterns are similar (Fig. 2.4). They both provide navigational support in the context of a medium size website, allowing users to navigate among items from the menu.

Fig. 2.4 Comparison of similar patterns

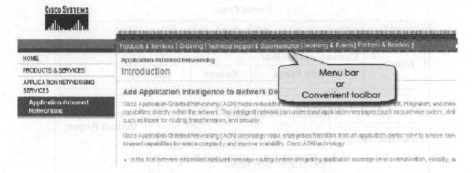

Fig. 2.5 Two competitor patterns

Therefore, the index browsing pattern can be replaced by the menu bar pattern and still solve the same design problem. Moreover, because both patterns provide different solutions to the same problem, they can be used at the same time in a design. In our example below, each pattern is used for a distinct set of navigation items.

2. **Competitor** (X, Y) if X and Y address the same problem within a similar context, by providing equivalent solutions. In other words, X and Y are competitors if they are similar and interchangeable. As a result, they cannot be used at the same time in a design. For example, the web convenient toolbar and menu bar patterns are competitors (see Fig. 2.5). The convenient toolbar solution states: "*Group* the *most common convenient action links*, such as home, site map help, etc." The convenient toolbar allows a user to directly access a set of common services from any web page. At the same time, the menu bar pattern, when used as a shortcut, provides an equivalent solution: "Provide a *collection* of *most frequently visited page links*." Both patterns provide the same solution of presenting a group or a collection of most frequently used links. Hence, making these patterns competitors.

3. **Super-ordinate** (X, Y) is a basic relationship to compose several patterns of different categories. A pattern X that is a superordinate of pattern Y means that Y is used as a building block to create X. For example, the home page pattern is a super-ordinate of convenient toolbar and index browsing patterns; because, both of them are used in home page pattern (see Fig. 2.6).

4. **Subordinate** (X, Y) if and only if X is embeddable in Y. Y is also called super-ordinate of X. This relationship is important in the mapping process of POD. For example, a home page pattern is composed of several other patterns, such as index browsing and convenient toolbar patterns (Fig. 2.6). All patterns used in a home page pattern will be sub-ordinate to it.

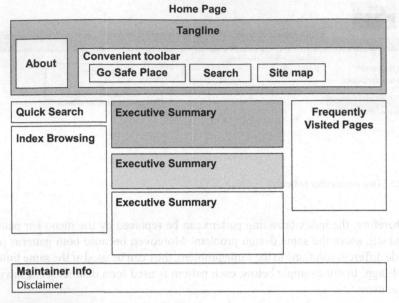

Fig. 2.6 Home page pattern with subordinate patterns

5. **Neighboring** (X, Y) if X and Y belong to the same pattern category (family). For example, the sequential and hierarchical patterns are neighboring as they belong to the category of architectural patterns.

Within the scope of the development of web-based applications using the UPADE language, POD allows for the exploitation of 48 pattern relationships, allowing even novice developers to use the underlying best practices to iterate through concrete and effective design solutions. As described in our pattern model, each pattern contains a list of related patterns. For example, the stack page pattern would contain the following information about related patterns: (1) super-ordinate: sequential, hierarchical, grid, composite. (2) sub-ordinate: Executive summary, on fly description, browsing index. (3) competitor: focus page, tiled page.

Let us illustrate how pattern composition (Fig. 2.7) can be applied to our website design for serge. We will use the POD model in combination with the patterns selected from existing collections.

During the second step, the designer applies *structural patterns* to establish a consistent physical and logical screen layout for each page that was defined in the previous step. This step involves applying *page manager patterns*, which are a type of structural pattern (Table 2.4). Different relationships exist between these patterns, and even between these patterns and those used in the previous design step. As an example, all the structural patterns are subordinate to the architectural patterns from the last step. In addition, to further illustrate some relationships, tiled page and stack page patterns are competitors (Fig. 2.8). This means that if you choose the tiled page pattern as a basic model for your home page, you cannot use the stack page pattern

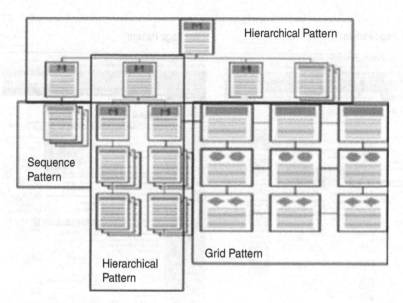

Fig. 2.7 The composite pattern

Table 2.4 Pattern examples used in the POD process

Pattern type	Pattern name	Description
Structural patterns: Page managers	Tiled page	Structures and presents content to the user from more general to specific by dividing the page into several surfaces
	Stack page	Groups content into categories that have no obvious hierarchy; this is done by designing several surfaces stacked together and labeling them appropriately
Structural patterns: Information containers	Executive summary	Provides an information preview or summary for a certain topic of choice
	On fly description	Provides the user with a short description of the object when the mouse hovers over it
Navigation support patterns	Dynamic path	Indicates the user's entire path starting from when the web application was initially accessed, and is similar to "breadcrumbs" in other pattern languages
	Index browsing	Allows the user to easily and promptly navigate among important content pages, and is located consistently throughout the website

for any of the subsequent pages. Such knowledge can be critical for pattern users because if it is not taken into consideration during design, it can compromise the benefits of the pattern.

The third step of the POD process involves employing *information container patterns*, the second type of structural patterns, to quickly "plug in" an information segment for each page. Long before the web was invented, authors of technical

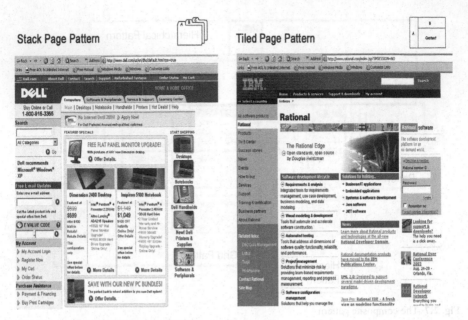

Fig. 2.8 Comparison of stack and tiled page patterns

documents discovered that users appreciate short segments of information. Such design practices should be embedded in the design process and presented to the designer. For example, for users, how long does it take to determine if a large document contains relevant information? This question is a critical design issue, and the executive summary pattern (Table 2.4), which provides an information preview, may be an appropriate design solution.

The fourth and final step consists of building the navigation support. It is possible to consider navigation elements earlier in conjunction with other patterns. *Navigation Support patterns* suggest different models for navigating between information segments and pages. To illustrate an example of existing relationships, the index browsing and dynamic path patterns (Table 2.4) are considered neighboring since they belong to the same design step. Although they are both used for navigation support, they are not used to solve the same usability problem and are applied in different contexts. Dynamic path is used to navigate between pages in an already taken path, and gives the user a sense of safety and control. Index browsing is generally used to navigate among important content pages, and allows the user to reach these pages safely.

Although all of the patterns can be applied independently, one of the main strengths of the POD approach is that developers can exploit pattern relationships and apply this knowledge to their design solutions. As an example, the executive summary pattern, combined with the index browsing pattern from navigation support, allows users to preview information about a certain topic before spending time to download, browse and, read different pages (Fig. 2.9). Executive summary is

Fig. 2.9 The index browsing and executive summary pattern

weighted as a highly recommended subordinate pattern when pattern users try to use the index browsing pattern.

Knowledge about context-oriented relationships, as described above, can be very useful to pattern users. They can be a guide in choosing the best solution for a specific user problem based on a particular context. Novice designers and software developers who are unfamiliar with user-centered design and usability engineering can especially benefit from such a systematic design process.

2.6   Key Contributions of the Chapter

Even the effort made to collect patterns by, both, practitioners and researchers, a universally accepted taxonomy for pattern is still missing in HCI. Patterns deal with different levels of abstraction and have to be considered at different stages. Therefore, if languages are not structured logically, it can be confusing for designers trying to work with them. Some authors have suggested their own partial classifications to facilitate the use of patterns. For example, (Welie 1999) discusses a taxonomy based on the domain of web application, GUI, or mobile UI design patterns. Tidwell (1997) organizes her patterns according to different facets of UI design; categories include content organization, navigation, page layout, and actions/commands.

Furthermore, pattern languages need to clearly define pattern relationships. Currently, pattern interrelationships are often incomplete and not context-oriented. This is, by far, the most serious drawback of current languages. For example, the experiences language describes some pattern relationships, but is incomplete. Other languages mention "related patterns" in their descriptions, but do not define the precise nature of the relationship. This is a limitation since relationship definitions are an important factor in determining the circumstances under which a pattern is applicable, having an effect on the pattern's context of use.

References

Billingsley PA (1995) Starting from scratch: building a usability program at union pacific railroad. Interactions 2(4):27–30

Coram, T, Lee J (1998) A pattern language for user interface design. http://www.maplefish.com/todd/papers/experiences. Accessed 14 April 2013

DSouza F, Bevan N (1990) The use of guidelines in menu interface design. Proceedings IFIP INTERACT '90, Cambridge, (27–31 August), pp 435–440

Duyne DK, Van Landay JA, Hong JI (2003) The design of sites: patterns, principles and processes for crafting a customer-centered web experience. Addison Wesley, Boston

Engelberg D, Seffah A (2002) A design patterns for the navigation of large information architectures. 11th Annual Usability Professional Association Conference, Orlando (Florida)

Erickson T (2000) Lingua Franca for design: sacred places and pattern language. In Proceedings of Designing Interactive Systems. ACM, New York

Gamma E, Helm R, Johnson R, Vlissides J (1995) Design patterns: elements of reusable object-oriented software. Addison Wesley, Boston

Gould JD, Boies SJ, Clayton L (1991) Making usable, useful, productivity-enhancing computer applications. Commun ACM 34(1):74–85. doi:10.1145/99977.99993

Granlund A, Lafreniere D (1999) A pattern-supported approach to the user interface design process. Workshop report, UPA'99 Usability Professionals' Association Conference. Scottsdale, AZ, June 29–July 2, 1999

Granlund Å Lafrenière D Carr DA (2001) A pattern-supported approach to the user interface design process. Proceedings of HCI International 2001 9th International Conference on Human–Computer Interaction. (August 5–10, 2001), New Orleans

Henninger S, Haynes K, Reith MW (1995) A framework for developing experience-based usability guidelines. Proceedings of the conference on designing interactive systems: processes, practices, methods, & techniques, Ann Arbor, pp 43–53. doi:10.1145/225434.225440

Javahery H, Seffah A (2002) A model for usability pattern-oriented design. Proceedings of TAMODIA 2002, Bucharest, pp 104–110

Javahery H, Sinnig D, Seffah A, Forbrig P, Radhakrishnan T (2006) Pattern-based UI design: adding rigor with user and context variables. Proceedings of the TAMODIA 2006, pp 97–108

Laakso SA (2003) Collection of user interface design patterns. University of Helsinki, Dept. of Computer Science, Helsinki

Landay JA, Myers BA (2001) Sketching interfaces: toward more human interface design. IEEE Comput 34(3):56–64

Macintosh (1992) Human interface guidelines. Apple Computer Company. Publisher Addison Wesley Professional. Cupertino. http://interface.free.fr/Archives/Apple_HIGuidelines.pdf. Accessed 14 April 2013

Microsoft (1995) The windows interface guidelines for software design. Microsoft Press. Redmond. http://www.ics.uci.edu/~kobsa/courses/ICS104/course-notes/Microsoft_Windows-Guidelines.pdf. Accessed 14 April 2013

Myers BA, Rosson MB (1992) Survey on user interface programming. Proceedings of the CHI 1992, New York, pp 195–202

Myers BA, McDaniel RG, Kosbie DS (1993) Marquise: creating complete user interfaces by demonstration. Proceedings of the INTERCHI 1993, New York, pp 293–300

Rosenzweig E (1996) Design guidelines for software products: a common look and feel or a fantasy? Interactions 3(5):21–26 (Sept/Oct. 1996). doi:10.1145/234757.234759

Sun Microsystems (2001) Java look and feel design guidelines. Publisher Addison Wesley Professional. http://java.sun.com/products/jlf/ed2/book/. Accessed 14 April 2013

Sutcliffe AG (2000) On the effective use and reuse of HCI knowledge. ACM Trans Comput Hum Interact 7(2):197–221

Taleb M, Javahery H, Seffah A (2006) Pattern-oriented design composition and mapping for cross-platform web applications. The XIII international workshop. DSVIS 2006, vol 4323/2007, doi:10.1007/978-3-540-69554-7. ISBN 978-3-540-69553-0. (July 26–28 2006. Trinity College Dublin Ireland. Publisher Springer-Verlag Berlin Heidelberg. Germany)

Tetzlaff L, Schwartz DR (1991) The use of guidelines in interface design. Proceedings of CHI'91, pp 329–333

Thovtrup H, Nielsen J (1991) Assessing the usability of a user interface standard. Proceedings of the ACM CHI'91 Conference Human Factors in Computing Systems, New Orleans, (28 April-2 May), pp 335–341

Tidwell J. Common Ground (1997) A pattern language for human-computer interface design. http://www.mit.edu/~jtidwell/common_ground.html. Accessed 14 April 2013

Weinschenk S, Yeo SC (1995) Guidelines for enterprise-wide GUI design. Wiley, New York

Welie MV (1999) The Amsterdam collection of patterns in user interface design. http://www.welie.com/patterns/. Accessed 14 April 2013

Welie MV, Van der Veer Gerrit C (2003) Pattern languages in interaction design. Proceedings of the INTERACT 2003

Yacoub S, Ammar H (2003) Pattern-oriented analysis and design: composing patterns to design software systems, 1st edn. Addison Wesley Professional, p 416

Zimmer W (1994) Relationships between design patterns. In: Coplien JO, Schmidt DC (eds) Patterns languages of program design. Addison-Wesley, Boston

Zimmerman J, Evenson S, Baumann K, Purgathofer P (2004) The relationship between design and HCI. Workshop of CHI Extended Abstracts 2004, pp 1741–1742

Chapter 3
HCI Design Patterns as a Building Block in Model-Driven Engineering

Abstract The main idea surrounding Model-Based User Interface (MBUI) engineering is to identify useful abstractions that highlight the core aspects and properties of an interactive system and its design. These abstractions are instantiated and iteratively transformed at different levels to create a concrete user interface. However, certain limitations prevent user interface (UI) developers from adopting model-based approaches for UI engineering. One such limitation is the lack of reusability of best design practices and knowledge within such approaches. With a view to fostering reuse in the instantiation and transformation of models, we introduce patterns as building blocks, which can be first used to construct different models and then instantiated into concrete UI artifacts. In particular, we will demonstrate how different kinds of patterns can be used as modules for establishing task, dialog, presentation, and layout models. Starting from an outline of the general process of pattern application, an interface for combining patterns and a possible formalization are suggested. The Task Pattern Wizard, tool we developed, uses an eXtensible markup language (XML approach. It is built on eXtensible user languages (XUL)-based. This tool helps designers for selecting, adapting, and applying patterns to task models. In addition, an extended example will illustrate the intimate complicity of several patterns and the proposed model-driven approach.

3.1 Motivations

The model-based methods are rarely used in practice (Trætteberg 2004). One major reason for this limitation is that creating various models, instantiating, and linking them together to create lower level models is a tedious and very time-consuming work, especially when most of the associated activities have to be done manually; tools provide only marginal support. This presents an overhead that is unacceptable in many industrial setups with limited resources, tough competition, and short time-to-market. This crippling overhead can be partially attributed to the fact that model-based methods (MOBI-D 1999; TERESA 2004)

© Springer International Publishing Switzerland 2015
A. Seffah, *Patterns of HCI Design and HCI Design of Patterns,*
Human-Computer Interaction Series, DOI 10.1007/978-3-319-15687-3_3

35

lack the flexibility of reusing knowledge in building and transforming models. At best, only few approaches offer a form of copy-and-paste reuse. Moreover, many of these reuses involve the "reuser" merely taking a copy of a model component and manually changing it according to the new requirements. No form of consistency with the original solution is maintained (Mens et al.1998). Copy-and-paste analysis and the concept of fragmented design models are clearly inadequate when attempting to integrate reuse in a systematic and retraceable way in the model-based user interface (MBUI) development life cycle.

This practical observation motivates the need for a more disciplined form of reuse. We will demonstrate that the reusability problems associated with current model-based approaches can be overcome through patterns. Patterns have been mainly known as proven solutions to well-known problems that occur in different situations. They are usually presented as a vehicle to capture the best practices and facilitate their dissemination. Because patterns are context-sensitive, the solution encapsulated in the pattern can be customized and instantiated to the current context of use before being reused (Alexander 1977). Nevertheless, in order to be an effective knowledge-capturing tool in model-based approaches, the following issues require investigation:

1. A classification of patterns according to models must be established. Such a classification would distinguish between patterns that are building blocks for models and patterns that drive the transformation of models, as well as create a concrete user interface (UI).
2. A tool support that can assist developers when selecting the proper patterns, instantiating them once selected, as well as when combining them to create a model.

These two aspects are the essence of this chapter. After a brief overview of existing model-based approaches, we will introduce how we have been combining model-based approaches and several patterns to build a framework for the development of user interfaces. A clear definition of the various models used and an outline of the UI derivation process are also given. Furthermore, we will suggest how to enhance this framework using patterns as a reuse vehicle. We will demonstrate how human-computer interaction (HCI) patterns can be used as building blocks when constructing and transforming the various models, and list which kind of HCI patterns lend themselves to this use. A brief case study is presented in order to validate and illustrate the applicability of our approach and the proposed list of pattern.

3.2   Patterns and User Interface Model-Driven Engineering

The HCI design patterns have the potential to provide a solution to the reuse problem while acting as driving artifacts in the development and transformation of models. However, in order to facilitate their reuse and applicability, patterns should be presented within a comprehensive framework that supports a structured design process, not just according to the structure of each individual aspect of the application (e.g., page layout, navigation, etc.), which is currently the case for most HCI patterns. This demonstrates the virtue of using model-based design approach in comparison to manual design practices. (Gaffar et al. 2005) is one attempt to seemingly integrate patterns in the design process. Based on the Usability Patterns-Assisted Design Environment (UPADE) Web Language, the approach aims to demonstrate when a pattern is applicable during the design process, how it can be used, as well as how and why it can or cannot be combined with other related patterns. Developers can exploit pattern relationships and the underlying best practices to devise concrete and effective design solutions.

Similarly, the "Pattern Supported Approach" (PSA) (Granlund and Lafrenière 1999) addresses patterns not only during the design phase, but throughout the entire software development process. In particular, patterns have been used to describe business domains, processes, and tasks to aid in early system definition and conceptual design. In PSA, HCI patterns can be documented according to the development lifecycle. In other words, during system definition and task analysis, it can be determined which HCI patterns are appropriate for the design phase, depending on the context of use. However, the concept of linking patterns together to put up a design is not tackled.

In addition, Molina et al. (2002) found that existing pattern collections focus on design problems, and not on analysis problems. As a result, he proposes the JUST-user interface (JUST-UI) framework, which provides a set of conceptual patterns that can be used as building blocks to create UI specifications during analysis. In particular, conceptual patterns are abstract specifications of elemental UI requirements, such as: *how to search, how to order, what to see,* and *what to do.* Molina also recognized that the relatively informal descriptions of patterns used today are not suitable for tool use. Within the Just-UI framework, a fixed set of patterns has been formalized so that they can be processed by the "OliverNova" tool (Oliver-Nova 2004). Eventually, the JUST-UI framework will use code generation to derive a UI implementation based on the analysis model.

Breedvelt et al. (1997) discuss the idea of using task patterns to foster design knowledge reuse while task modeling. Task patterns encapsulate task templates for common design issues. This means that whenever designers realize that the issue with which they are contending is similar to an existing issue that has already been detected and resolved, they can immediately reuse the previously developed solution (as captured by the Task patterns). More specifically, Task patterns are used as templates (or task building blocks) for designing an application's task model. According to Breedvelt, another advantage of using Task patterns is that they facilitate reading and interpreting the task specification. Patterns can be employed as placeholders for common, repetitive task fragments. Instead of thinking in terms of tasks, one can think in terms of patterns at a more abstract level. Such an approach renders the task specification more compact and legible.

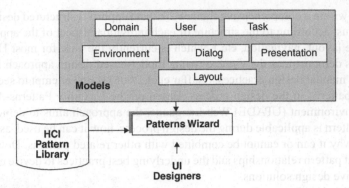

Fig. 3.1 PD-MUI framework

However, Breedvelt et al. (2007) consider Task patterns as individual static en-capsulations of a (task) design issue in a particular context of use. Concepts for a more advanced form of reuse, including customization and combination, are not presented. The (Gaffar et al. 2005) approach has highlighted another important aspect of the pattern concept: *pattern combination*. By combining different patterns, developers can utilize pattern relationships and combine them in order to produce an effective design solution. We will consider this principle in Sect. 3.5.2 and suggest an interface for combining patterns. As a result, patterns become a more effective vehicle for reuse.

3.3   Pattern-Driven and MBUI (PD-MBUI) Framework

3.3.1   Basic Concepts and Terminology

PD-MBUI (Pattern-Driven and MBUI) aims to reconcile and unify in a single framework the pattern-driven and model-based approaches, two powerful methods for UI and software engineering as in Fig. 3.1:

1. A library of HCI patterns that can be used, as building blocks, in this construction and transformations. A taxonomy and examples of patterns are given in Sect 3.3.2.
2. A method of identifying, instantiating, and applying patterns during the construction and refinement of these models. This method is summarized in Sect. 3.4.1.
3. A set of models including domain, task, user, environment, dialog, presentation, and layout models. These models as well as the process of constructing them are detailed in Sect. 3.5.2.
4. A tool, the Pattern Wizard, which helps user interface developers in selecting and applying patterns when constructing and transforming the various models to a concrete user interface. This tool aims to combine all the ingredients of the

PD-MBUI in a single and integrative framework for the engineering of pattern-driven and MBUI's.

Within our approach, we will be using the following notions as defined here:

1. UI or HCI design patterns as proven solutions to a user problem that occurs in various contexts and projects. We take for granted that the proposed library of patterns and the pattern-driven approach are valid. This aspect has been largely debated by others including our preliminary work (Gaffar et al. 2005; Sinnig 2004). An example of pattern is *Multi-Value Input Form* (Paternò 2000). This task pattern provides a solution to the typical user problem of entering a number of related values. These values can be of different data types, such as "date," "string," or "real."
2. User interface component or widgets such as buttons, windows, and dialog boxes are generally defined as object–oriented classes in UI toolkits such as Java swing, etc.
3. An artifact is an object that is essential in order for a task to be completed. The state of this artifact is usually changed during the course of the task performance. In contrast to an artifact, a tool is merely an object that supports performing a task. Such a tool can be substituted without changing the task's intention (Sinnig 2004).
4. Within our framework, several notations have been used including XUL, Unified Modeling Language (UML) as well as Concurrent Task Tree (CTT). We feel it is beyond the scope of this work to deal with these notations in any substantive detail. Readers unfamiliar with these notations can find more details at (XUL 2014), (OMG 2009) and CTT Environment (CTTE) (Paternò 2005).

3.3.2 PD-MBUI Major Models

Figure 3.2 depicts the models considered in this book within our approach. We have selected these models based on the fact that they have been largely cited in scientific literature (Puerta 1997; Schlungbaum 1996; Trætteberg 2002). We put in some effort to define them in such a way that they do not overleap and that the flow of transformation is also clearly stated, as detailed in Fig. 3.1. This is fundamental in order to know precisely which type of pattern is needed and when it applies.

The process of constructing these variety of models distinguishes three major phases.

The starting point of phase I is the domain model. This model encapsulates the important entities of an application domain together with their attributes, methods, and relationships (Schlungbaum 1996). Within the scope of UI development, it defines the objects and functionalities accessed by the user via the interface. Such a model is generally developed using the information collected during the business and functional requirements stage. Two other models are then derived from this model: user and task models.

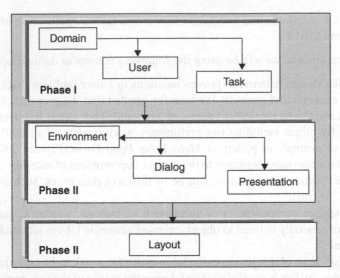

Fig. 3.2 Models and their relationships in the PD-MBUI framework

The user model captures the essence of the user's static and dynamic characteristics. Modeling the user's background knowledge is useful when personalizing the format of the information (e.g., using an appropriate language that is understood by the user). The task model specifies what the user does or wants to do, and why. It describes, an abstract meaning without any knowledge of the tasks that users perform while using the application, as well as how the tasks are interrelated. In simple terms, it captures the user tasks and system behavior with respect to the task set. Beside natural language, notations such as Goals, Operators, Methods, and Selection rules (GOMS) and CTT are generally used to document task models. The task model is constructed in mutual relationship to the user model, representing the functional roles played by users when accomplishing tasks, as well as their individual perception of the tasks. The user model is also related to the domain since the user may require different views of the same data while performing a task. Moreover, a relationship must be formed between the domain model and the task model, because objects of the domain model may be needed in the form of artifacts and tools for task accomplishment.

The second stage starts with the development of the environment model. This model specifies the physical and organizational context of interaction (Trætteberg 2002). For example, in the case of a mobile user application, an environmental model would include variables such as the user's current location, the constraints and characteristics presented by this location, the current time and any trigger conditions specified or implied by virtue of the location type. This model also describes the various computer systems that may run a UI (Prasad 1996). The platform model describes the physical characteristics of the target platforms, such as the target devices' input and output capabilities. Based on this model and those developed in the first stage, the dialog and the presentation model can be developed.

The dialog model specifies when the end user can invoke functions and interaction media, when the end user can select or specify inputs, and when the computer can query the end user and present information (Puerta 1997). In particular, this model specifies the user commands, interaction techniques, interface responses, and command sequences permitted by the interface during user sessions. The presentation model describes the visual appearance of the user interface (Schlungbaum 1996). The presentation model exists at two levels of abstraction: the abstract and the concrete presentation model. The former provides an abstract view of a generic interface, which represents a corresponding task and dialog model.

In the last stage, the "Layout Model" is realized as a concrete instance of an interface. This model consists of a series of UI components that defines the visual layout of UI and the detailed dialogs for a specific platform and context of use. There may be many concrete instances of layout model that can be derived from a presentation and dialog model.

3.4 Examples of Patterns

3.4.1 HCI Patterns Taxonomy and Samples

Figure 3.3 portrays which types of patterns are used to construct and transform each type of model and how this happens in the model-driven engineering process.

The following are the major types of patterns we considered:

1. Task and feature patterns are used to describe hierarchically structured task fragments. These fragments can then be used as task building blocks for gradually building the envisioned task model.
2. Patterns for the dialog model are employed to help with grouping the tasks and to suggest sequences between dialog views.
3. Presentation patterns are applied to map complex tasks to a predefined set of interaction elements that were identified in the presentation model.
4. Layout patterns are utilized to establish certain styles or "floor plans" which are subsequently captured by the layout model.

The following Table 3.1 summarizes some of the considered patterns.

3.4.2 Patterns Instantiation and Application

In this book, we stated that patterns can be used as building blocks for different models throughout the UI development approach. For the construction of models,

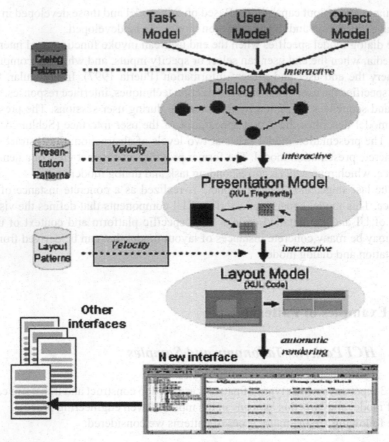

Fig. 3.3 PD-MUI framework revisited (putting it all together) *Patterns* as building blocks within a model based methodology

the following process, which is a part of the PD-MBUI, was proposed to instantiate and apply patterns:

1. **Identification**: A subset M' of the target model M is identified thus: $M' \supseteq M$. This relationship should reduce the domain size and help focus attention on a smaller, more pertinent subset for the next step.
2. **Selection**: An appropriate pattern P is selected to be applied to M'. By focusing on a subset of the domain, the designer can scan M' more effectively to identify potential areas that could be improved through patterns. This step is highly dependent on the experience and creativity of the designer.
3. **Adaptation**: A pattern is an abstraction that must be instantiated. Therefore, this step has the pattern P adjusted according to the context of use, resulting in the pattern instance S. In a top–down process, all variable parts are bound to specific values, which yield a concrete instance of the pattern.

Table 3.1 Pattern summary

Pattern name	Type	Problem
Browse	Task	The user needs to inspect an information set and navigate a linear ordered list of objects such as images or search results.
Dialog	Task	The user must be informed about something that requires attention. The user must make a decision that will have an impact on further execution of the application, or the user must confirm the execution of an irreversible action.
Find	Task	The user needs to find any kind of information provided by the application.
Login	Task	The user needs to be authenticated in order to access protected data and/or to perform authorized operations.
Multi-value input form (Paternò 2000)	Task	The user needs to enter a number of related values. These values can be of different data types, such as "date," "string" or "real."
Print object	Task	The user needs to view the details related to a particular information object
Search	Task	The user needs to extract a subset of data from a pool of information.
Wizard (Welie 2004)	Dialog	The user wants to achieve a single goal, but several consecutive decisions and actions must be carried out before the goal can be achieved.
Recursive activation (Paternò 2000)	Dialog	The user wants to activate and manipulate several instances of a dialog view.
Unambiguous format	Presentation	The user needs to enter data, but may be unfamiliar with the structure of the information and/or its syntax.
Form	Presentation	The user must provide structured textual information to the application. The data to be provided is logically related.
House style (Tidwell 2004)	Layout	Applications usually consist of several pages/windows. The user should have the impression that it all shares a consistent presentation and appears to belong together.

4. **Integration**: The pattern instance S is integrated into M' by connecting it to the other elements in the domain. This may require replacing, updating or otherwise modifying the other objects to produce a seamless piece of design.

Variables are used as placeholders for the context of use. During the process of pattern adaptation, these placeholders are replaced by concrete values representing the particular consequences of the current context of use.

Fig. 3.4 Interface of a
pattern

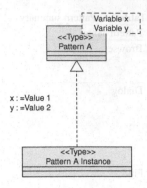

Figure 3.4 shows the interface of "Pattern A". The UML notation for parametric classes is used to convey that the pattern assumes two parameters (variables x and y). In order to instantiate the pattern, both variables must be assigned concrete values. In practical terms, the interface informs the user of the pattern that the values for variables x and y must be provided in order for the pattern to be used. In the figure, pattern A has been instantiated, resulting in "Pattern A Instance". In addition, UML stereotypes are used to signal the particular type (role) of the pattern.

Patterns are often implemented using other patterns, i.e., a pattern can compose of several subpatterns. This pattern–subpattern relationship, based on the concept of class aggregation, is presented in Fig. 3.3. Pattern A consists of the subpatterns B and C. If we place patterns in this kind of relationship, special attention must be given to the pattern variables. A variable defined at the super-pattern level can affect the variables used by the subpatterns.

In Fig. 3.5, variable x of pattern A affects the variables yy and zz of subpatterns B and C. During the process of pattern adaptation, variables yy and zz will be bound to the value of x. As such, we observe how modifying a high-level pattern can affect all subpatterns.

3.5 Examples of Models Construction Using Patterns

In previous sections of this book, it was shown how patterns can generally be applied to models and how they can be aggregated. This section provides an in-depth discussion of how different categories of patterns can be used together when constructing the task, dialog, presentation, and layout model.

3.5.1 Patterns in Task Modeling

Patterns for the task model describe generic reusable task fragments that can serve to establish the task model. In particular, instances of task patterns (*i.e.*, already

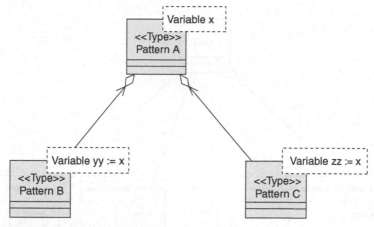

Fig. 3.5 Pattern aggregation

customized patterns) can be used as building blocks for the task model. Examples of such patterns for the task model include: *Find* something, *Buy* something, *Search for* something, *Login* to the system or *Fill out* an input form.

A typical example of a task pattern is *Search* (Gaffar et al. 2005). The pattern is suitable for interactive applications that manage considerable amounts of user-accessible data. The user wants to have fast access to a subset of this data.

As a solution, the pattern suggests giving the user the possibility to enter search queries. On the basis of these queries, a subset of the searchable data (*i.e.*, the result set) is calculated and displayed to the user. The *Multi-Value Input Pattern* (Paternò 2000; Sinnig 2004) may be used for the query input. After submission, the results of the search are presented to the user and then they can either be browsed (*Browse Pattern*; Sinnig 2004) or used as input for refining the search.

Figure 3.6 illustrates how the *Search* pattern is composed of the subpatterns *Multi-Value Input* and *Browse*, as well as of recursive references to itself (*Search*). It also demonstrates how the variables of each pattern are interrelated. The value of the "Object" variable of the *Search Pattern* will be used to assign the "Object" variable of the *Browse* and *Sub-Search Patterns*. In addition, a subset of the "Search" object attribute is used to determine the various "Input Fields" of the *Multi-Value Input Pattern*, which is in turn responsible for capturing the search query. During the adaptation process, variables of each pattern must be resolved in a top-down fashion and replaced by concrete values.

The suggested task structure of the *Search Pattern* is illustrated in Fig. 4.7. In order to apply and integrate the task structure, the pattern and all its subpatterns must be instantiated and customized to the current context of use (Fig. 3.7).

The top-down process of pattern adaptation can be greatly assisted by tools such as wizards. A wizard moves through the task pattern tree and prompts the user whenever it encounters an unresolved variable. The Sect. 4.6 introduces the Task

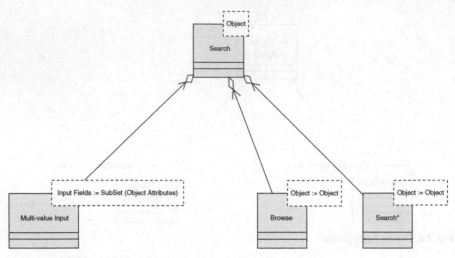

Fig. 3.6 Interface and composition of the *Search Pattern*

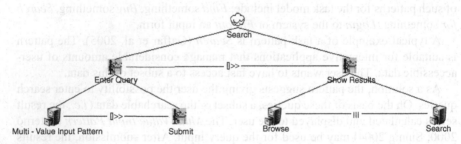

Fig. 3.7 Structure of the *Search Pattern*

Pattern Wizard, a tool that assists the user in selecting, adapting and integrating task and feature patterns.

3.5.2 Patterns in Dialog Modeling

Our framework's dialog model is defined by a so-called dialog graph. Formally speaking, the dialog graph consists of a set of vertices (dialog views) and edges (dialog transitions). Creating the dialog graph is a two-step process: first, related tasks are grouped together into dialog views. Second, transitions from one dialog to another, as well as trigger events are defined.

In order to foster establishing the dialog model, we believe that patterns can help with both grouping tasks to dialog views and establishing the transition between the various dialog views.

A typical dialog pattern is the *Recursive Activation Pattern* (Breedvelt et al. 1997). This pattern is used when the user wishes to activate and manipulate several instances of a dialog view. In practical terms, it suggests a dialog structure where,

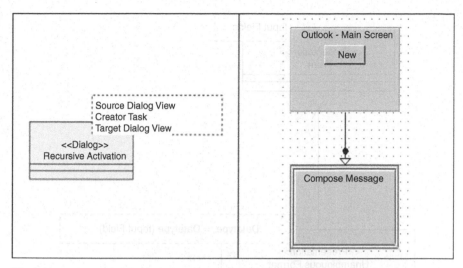

Fig. 3.8 Interface and "Microsoft Outlook" instance of the *Recursive Activation Pattern*

starting from a source dialog, a specific creator task can be used to instantiate a copy of the target dialog view. The pattern is applicable in many modern interfaces where several dialog views of the same type and functionality are concurrently accessible. A typical example of an application scenario is an e-mail program that supports editing several e-mails concurrently during a given session.

In the left pane of Fig. 3.8, we observe that in order to adapt (instantiate) the pattern, the source dialog view and the corresponding creator task, as well as the target dialog view must all be set. A specific instance of the pattern is shown in the right part of Fig. 3.8, simulating the navigational structure of Microsoft Outlook when composing a new message. For this particular example, the visual notation of a tool called the Dialog Graph Editor (Sinnig 2004) was used.

3.5.3 Patterns in Presentation Modeling

The abstract delineation of a user interface is determined in the presentation model through a defined set of abstract UI elements. Examples of such UI elements are Buttons, Lists or more complex aggregated elements such as trees or forms. Note that all interaction elements should be described in an abstract manner without reference to any particular interface components. Likewise, style attributes such as size, font, and color remain unset, pending definition by the layout model. Abstraction is a key to the success of presentation model as it frees the designers from unneeded details and allows for more efficient reuse on different platforms

Patterns for the presentation model can be applied when describing the abstract UI elements. However, they can be more effective when applied for defining and mapping complex tasks (such as advanced search) to a predefined set of interaction

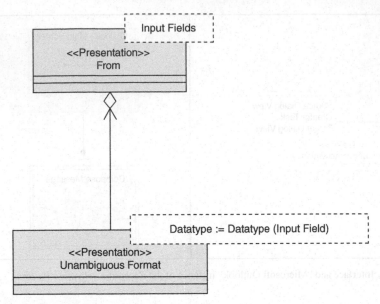

Fig. 3.9 Interface of the *Form Pattern*

elements. In this many-to-many interaction, patterns can provide insight into proven solutions ready to reuse.

One illustrative example of a presentation pattern is the *Form Pattern*. It is applicable when the user must provide the application with structural and logically related information. In Fig. 3.9, the interface of the *Form Pattern* is presented, indicating that the various Input Fields to be displayed are expected as parameters. It is also shown that the *Unambiguous Format Patterns* can be employed in order to implement the *Form Pattern*.

In particular, the *Unambiguous Format Pattern* is used to prevent the user from entering syntactically incorrect data. In conjunction with the *Form Pattern*, it determines which interaction elements will be displayed by the input form. XUL code will be produced for the most suitable interaction element, depending on the data type of the desired input as shown in Fig. 3.10. Three different instances of the *Unambiguous Format Pattern are presented*.

3.5.4   *Patterns in Layout Management Modeling*

In this step, the abstract UI elements of the presentation are physically positioned following an overall layout or floor plan, which yields the layout model. Furthermore, the visual appearance of each interaction element is specified by setting fonts, colors, and dimensions.

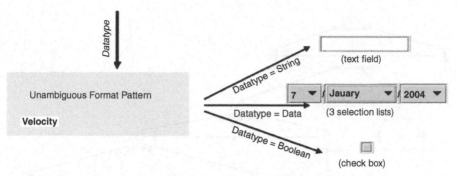

Fig. 3.10 The *Unambiguous Format Pattern* with three unique instances

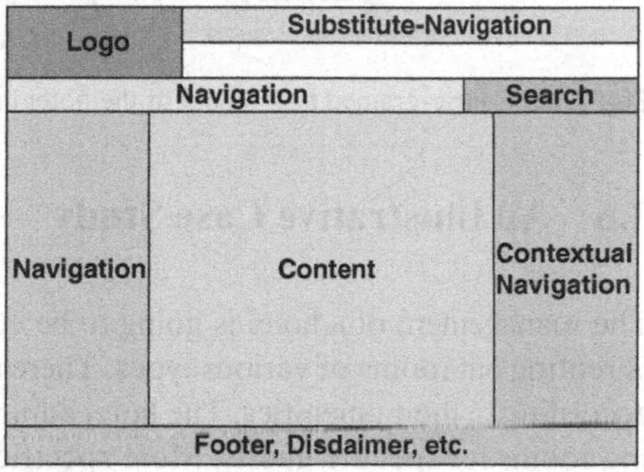

Fig. 3.11 Floor plan suggested by the *Portal Pattern*

Logo	Substitute-Navigation		
	Navigation		Search
Navigation	Content		Contextual Navigation
Footer, Disclaimer, etc.			

There are two different ways in which patterns can be employed when defining the layout model: (1) by providing a floor plan for the UI and (2) by setting the style attributes of the various widgets of the UI. The proposed solutions and the criteria of selecting between different designs depend—among other factors—on the context of use, nature of the application and satisfaction of the users. Aesthetic and human behavior aspects can complicate the design and make the final results unpredictable. Patterns come in handy as shortcuts to analyzing some of these considerations by offering solutions that have been used before with good results.

The layout planning consists of determining the composition of the UI by providing a floor plan. Examples of such patterns are the *Portal Pattern* (Welie 2004), *Card Stack* (Tidwell 2004), *Liquid Layout* (Tidwell 2004) and *Grid Layout* (Welie 2004). Figure 3.11 presents the floor plan suggested by the *Portal Pattern*, which is applicable for web-based UIs.

In the style planning, *Layout Patterns* are beneficial when the style attributes of the various widgets of the UI must be configured. For instance, the *House Style Pattern* suggests maintaining an overall look-and-feel for each page or dialog in order to mediate the impression that all pages share a consistent presentation and appear to belong together.

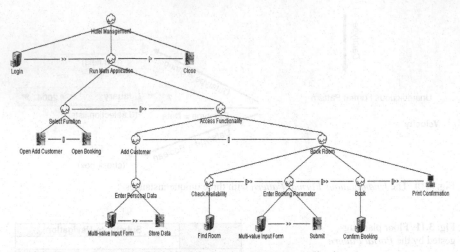

Fig. 3.12 Course-grained task model of the hotel management application

3.6   An Illustrative Case Study

The management of a hotel is going to be computerized. The hotel's main business is renting out rooms of various types. There are a total of 40 rooms available, priced according to their amenities. The hotel administration needs a tool capable of booking rooms for specific guests. More specifically, the application's main functionality consists of adding a guest to the internal database and booking an available room for a registered guest. Moreover, only certified guests have access to the main functionality of the program. Eventually, the application would be running on windows, icons, menus, pointer (WIMP)-based systems.

Note that only a simplified version of the hotel management system will be developed. The application and corresponding models will not be tailored to the different platform and user roles. The main purpose of the example is to show that MBUI design consists of a series of model transformations, in which mappings from the abstract to the concrete models must be specified. Furthermore, it will be shown how patterns are used to establish the various models, as well as to transform one model into another. A summary of all patterns used in this article can be found in Table 4.2. For a more detailed description, refer to (Sinnig 2004).

3.6.1   The Task Model

Figure 3.12 depicts the coarse-grained task structure of the envisioned hotel management application. Only high-level tasks and their relationships are portrayed. An impression about the overall structure and behavior of the applications is given. The structure provided is relatively unique for a hotel management application; the

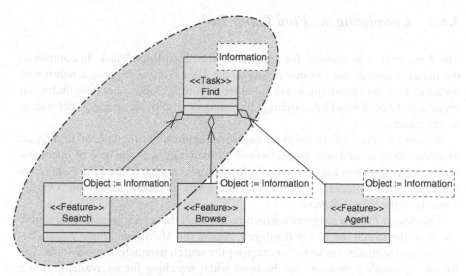

Fig. 3.13 Interface and structure of the *Find Pattern*

concrete "realization" of the high-level tasks has been omitted. The Pattern Task symbol is used as a placeholder representing the suppressed task fragments.

A large part of many interactive applications can be developed from a fixed set of reusable components. If we decompose the application far enough, we will encounter these components. In the case of the task model, the more the high-level tasks are decomposed, the easier the reusable task structures (that have been gained or captured from other projects or applications) can be employed. In our case, these reusable task structures are documented in the form of patterns. This approach ensures an even greater degree of reuse, since each pattern can be adapted to the current context of use.

The main characteristics of the envisioned hotel management application, modeled by the task structure of Fig. 3.13, can be outlined as follows:

Accessing the application's main functionality requires logging in to the system (the login task enables the management task). The key features are "adding a guest" by entering the guest's personal information and "booking a hotel room" for a specific guest. Both tasks can be performed in any order. The booking process consists of four consecutively performed tasks (related through "Enabling with Information Exchange" operators):

1. Locating an available room.
2. Assigning the room to a guest.
3. Confirming the booking.
4. Printing a confirmation.

As shown in Fig. 3.12, the *Login, Multi-Value Input Form, Find* and *Dialog* patterns can be used in order to complete the task model at the lower levels. In the next section, the application of the *Find Pattern* will be described in greater detail.

3.6.2   Completing the Find Room Task

The *Find Pattern* is essential for completing the "Find Room" task. In contrast to the patterns already used in this example, the *Find Pattern* suggests a number of options rather than providing a task structure. Figure 3.13 illustrates how finding an object can be performed by searching, browsing or employing an agent, depending on the pattern.

Within the scope of the hotel management application, the task of finding an available room should only be performed by searching with the help of query parameters. As shown in Fig. 3.13, the "Information" variable of the *Find Pattern* (in this case, a placeholder for the "Hotel Room" value) is used to assign the "Object" variable of the *Search Pattern*.

The *Search Pattern* suggests a structure in which the search queries are entered, and then the search results are displayed. Again, the *Multi-Value Input Form Pattern* is used to model the tasks for entering the search parameters into a form. The following search parameters can be used when searching for an available room: "Arrival Date," "Departure Date," "Non-Smoking," "Double/Single," and "Room Type." After submitting the search queries, the search results (*i.e.*, the available hotel rooms) can be manually scanned using the *Browse Pattern* or, based on the search results; a refinement search can be performed by employing the *Search Pattern* recursively. For the scope of this case study, refinement searches are unnecessary, and the search results should only be browsed.

According to the *Browse Pattern,* the list of objects (the hotel rooms) is printed, after which it can be interactively browsed as an option. Details of the hotel room can be viewed by selecting it. The *Print Object Pattern* is used to print out object's properties. It suggests using application tasks to print the object values that can be directly or indirectly derived from the object's attributes. In the case of the hotel management application, the following hotel room attributes should be printed: "Room Number," "Smoking/Non-Smoking," "Double/Single," "Room Type," and "Available Until."

After adapting all patterns to suit the hotel management application, the task structure displayed in Fig. 3.14 is derived. Note that the "Make Decision" task has been added manually, without pattern support.

A first draft of the envisioned task model can be derived once all patterns have been adapted and instantiated. At this point, first evaluations can be carried out. For instance, the XUL-Task-Simulator (Sinnig 2004) can be used to simulate and animate possible scenarios. Results of the evaluation indicate that preliminary modifications and improvements of the task model are possible.

3.6.3   Designing the Dialog Structure

After establishing the task model for our example application, the dialog models can be interactively derived. In particular, the various tasks are grouped to dialog

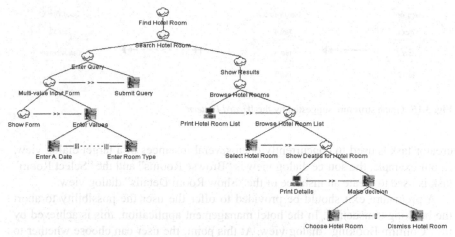

Fig. 3.14 Concrete Task Structure Delivered by the *Find Pattern*

views, then transitions are defined between the various dialog views. Since the desired target platform of the hotel management application is a WIMP-based system, a dialog view will subsequently implemented as either a window or a container in a complex window.

When designing the dialog graph for the hotel management application, we designated the login dialog view as both modal and the start-up dialog. After executing Submit, the "Main Menu" dialog will be opened. As such, a sequential transition between both dialog views is defined. From the main menu, either the "Add Guest" or "Search Applicable Room" dialog view can be opened by a sequential transition. After completing the "Add Guest" dialog view, the main menu will be reopened. For this reason, a sequential transition to the "Main Menu," initiated by the "Store Data" task, must be defined.

The application's booking functionality consists of a series of dialog views that must be completed sequentially. The *Wizard* dialog pattern emerges as the best choice for implementation. It suggests a dialog structure where a set of dialog views is arranged sequentially and the "last" task of each dialog view initiates the transition to the following dialog view. Figure 3.15 depicts the *Wizard Pattern's* suggested graph structure.

After applying the *Wizard Pattern*, the dialog views "Search Applicable Room," "Browse Results," "Show Details," "Enter Booking Parameters," "Confirm Booking," and "Print Confirmation" are connected by sequential transitions.

However, the sequential structure of the booking process must be slightly modified in order to enable the user to view the details of multiple rooms at the same time. Specifically, this behavior should be modeled using the *Recursive Activation* dialog pattern. This pattern is used when the user wishes to activate and manipulate several instances of a dialog view. In this particular case, the user will be able to activate and access several instances of the "Show Room Details" dialog view. This pattern suggests the following task structure: starting from a source dialog view, a

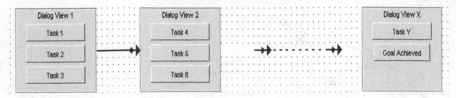

Fig. 3.15 Graph structure suggested by the *Wizard Pattern*

creator task is used to concurrently open several instances of a target dialog view. In our example, the source dialog view is "Browse Rooms" and the "Select Room" task is used to create an instance of the "Show Room Details" dialog view.

A premature exit should be provided to offer the user the possibility to abort the booking transaction. In the hotel management application, this is achieved by the "Confirm Booking" dialog view. At this point, the user can choose whether to proceed with the booking or to abort the transaction. Another sequential transition must therefore be defined: one which is initiated by the "Select Cancel Booking" tasks and leads back to the main menu. The hotel management application's complete dialog graph, as visualized by the Dialog Graph Editor is depicted in Fig. 3.16.

The next step is to evaluate the defined dialog graph. The dialog graph can be animated using the Dialog Graph Editor to generate a preliminary abstract prototype of the user interface. It is possible to dynamically navigate through the dialog views by executing the corresponding tasks. This abstract prototype simulates the final interface's navigational behavior. It supports communication between users and software developers: design decisions are transparently intuitive to the user, and stakeholders are able to experiment with a dynamic system.

3.6.4 Defining the Presentation and Layout Model

In order to define the presentation model for our example, the grouped tasks of each dialog view are associated with a set of interaction elements, among them forms, buttons, and lists. Style attributes such as size, font, and color remain unset and will be defined by the layout model.

A significant part of the user's tasks while using the application revolves around providing structured textual information. This information can usually be split into logically related data chunks. At this point, the *Form Presentation Pattern*, which handles this exact issue, can be applied. It suggests using a form for each related data chunk, populated with the elements needed to enter the data. Moreover, the pattern refers to the *Unambiguous Format Pattern*, in conjunction with which it can be employed.

The purpose of the *Unambiguous Format Pattern* is to prevent the user from entering syntactically incorrect data. Drawing on information from the business object model, it is able to determine the most suitable input element. In other words, depending on the domain of the object to be entered, the instance of the pattern

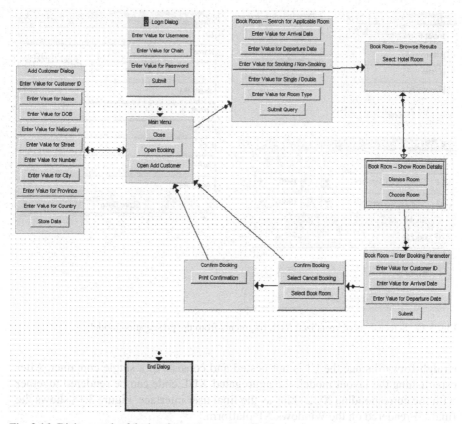

Fig. 3.16 Dialog graph of the hotel management application

provides input interaction elements chosen in such a way that the user cannot enter syntactically incorrect data.

Figure 3.17 shows the windows prototype interfaces rendered from the XUL fragments of the hotel management application's presentation model for the "Login," "Main Menu," "Add Guest," and "Find Room" dialog views. All widgets and UI components are visually arranged according to the default style.

In the layout model, the style attributes that have not yet been defined are set in keeping with the hotel management application's standards. According to the *House Style Pattern* (which is applicable here), colors, fonts, and layouts should be chosen so that the user has the impression that all windows of the application share a consistent presentation and appear to belong together. Cascading style sheets have been used to control the visual appearance of the interface. In addition, to assist the user when working with the application, meaningful labels have been provided. The *Labeling Layout Pattern* suggests adding labels for each interaction element. Using the grid format, the labels are aligned to the left of the interaction element.

The layout model determines how the loosely connected XUL fragments are aggregated according to an overall floor plan. In the case of this example, this is fairly

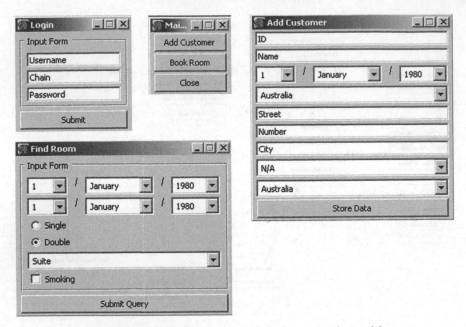

Fig. 3.17 Screenshots of visualized XUL fragments from the presentation model

straightforward since the UI is not nested and consists of a single container. After establishing the layout model, the aggregated XUL code can be rendered together with the corresponding XUL skins as the final user interface. Figure 3.18 shows the final UI rendered on the Windows XP platform.

3.7   Key Contributions of This Chapter

In this chapter, we demonstrated how patterns can be delivered and applied within be MBUI development approaches. Within our proposed framework PD-MBUI, patterns were introduced to overcome the lack of reuse in model construction and transformation. This represents one of the major limitations of the existing MBUI development frameworks. In particular, we illustrated how different kinds of patterns can be used as building blocks for the establishment of task, dialog, presentation, and layout model. In order to foster reuse, we proposed a general process of pattern application, in which patterns are seen as abstractions that must be instantiated. In addition, we described an interface for combining patterns and a possible model-based formalization. The applicability of the proposed pattern-driven model-based development approach has been demonstrated through a comprehensive case study. Furthermore, we introduced the Task—Pattern Wizard tool for using, selecting, adapting, and applying patterns.

A major contribution of this work is the use of patterns to support model reuse in the construction of specific models and their transformations. Traditionally, patterns

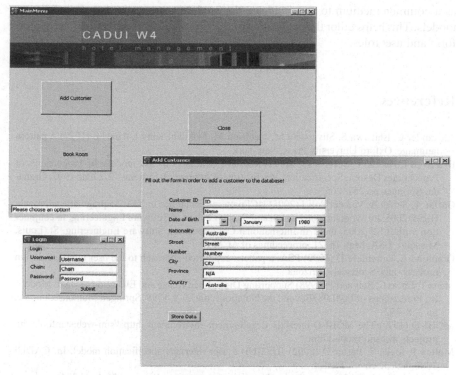

Fig. 3.18 Screenshots from the hotel management application

are encapsulations of a solution to a common problem. In this research, we extended the pattern concept by providing an interface for patterns in order to combine them. In this vein, we proposed the general process of pattern application, in which patterns can be customized for a given context of use. We then transferred the pattern concept to the domain of MBUI development. In order to foster reuse and avoid reinventing the wheel, we demonstrated how task, dialog, presentation, and layout patterns can be used as building blocks when creating the corresponding models, which are the core constituents of our development approach.

In order to demonstrate the applicability of our approach, we developed a UI prototype for a hotel management application. In this, elaborate case study patterns were identified and applied for each of the models that were used during development. The main purpose of the example is to show that MBUI development consists of a series of model transformations, in which mappings from the abstract to the concrete models must be specified and—more importantly—automatically supported by tools.

We are currently expanding the modeling concept into an integrated pattern environment (IPE), which integrates this and other tools into a generalized pattern driven development environment that is independent of platform and programming languages. The transformation between models is automated by the use of XML as a common medium to communicate the modeling semantics between different models. This helps tailor the application and corresponding models to different platform and user roles.

References

Alexander C, Ishikawa S, Silverstein M, Jacobson M, Fiskdahl-King I, Angel S (1977) A pattern language. Oxford University Press, New York

Breedvelt I, Paternò F, Severiins C (1997) Reusable structures in task models. In: Proceedings of Proceedings Design, Specification, Verification of Interactive Systems '97, June 1997, Granada, Springer, pp 251–265

Gaffar A, Seffah A, Van der Poll J (2005) HCI patterns semantics in XML: a pragmatic approach, HSSE 2005. In: Workshop on Human and Social Factors of Software Engineering, in conjunction with ICSE 2005, the 27th International Conference on Software Engineering, St. Louis, Missouri, USA, May 15–21, proceedings of ACM

Granlund A, Lafreniere D (1999) PSA: a pattern-supported approach to the user interface design process, July, Scottsdale, Arizona

Mens T, Lucas C, Steyaert P (1998) Supporting Disciplined Reuse and Evolution of UML Models. In: Proceedings of UML98: Beyond the Notation, June 3–4, 1998, Springer, Mulhouse, France, pp 378–392

MOBI-D (1999) The MOBI-D interface development environment. http://smi-web.stanford.edu/projects/mecano/mobi-d.htm

Molina P, Meliá S, Pastor O (2002) JUST-UI: a user interface specification model. In: CADUI 2002, Valenciennes, France

OliverNova (2004) CARE technologies. http://www.care-t.com. Accessed 20 April 2015

OMG (2009) Unified modeling language. http://www.omg.org/spec/UML/index.htm. Accessed 20 April 2015

Paternò F (2000) Model-based design and evaluation of interactive applications. Springer, London

Paternò F (2005) Model-based tools for pervasive usability. Interact Comput 17(3):291–315

Prasad S (1996) Models for mobile computing agents. Special Issue: position statements on strategic research directions in computing research. ACM Computing Survey 28(4), Dec 1996

Puerta A (1997) A model-based interface development environment. IEEE Software 14(1997):41–47

Schlungbaum E (1996) Model-based user interface software tools—current state of declarative models. Technical Report 96–30. Graphics, Visualization and Usability Center Georgia Institute of Technology. (Georgia). USA.

Sinnig D (2004) The complicity of patterns and Model-Based UI Development. Master of Computer Science, Montreal, Concordia University, p 148

TERESA (2004) Transformation environment for interactive systems representations. http://giove.cnuce.cnr.it/teresa.html. Accessed 20 April 2015

Tidwell J (2004) UI patterns and techniques. http://time-tripper.com/uipatterns/index.php

Trætteberg H (2002) Model-based user interface design in computer and information sciences. Norwegian University of Science and Technology, Trondheim

Trætteberg H (2004) Integrating dialog modelling and application development. In: Making Model-based UI Design Practical: Usable and Open Methods and Tools: A Workshop at IUI 2004, January, Madeira, Portugal

Welie M (2004) Patterns in interaction design. http://www.welie.com. Accessed 20 April 2015

XUL (2014) https://developer.mozilla.org/en-US/docs/Mozilla/Tech/XUL. Accessed 20 April 2015

Chapter 4
Adding Usability Quality Attributes into Interactive Systems Architecture: A Pattern-Based Approach

Abstract Traditional interactive system architectures such as MVC (Model, View, Controller) and PAC (Presentation, Abstraction and Control) decompose the system into subsystems that are relatively independent, thereby allowing the design work to be partitioned between the user interfaces (UI) and underlying functionalities. Such architectures also extend the independence assumption to usability, approaching the design of the UI as a subsystem that can be designed and tested independently from the underlying functionality. This Cartesian dichotomy can be dangerous, as functionalities buried in the application's logic can sometimes affect the usability of the system. Likewise, in a design process where usability aspects are incorporated early on, they can affect the architecture of the system.

Our investigations model the relationships between internal software attributes and externally visible usability factors. We propose a pattern approach for modeling these relationships and for providing an effective solution. We conclude by discussing how these enhanced patterns with usability measures can lead to development approach for improving interactive system architectures, and how these patterns can support the integration of usability in the software design process.

4.1 Software Architecture—A Definition

Software architecture is a fundamental design concept of any system, embodied in its components, their relationships to each other, and the principles governing its design, development, and evolution (ANSI/IEEE 1471–2000). In addition, it encapsulates the fundamental entities and properties of the application that generally ensure the quality of application including reliability, robustness, and reusability. However, usability that is more and more recognized as important quality factor has been neglected in these architectural models (ISO 9126 2003).

In the field of human–computer interaction (HCI), interactive systems architectures of the 1980s and 1990s such as MVC (Model, View, Controller) and PAC (Presentation, Abstraction and Control) are based on the principle of separating the core functionality from the UI. The functionality is what the software actually does and what data it processes, thereby offering behavior that can be exploited to

© Springer International Publishing Switzerland 2015

A. Seffah, *Patterns of HCI Design and HCI Design of Patterns,*
Human-Computer Interaction Series, DOI 10.1007/978-3-319-15687-3_4

achieve some user needs. The UI defines how the functionality is presented to end-users and how the users interact with it. The underlying assumption is that usability, the ultimate quality factor, is primarily a property of the UI. Therefore, separating the UI from the application's logic makes it easy to modify, adapt, or customize the interface after user testing. Unfortunately, this assumption does not ensure the usability of the system as a whole.

We now realize that system features can have an impact on the usability of the system, even if they are logically independent from the UI and not necessarily visible to the user. For example, Bass observed that even if the presentation of a system is well designed, the usability of a system can be greatly compromised if the underlying architecture and designs do not have the proper provisions for user concerns (Bass et al. 2001). We propose that the software architecture should define not only the technical issues needed to develop and implement the functionality, but also dialogs with the users.

At the core of our vision are those invisible components that are the implementations of functionality can affect usability. By invisible components, we mean precisely any software entity that does not have visible cues on the presentation layer. They can be an operation, data, or a structural attribute of the software. Examples of such phenomena where invisible component affects usability are commonplace in database modeling. Queries that were not anticipated by the modeler, or that turn out to be more frequent than expected, can take forever to complete because the logical data model (or even the physical data model) is inappropriate. Clientserver and distributed computer architectures are also particularly prone to usability problems stemming from their "invisible" components.

Another example came from the Web where designers of distributed applications with web browser-based UI are often faced with these concerns. They must carefully weigh what part of the application logic will reside on the client side and what part will be on the server side in order to achieve an appropriate level of usability. User feedback information, such as application status and error messages, must be carefully designed and exchanged between the client and server part of the application, anticipating response time of each component, error conditions and exception handling, and the variability of the computing environment. Sometimes, the web UI becomes crippled by the constraints imposed by these invisible components because the appropriate and required style of interactions is too difficult to implement.

Like other authors (Bass et al. 2001; Folmer et al. 2003), we argue that both software developers implementing the system's features and usability engineers in charge of designing the user interfaces should be aware of the importance of this intimate relationship between the way that the features are implemented and the user interfaces. This relationship can inform architecture design for usability. As discussed in this chapter, with the help of patterns that incorporate the attributes that quantify usability, this relationship can help to integrate the usability concerns in software architecture while ensuring the usability of the product. We will identify scenarios where invisible components of an interactive application will impact on usability; we will also propose solutions to each scenario. The solutions are presented in the form of patterns. Beyond proposing a list of patterns to solve specific problems, we will detail a measurement-oriented framework for studying and integrating usability concerns in interactive software architecture via patterns and usability measures.

4.2 Drawbacks and Fundamentals

The concept of separating the view from the real object is relatively old. It reflects the fundamental need of reducing system complexity while improving its scalability, reusability, and other quality concerns. In the field of database engineering, a clear separation between table and view help achieve many goals (Gaffar 2001):

- Increase security by masking classified information in tables from the views presented to unauthorized users.
- Reduce redundancy by storing atomic, normalized data in efficiently designed tables while displaying them in different views according to users' needs.
- Increase system flexibility by allowing the addition of new views as needed without the need to change the actual tables which is a costly and risky task.
- Increase data integrity by limiting the changes to normalized tables and simply updating the views as needed.

This principle of concerns separation is so deeply rooted in database engineering that it is supported not only at the design level but also at the language level. Most query languages offer direct manipulation to creating and manipulating tables and views separately.

The same need for separation has been identified in software interfaces. Large number of architectures for interactive systems have been proposed, e.g., Seeheim model, MVC, Arch/Slinky, Presentation PAC, PAC-Amadeus and Model-View-Presenter (MVP) (Bass et al. 1998). Most of these architectures distinguish three main components: (1) abstraction or model; (2) control or dialog; and (3) presentation. The model contains functionality of the software. The view provides graphical user interface (GUI) components for a model. It gets the values that it displays by querying or receiving notification from the model of which it is a view. A model can have several views. When a user manipulates a view of a model, the view informs a controller of the desired change. Figure 4.1 summarizes the role of each one of these three components for an MVC-based application.

The motivation behind these architecture models is to improve, among others, the adaptability, portability, and complexity concerns. However, even if the principle of separating interactive software in components has its design merits, it can be the source of serious adaptability and usability problems in software that provides fast, frequent, and intensive semantic feedback. The communication between the view and the model makes the software system highly coupled and complex.

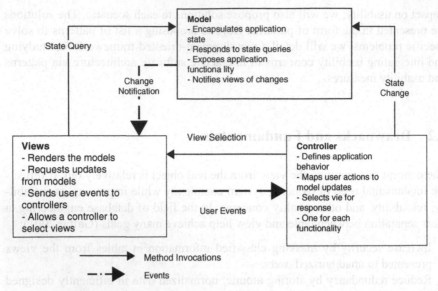

Fig. 4.1 The separation of concerns in the MVC architecture

Design patterns such as the observer pattern (Gamma et al. 1995) have emerged to reduce this complexity, but they do not acknowledge the presence of dependencies between the model and the views (Gamma et al. 1993).

In general, these architectures lack provisions for integrating usability in the design of the model or abstraction components. For example, Bass et al. (2001) identified specific connections between the aspects of usability (such as the ability to "undo") and the model response (processed by an event-handler routine).

4.3 A Pattern-Based Integration of Usability in Architecture

To quantify and model this intimate relationship that exists between the model and the interface, we proposed the following methodological approach to (Fig. 4.2):

1. Identify and categorize typical design scenarios that illustrate how invisible components and their intrinsic quality properties might affect the usability and UI components. Samples of the scenarios we identified are detailed in Sect. 4.4.
2. Detail each scenario while specifying the cause/effect relationship between the measures that quantify the quality of an invisible software entity and usability factors such as efficiency, effectiveness, and satisfaction. As it will be discussed in Sect. 5.5, we have been using an enhanced version of ISO 9126 quality model and the related measures (Seffah et al. 2003).

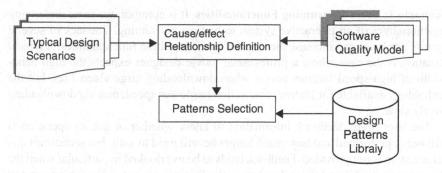

Fig. 4.2 Proposed methodological framework

3. Identify and select design patterns, ones that can solve the problem described in similar scenarios. Some patterns we proposed are detailed in Sect. 4.5. However, the detailed description of the whole library of patterns and the related pattern-oriented design approach goes beyond the scope of this chapter. The interested reader can find more details in Sinnig (2004); Gaffar (2005).
4. Incorporate these patterns to enhance existing architectural models such as MVC. An example is given in Sect. 4.7.

4.4 Identifying and Categorizing Typical Scenarios

The first step in our approach for achieving usability via software architecture and patterns is to identify typical situations that illustrate how invisible components of the model might affect usability. Each typical situation is documented using a scenario. Scenarios are widely used in HCI and software engineering (Carroll 2000). Scenarios can improve communication between user interface specialists and software engineers who design invisible components—this communication is essential in our approach to patterns. In this context, we define a scenario as a narrative story written in natural language that describes a usability problem (effect) and that relates the source of this problem to an invisible software entity (cause). The scenario establishes the relationship between internal software attributes that are used to measure the quality of the invisible software entity and the external usability factors that we use for assessing the ease of use of the software systems.

The following are some typical scenarios we extracted from our empirical studies and from a literature review. Other researchers also proposed other scenarios (Bass et al. 2001). The goal of our research is not to build an exhaustive list of scenarios, but rather to propose a methodological framework for identifying such scenarios and to define patterns that can be used by developers to solve such problems. The scenarios are therefore intended as illustrative examples.

Scenario 1: Time-Consuming Functionalities It is common for some underlying functionalities of an interactive system to be time consuming. The lack of several quality attributes can increase the time for executing these functionalities. A typical situation is the case where a professional movie designer expects the high bandwidth of high-speed Internet access when downloading large video files, but the technology available for Internet connection has lower speed, making downloading overly slow.

The user needs feedback information to know whether or not an operation is still being performed and how much longer he will need to wait, but sometimes this information is not provided. Feedback tends to be overlooked in particular when the designers of the UI and those developing the features are not in the same team and that there is a lack of communication between them.

Scenario 2: Updating the Interface When the Model Changes Its State Usability guidelines recommend helping users understand a set of related data by allowing them to visualize the data from different points of view. A typical method is to provide graphical and textual representations of the same underlying data model.

Whenever the data model changes, the underlying model should update the graphical and the textual representations. Two main techniques to deal with this issue are *polling*—where interfaces are designed to poll the system periodically for changes, and *broadcasting*—where the system notifies the interfaces of new changes. Depending on the nature and rate of changes, the cost of notification, and the overall context of use, designers choose an optimal updating technique, and select the rate of polling or broadcasting if applicable. In certain cases, the system might not be designed to automatically update all views when one view changes. This can result in inconsistent views that can in turn increase the user's memory load, frustration, and errors.

Scenario 3: Performing Multiple Functionalities Using a Single Control It is easier and more straightforward to use a dedicated control for each functionality and in particular for critical functions, even at the expense of more buttons and menus. This is the current practice in much standard functionality like *File Save*, *Save As*, and *Print* options. However, for complex domain-specific functionality, this is not always the case. When a single control performs multiple operations, it requires a complex menu structure and choice of modes, which increases the likelihood of mode errors and other usability problems.

Unfortunately, there is a design trade-off between simplicity in appearance and simplicity in use. Aggregating several related functionalities under one control or in one procedure makes it easier for users to find and use them in one "click," and offer a lower number of total controls, increasing the learnability of the system. This is a dangerous design trap as it clearly limits the flexibility of interacting with the system and the effectiveness of accomplishing unforeseen complex tasks. Alas, consumers (and organizations) make purchase decisions based on appearance first, so this is a fundamental conflict (Norman 2002).

Scenario 4: Invisible Entities Keep the User Informed We know that providing the user with an unclear, ambiguous, or inconsistent representation of the system's modes and states can compromise the user's ability to diagnose and correct failures, errors, and hazards, or even simply interact with the system. This can happen when a system functionality allows the user to visualize information that competes or conflicts with currently or previously displayed information in other views. A well-known example is when a user opens a Microsoft explorer window to navigate the file system and the available drives on the computer, and then adds a USB memory stick (external storage device) to the system. Depending on the version of the software, the user may not be able to see the new addition in current explorer window at all, and they may have to open a new explorer window.

In other cases, they might not see it in the main window, but can see it under "My Computer" within the main window, which is an inconsistency in displaying the system state. In older systems that are batched up to support this new technology, the user can eject the added USB storage device but it remains displayed in the explorer window, even if it is no more functional. All these cases vary by the version of the operating system, and are especially seen in older versions where "true plug and play" feature was not available. This feature is indeed challenging to implement and requires modifications to the file explorer software to dynamically detect the system state and consistently refresh user's views. It is even more challenging to modify older versions by new batches to accommodate this feature. Without going into technical details, we can see the intricate relationship between the interface and the underlying system, and the confusion the inexperienced users might go through in these situations.

To avoid such situations, it is important for the functionality developers to accurately communicate the system's modes and states to the user interface designer. Ignoring this informative feedback can lead to users making wrong assumptions that may lead to inefficient or incorrect interaction. User interface designers should inform the developers about all the tangible consequences related to the states and modes of the systems.

Scenario 5: Providing Error Diagnostics When Features Crash When a feature failure occurs due for example to exception handling, the interface sometimes provides unhelpful error diagnostics to the user.

The user should be notified of the state that the system is currently in and the level of urgency with which the user must act. The system feature should help the user to recognize potential hazards and return the system from a potentially hazardous state to a safe state. Messages should be provided in a constructive and correct manner that helps restore the system to a safe state.

Scenario 6: Technical Constraints on Dynamic Interface Behavior Particularly in web-based transactional systems, technical and logistic constraints can severely limit dynamic behavior of the interface within a highly interactive page. It can therefore be difficult or impossible to design elements that automatically update as a result of an action elsewhere on the same page. For example, in a series of dependent drop-down lists "Country," "Province," and "City," it may be challenging to automatically update "Province" as a function of the "Country" selection without referring back to the server after each selection to download the next dependant list. The complexity increases when combined with business rules and restrictions. For example in an e-banking system, a user who transfers money from her checking account to pay her credit card of the same bank can see the new balance on the checking account immediately but keep seeing the old credit card balance without update.

While it might look like an interface problem and the user might become upset when seeing the money deducted from the checking account but not added to the credit card, the fact might be that the bank policy explicitly prevents displaying credit card account updated until they are manually verified; within 36 h. A perfectly correct interface would still display this inconsistency for the next 36 h. A usable interface would be aware of some business rules and hence of this potential inconvenience. The UI (client side) would simply notify the user of the reason, saving her a lot of frustration, especially when many users are weary of technology glitches or have less trust on web-based transactions than on teller-based interactions.

These technical constraints against dynamism are often imposed in web-based client-server contexts due to the dictum that the business rules must be separate from the UI. Dynamic interface behavior of an interactive system can require the UI to have a degree of intelligence that incorporates certain business rules, which conflicts with the "separate layers" dictum. In few cases, the alternative is for the client to call the server more frequently to refresh the page dynamically, but architects tend to avoid this approach because of the presumed extra demand on bandwidth. In other cases, the only alternative is for the client to call or visit the bank to inquire about the allegedly missing money. We can see that a usable interface can be much more useful.

There is no easy solution to this problem. The most important principle in this situation is to analyze user needs relating to dynamism before making technology decisions that could have an impact on dynamism. Transactional systems often require considerable dynamism, whereas purely informational systems can often get by without dynamism in the UI. If it is unacceptable for business rules to immediately incorporate electronic transactional changes (as one example), which will have an impact on the interface behavior, then the interface should be aware of this business rule. It would help to incorporate some business rules into the client side. In other cases, business rules are confidential and cannot be incorporated in client interfaces, reducing the usability of interface. When fully dynamic behavior is not possible, it would help to increase the network bandwidth to better support pseudo-dynamic behavior, involving more frequent page refreshes through calls to the server.

The preceding scenarios are used as an illustrative sample. In total, we have identified more than 24 scenarios. Len Bass also described a list of 26 scenarios, some of which were a source of inspiration for our work. Providing an exhaustive list of scenarios is certainly useful from the industry perspective. However, our goal for this research is to better understand and validate how software features affect usability in general and as such our focus is to model the scenarios in term of a cause/effect relationship. This relationship connects the quality attributes of invisible components with recognized usability factors. Section 5.6 details this perspective.

4.5 From Scenario to Design Patterns

As defined in the previous section, a design scenario illustrates a category of problem that may occur in different situations. Here, we look at solutions to these problems while introducing patterns as vehicle for representing the problem, the situation, and the solution in an integrative manner. Each design pattern is defined as a solution to the problem described in a scenario. Within our methodological approach, we have been considering two types of patterns:

- **System Design Patterns**. The aim of these design patterns is to propose software designs and architectures for building portable, modifiable, and extensible interactive systems. A classical pattern of this category is the observer that acts as a broker between the UI (views) and the model (Gamma et al. 1995). When the observers receive notification that the model has changed, they can update themselves. This pattern provides a basic solution to the problem described in scenario 3 in Sect. 4.4;
- **Interaction Design Patterns**, Defined at the level of GUI. These are proven user experience patterns and solutions to common usability problems. A number of pattern languages have been developed over the last few years (Tidwell 1997; Welie 1999).

We believe that these two categories of patterns need to be applied and combined in order to provide an integrated design framework to problems described in our scenarios. System design patterns, widely used by software engineers, are a top-down design approach that organizes the internal structure of the software systems. Interaction design patterns, promoted by human–computer interaction practitioners, are used as a bottom-up design approach for structuring the UI.

To illustrate how these diverse system and interaction patterns can be combined to provide comprehensive solutions, in the following sections we describe our five scenarios using interaction and design patterns. Although a number of de facto standards have emerged to document patterns, we use a simple description with the following format:

- "Name" is a unique identifier.
- "Context" refers to a recurring set of situations in which the pattern applies.
- "Force": The notion of force generalizes the kind of criteria that we use to justify designs and implementations. For example, in a straightforward manner, simple study of functionality, the main force to be resolved is efficiency (resources complexity) or effectiveness (task complexity). However, patterns deal with the larger, harder to measure and conflicting sets of goals and constraints encountered in the design of every component of the interactive system.
- "Problem" refers to a set of constraints and limitations to be overcome by the pattern solution.
- "Solution" refers to a canonical design form or design rule that someone can apply to resolve these problems.

- "Resulting context" is the resulting environment, situation, or interrelated conditions. Again, in a simple system this can be easily predictable, while in complex interactive system it can be hard to find out in a deterministic way.
- "Effects of invisible components on usability" which defines the relationship between the software quality attributes and usability factors.

4.5.1   System Design Patterns

The first pattern is Observer pattern proposed by Gamma et al. (1995). Within the MVC architecture, this largely used pattern ensures the separation between the code related to UI and the invisible components that form the model. This pattern defines a one-to-many dependency between objects, mainly a model and several views with the MVC model, so that when one object changes state, all its dependents are notified and updated automatically (Fig. 4.3). This pattern establishes the basis for separating the UI and functionality.

The second pattern that we have considered is the Abstract Factory pattern that complements the previous. It provides an interface for creating families of related or dependent objects (mainly views) without specifying their concrete implementations (e.g. The Toolkit class). Given a set of related views that forms the user interfaces, the Abstract Factory pattern provides a way to create instances of those abstract classes from a matched set of concrete subclasses.

Figure 4.4 illustrates the enhanced MVC architecture that includes two system design patterns.

We also used several other system design patterns. An example is the Working Data Visualization pattern that copes with the specific usability problem described in scenario 2 in the Sect. 4.4.

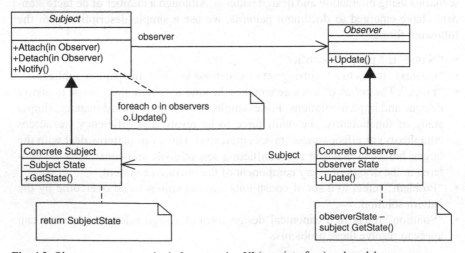

Fig. 4.3 Observer pattern as a basis for separating UI (user interface) and model concerns

Name: Working Data Visualization
(*Scenarios addressed:* 2. *Updating the Interface When the Model Changes its State*)

Problems

If the user cannot see working data in different view modes so as to get a better understanding of it, and if switching between views does not change the related manipulation command, then usability will be compromised.

Context

Sometime users want to visualize a large set of data using different point of view, to better understand what they are doing and what they need to edit to improve their documents.

Forces

- Users like to gain additional insight about working data while solving problems;
- Users like to see what they are doing from different viewpoints depending on the task and solution state;
- Different users prefer different viewpoints (modes)
- Each viewpoint (mode) should have related commands to manipulate data

Solution

Data that is being viewed should be separate from the data view description, so that the same data can be viewed in different ways according to the different view descriptions. The user gets the data and commands according to the user-selected view description.

Effects of invisible components on usability

- Quality attributes of invisible components: Integrity
- Usability factors affected: Visual consistency

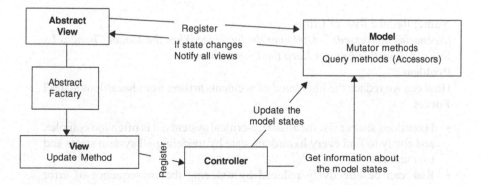

Fig. 4.4 An enhanced version of the basic MVC model

Table 4.1 Example of design patterns

Pattern	Problem	Solution
Event Handler	How should an invisible component handle an event notification message from its observable visual components?	Create and register a handler method for each event from observable visual components
Complete Update	How to implement behavior in the user interface to update the (observer) visual component from the model	Assume all (observer) visual components are out-of-date and update everything
Multiple Update	How to implement changes in the model of subform to reflect parent of subform, child of subform, siblings of subform	Each subform should notify its parent when it changes the model. The parent should react to changes in the subform via the Event Handler and update its children components via Complete Update
Subform	How to design parts of user interfaces to operate on the model in a consistent manner	Groups the components that operate on the same model aspect into subforms

Other relevant patterns we used include Event Handler, Complete Update, and Multiple Update (Sandu 2001). We use them to notify and update views (scenario 1- Sect. 4.4) using traditional design patterns such as Observer and Abstract Factory. We incorporated these patterns into the subform pattern that groups the different views in the same container, called the Form (Table 4.1). The Event Handler, Complete Update, and Multiple Update patterns can be applied in two phases. The first phase changes the states of the user interface models in response to end user events generated by the visual components, and the second phase updates the visual components to reflect the changes in the UI model. Since the update phase immediately follows the handling phase, the UI always reflects the latest changes.

The next example of software design patterns we propose is the Reduce Risk of Errors pattern.

Name: Reduce Risk of Errors
(*Scenarios addressed: 2. Updating the Interface When the Model Changes Its State; 4. Invisible Entities Keep the User Informed*)
Problem
How can we reduce the likelihood of accidents arising from hazardous states?
Forces

- Hazardous states exist for all safety-critical systems; it is often too complex and costly to find every hazardous state by modeling all system states and user tasks.
- Risk can be effectively reduced by reducing the consequence of error rather than its likelihood.

- When a hazardous state follows a nonhazardous state, it may be possible to return to a nonhazardous state by applying some kind of recovery operation.

Solution
Enable users to recover from hazardous actions they have performed. Recovering a task is similar to undoing it, but promises to return the system to a state that is essentially identical to the one prior to the incorrect action. This pattern may be useful for providing a recover operation giving a fast, reliable mechanism to return to the initial state. Recovering a task undoes as much of the task as is necessary (and possible) to return the system to a safe state.

Resulting Context
After applying this pattern, it should be possible for users to recover from some of their hazardous actions. Other patterns can be used to facilitate recovery by breaking tasks into substeps, each of which may be more easily recovered than the original task. The user should be informed of what the previous state is that the system will revert to.

Effects of invisible components on usability
Effects 1:

- Quality attributes of invisible components: Integrity
- Usability factors affected: Visual consistency

Effects 2:

- Quality attributes of invisible components: Suitability
- Usability factors affected: Operability

The last example of software design patterns is the Address Dynamic Presentation pattern.

Name: Dynamic Presentation in User Interface
(*Scenarios addressed: 6. Technical Constraints on Dynamic Interface Behavior*)
Problem
How can we avoid technical constraints on dynamic behavior of the user interface?
Forces

- Users benefit from immediate feedback on their actions
- Dynamically updating fields can reduce the time required to accomplish a task

Solutions

- Analyze user needs relating to dynamism before making technology decisions that could have an impact on dynamism. Transactional systems often require considerable dynamism.
- If it is unacceptable for business rules to be incorporated into the client, then it might be possible to make a business case for increasing the network bandwidth so as to better support pseudo-dynamic behavior, involving more frequent page refreshes through calls to the server.

Resulting Context

After applying this pattern, users will have more immediate feedback on the consequences of their actions, increasing the understandability of the UI and reducing errors; in addition, time and effort to accomplish a task will be reduced in certain cases.

Effects of invisible components on usability

Effects 1:

- Quality attributes of invisible components: Functionality
- Usability factors affected: Understandability

Effects 2:

- Quality attributes of invisible components: Suitability
- Usability factors affected: Operability

4.5.2   Interaction Design (HCI) Patterns

Over the last 5 years, several HCI patterns languages have been proposed to facilitate the design of user interfaces and ensure their usability (Tidwell 1997; Welie 1999; Sandu 2001). Examples include Amsterdam collection (Tidwell 1997) and common ground (Welie 1999). Within our approach, we adapted and used some of these patterns to solve some of user problems reported in one of the five design scenarios.

The first basic HCI pattern that we used is the progress indicator pattern (Tidwell 1997). It provides a solution for the time-consuming features scenario (scenario 1, Sect. 4.4).

Name: Progress Indicator
(*Scenarios addressed: 1. Time-Consuming Functionalities*)
Problem
A time-consuming functionality is in progress, the results of which are of interest to the user. How can the artifact show its current state to the user, so that the user can best understand what is happening and act on that knowledge?

Forces

- The user wants to know how long they have to wait for the process to end.
- The user wants to know that progress is actually being made, and that the process has not just "hung."
- The user wants to know how quickly progress is being made, especially if the speed varies.
- Sometimes it is impossible for the artifact to know how long the process is going to take.

Solution

Show the user a status display of some kind, indicating how far along the process is in real time. If the expected end time is known, or some other relevant quantity (such as the size of a file being downloaded), then always show what proportion of the process has been finished so far, so the user can estimate how much time is left. If no quantities are known—just that the process may take a while—then simply show some indicator that the process is ongoing.

Resulting Context

A user may expect to find a way to stop the process somewhere close to the progress indicator. It's almost as though, in the user's mind, the progress indicator acts as a proxy for the process itself. If so, put a "stop" command near the progress indicator if possible.

Effects of invisible components on usability

Effects 1:

- Quality attributes of invisible components: Performance
- Usability factors affected: User satisfaction

The second pattern we integrated in our framework is the keep the user focused pattern, which brings an integrated solution to the problems described in scenarios 2, 3, and 4 in the Sect. 4.4.

Name: Keep the User Focused
(**Scenarios addressed:** *2. Updating the Interface When the Model Changes its State; 3. Performing Multiple Functionalities Using a Single Control; 4. Invisible Entities Keep the User Informed*)

Context

An application where several visual objects are manipulated, typically in drawing packages or browsing tools

Problem

How can the user quickly learn information about a specific object they see and possibly modify the object?

Forces

- Many objects/views can be visible but the user usually works on one object/view at a time.
- The user wants both an overview of the set of objects and details on attributes and available functions related to the object he or she is working on.
- The user may also want to apply a function to several objects/views.

Solution

Introduce a focus in the application. The focus always belongs to an object present in the interface. The object of focus on which the user is working determines the context of available functionality. The focus must be visually shown to the user, for example, by changing its color or by drawing a rectangle around it. The user can change the focus by selecting another object. When an object has the focus, it becomes the target for all the functionality that is relevant for the object. Additionally, windows containing relevant functionality are activated when the focus changes. This reduces the number of actions needed to select the function and execute it for a specified object. The solution improves the performance and ease of recall.

Resulting Context

The "Keep the User Focused" pattern complements the software design patterns in the following situations:

- Helping users anticipate the effects of their actions, so that errors are avoided before calling the underlying features
- Helping users notice when they have made an error (provide feedback about actions and the state of the system)
- Providing time to recover from errors
- Providing feedback once the recovery has taken place

Effects of invisible components on usability
Effects 1:

- Quality attributes of invisible components: Integrity
- Usability factors affected: Visual consistency

Effects 2:

- Quality attributes of invisible components: Functionality
- Usability factors affected: Understandability

Effect 3:

- Usability factors affected: Operability
- Quality attributes of invisible components: Suitability

There is not a one-to-one mapping between software design patterns and HCI patterns. The problems described in a specific scenario can require any number of HCI and software design patterns, and each pattern may be affected by a number of problems described in different scenarios. In our approach, we argue that using a few patterns can be very valuable, even without an entire pattern language.

Our list of patterns is not intended to be exhaustive. We are considering some of the existing patterns (Newman and Lamming 1995; Buschmann et al. 1996). However, most of the existing patterns have not originally been proposed to cope with the problem we are addressing. We are therefore adapting them as we did with the ones we introduced in these sections.

4.6 Modeling the Cause–Effect Relationships Between the Model and User Interface

In this chapter, we focused on specific ways in which internal software properties can have an impact on usability. In this section, we attempt to provide a more general, theoretical framework for modeling the relationships between usability and invisible software attributes. In particular, among the huge or potentially infinite number of ways that invisible components can affect usability, our main goal is to understand whether there are specific places where we are more likely to find these relationships or effects. Another goal is to verify whether there is any structure underlying these relationships, which would allow us to define a taxonomy of how usability issues arise from invisible components.

Usability is often thought of as a modular tree-shaped hierarchy of usability concepts, starting at the level of GUI objects, and abstracting progressively up toward low-level usability criteria or measures and then into high-level usability factors. Figure 4.5 illustrates this definition of usability and its relationship to parallel "towers" of other software attributes.

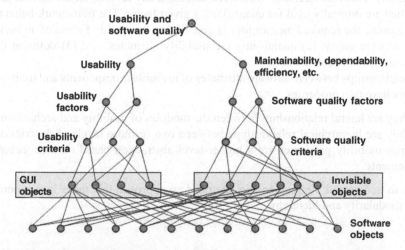

Fig. 4.5 Traditional "twin towers" model of usability and other software quality factors

Table 4.2 A partial vision of the ISO 9126 measurement framework. Taxonomy of usability issues arising from invisible components

Software quality factor	Measurement criteria
Functionality	Suitability Accuracy Interoperability Security
Reliability	Maturity Fault tolerance Recoverability
Usability	Understandability Learnability Operability Attractiveness
Efficiency	Time behavior Resource Utilization
Maintainability	Analyzability Changeability Stability Testability
Portability	Adaptability Instability Co-existence Replaceability

Table 4.2 provides more detailed information on the software quality factors and criteria referred to schematically in the right-hand branch of Fig. 4.2. (In principle, each quality factor would form a separate branch.). In our work, we have adopted the software quality model proposed by ISO 9126. Table 4.2 is an overview of the consolidated framework we have been using (Seffah et al. 2003).

The table shows the criteria for measuring usability as well as five other software quality factors including functionality, reliability, efficiency, maintainability, and portability. This measurement framework automatically inherits all the metrics and data that are normally used for quantifying a given factor. The framework helps us to determine the required metrics for (1) quantifying the quality factors of an invisible software entity, (2) quantifying the usability attributes, and (3) defining the relationships between them.

Relationships between software attributes of invisibles components and usability factors have two properties:

1. They are lateral relationships between the modules of usability and architecture.
2. They are hierarchical relationships between two or more levels of description, since usability properties are a higher-level abstraction based on architectural elements.

Thus to understand the relationship, we need an approach that takes into account both modularity and hierarchy.

In software engineering, software modules have two features that need to be considered during design, namely, coherence and coupling. Coherence refers to how relevant the components of a subsystem are to each other, and it needs to be maximized. On the other hand, coupling refers to how dependent a subsystem is on other subsystems, and it needs to be minimized.

In a similar approach in "The Architecture of Complexity", Simon (1962) discusses "nearly decomposable systems." In hierarchic systems, interactions can be divided into two general categories: those among subsystems, and those within subsystems. In a simplified approach, we can describe a system as being "decomposable" into its subsystems by basically assuming that we are fully aware of all interactions between subsystems and that everything has been "taken care of." At this stage we can go on with the studying and development of each subsystem separately, relying on our limited model of interaction. However, as a more refined approximation, it is more accurate to speak of a complex system as being "nearly decomposable," meaning that there are complex interactions between the subsystems, and that after separation, these interactions remain active and nonnegligible.

Nearly decomposable systems have two properties:

- Modularity: In the short run, the behavior of each subsystem is approximately independent of the other subsystems.
- Hierarchy (or aggregation): In the long run, the behavior of any one subsystem depends in only an aggregate way on the other subsystems.

These properties indicate that in reality, the traditional model of usability is oversimplified. Although the usability subsystem is fundamentally different from the architecture, Simon's principle of nearly decomposable systems predicts that it is possible for usability properties to be affected to some degree by architectural properties. Figure 4.6 illustrates an interpretation of this alternative model of usability.

In this Fig. 4.6, a node (usability property) at any level of usability can potentially be influenced by nodes at any lower level of architecture, or conceivably

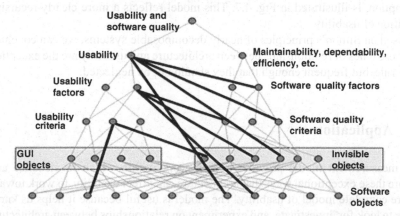

Fig. 4.6 Revised model of usability, including possible types of cross relationships with architecture (*bold* links)

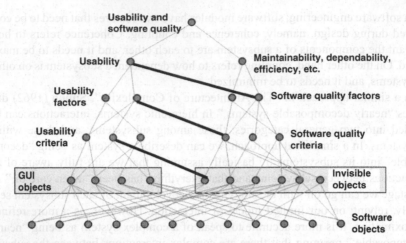

Fig. 4.7 Most probable types of cross relationships between usability and architecture (*bold* links)

even by combinations of several different levels of architecture. Figure 4.6 is a first approximation. Simon's second principle of near decomposability states that subsystems depend in only an aggregate way on other subsystems.

This principle implies that if architecture has an effect on usability, it will tend to be in an aggregate way and therefore at a higher level of architecture, rather than through the effect of an individual low-level architectural component. We interpret this principle to mean that the effects of architecture on usability will tend to propagate from levels of architecture that are closer to the level of usability, rather than farther away.

Therefore to refine the model, we will assume that the most likely relationships occur between usability properties and the immediately closest lower architectural level, and that more distant architectural levels have an exponentially decreasing probability of having an effect on usability. The revised model, based on this assumption, is illustrated in Fig. 4.7. This model reflects a more clearly recursive definition of usability.

Based on Simon's principles of nearly decomposable systems, we can conclude that these types of relationships between architecture and usability are the exception to the rule, but frequent enough that they should not be neglected.

4.7   Application

This measurement model provides a framework within which to visualize and explore these exceptional ways that architecture can affect usability, to work toward a more complete model of usability. The model is useful because it helps us know where to look for, investigate, and experiment on relationships between architecture and usability. Further progress will require detailing the hierarchies on both sides of the tree, and considering each possible relationship between nodes at proximate levels. Another goal will be to provide other heuristic principles to further narrow down the likely interrelationships between these two branches.

Table 4.3 provides examples of the specific types of relationships that occur in the scenarios described in Sect. 4.2. The second column refers to the invisible object's properties and software qualities identified in the right-hand branch of Figs. 4.5 through Fig. 4.7, and the third column represents the usability properties identified in the left-hand branch of those figures.

For example, the scenario 1 (Sect. 4.4) can be modeled as a relationship that connects the performance of the software feature with certain usability attributes such as user satisfaction. It can lead to the following requirement related to scenario 1 (Sect. 4.4): "To ensure an 80% level of satisfaction, the maximum acceptable response time of all the underlying related feature should not exceed 10 s; if not the user should be informed and a continuous feedback needs to be provided."

4.8   Key Contributions of this Chapter

In this book, we first identified specific scenarios of how invisible software components can have an effect on the usability of the interactive system. Then, we provided a list of patterns that solved the problems described in the scenarios. This research effort can benefit software architecture designers and developers, who can use our approach in two different ways. First, the scenarios can serve as a checklist to determine whether important usability features (external attributes) have been considered in the design of features and the related UI components. Second, the patterns can help the designer incorporate some of the usability concerns in the design.

More than defining a list of scenarios and patterns that describe the effects of invisible software attributes on software usability, the long-term objective is to build and validate a comprehensive framework for identifying scenarios. The goal of the framework is to define these patterns as a relationship between software quality factors and usability factors. In this chapter, we have suggested different HCI and software design patterns as solutions to the problems described in these scenarios and in similar ones. Every pattern has a set of problems to be solved and a set of goals to be achieved.

As designers gain a better understanding of the relationship between interaction design patterns and software architecture patterns, this knowledge will affect the evolution of standards in architecture design and GUI software libraries. Some developers are making proper use of standard GUI libraries and respecting interface design guidelines in a way that considerably increases the usability of interactive applications. However, more can be done in this direction, and the approach we have outlined in this chapter is an attempt to build a better and more systematic understanding of how usability can be incorporated into software architecture.

References

ANSI/IEEE Std (1471–2000) Recommended practice for architectural description of software-intensive systems

Bass L, Clements P, Kazman R (1998) Software architecture in practice. Addison- Wesley, Reading

Bass L, John BE, Kates J (2001) Achieving usability through software architecture, SEI Report. Carnegie Mellon University, Pittsburgh, PA 15213–3890

Buschmann F, Meunier H, Rohnert P, Sommerlad Stal M (1996) Pattern-oriented software architectures: a system of patterns. Wiley, West Sussex

Carroll JM (2000) Scenario-based design of human–computer interactions. MIT Press, Cambridge

Gaffar A (2001) Design of a framework for database indexes. Master thesis, Concordia University, Montreal

Gaffar A, Seffah A, Van der Poll J (2005) HCI patterns semantics in XML: a pragmatic approach, HSSE 2005. In: Workshop on Human and Social Factors of Software Engineering, in conjunction with ICSE 2005, the 27th International Conference on Software Engineering, St. Louis, Missouri, USA, May 15–21, proceedings of ACM

Gamma E, Helm R, Johnson R, Vlissides J (1995) Design Patterns: elements of reusable object-oriented software. Addison Wesley

Folmer E, van Gurp J, Bosch J (2003) A framework for capturing the relationship between usability and software architecture. Softw process: improv pract 8(2):67–87

ISO/IEC TR 9126-3:2003. Software engineering—product quality—part 3: internal metrics, ISO 2003

Newman W, Lamming MG (1995) Interactive system design. Addison-Wesley, Harlow

Norman BD (2002) The computer industry. CACM 45(July), 7

Sandu D (2001) User interface patterns. In: 8th Conference on Pattern Languages of Programs September 11–15, llerton Park Monticello, Illinois, USA

Seffah A, Abran A, Khelifi A, Suryn W (2003) Usability meanings and interpretations in ISO standards. Soft Quality J 11(4)

Simon HA (1962) The architecture of complexity. Proceedings of the American Philosophical Society, Vol 106, No. 6. (Dec. 12, 1962), pp. 467–482

Sinnig D (2004) The complicity of patterns and Model-Based UI Development. Master of Computer Science, Montreal, Concordia University, 148 p

Tidwell J (1997) Common ground: a pattern language for human–computer 848 interface design. http://www.mit.edu/~jtidwell/common_ground.html. Accessed 20 April 2015

Welie MV (1999) Patterns in interaction design: the Amsterdam Collection. http://www.welie.com/patternl. Accessed 20 April 2015

Chapter 5
A Pattern Framework for Task Modeling in Smart Environments

Abstract Although, the wide range of tools that exist to support model-based approaches, creating various models, transforming, and linking them is still a time consuming and complex activity. In addition, model-based approaches lack an advanced concept of reuse of already modeled solutions. In this chapter, an attempt to overcome the high complexity of the modelling process of applications is presented. It will be shown that patterns may be employed to avoid these disadvantages, since they provide an advanced concept of reuse by definition. After introducing the concept of pattern-driven and task-based development in general concrete tool support will be discussed. In addition, the role of task models for smart environments will be discussed. Specific task patterns for this domain will be discussed as well.

5.1 Task Modeling for User Interface

One of the first popular modelling methods for user interface design was Task Knowledge Structure (TKS) Johnson et al. 1985. Tool support was later provided by the ADEPT system Johnson et al. 1993. Some years later Mobi-D (Model-based Interface Designer) Paternó and Santoro 2002 provided even more successful results in developing task-based user interfaces. It is based on a user task, a domain, a user, a dialog, and a presentation model. Extensible Interface Markup Language (XIML 2012) was developed to use this model-based approach together with XML technology. Tool support was provided accordingly.

The idea got more momentum with the appearance of mobile devices. The *One Model Many Interfaces* approach Paterno 2001 suggests to use task models as well as abstract and concrete user interface models. It aims to support the development of multimodal user interfaces. For the purpose of specifying the single models, it contains the Teresa XML notation TeresaXML 2012. The *User Interface Extensible Markup Language* (UsiXML) approach UsiXML 2014 is based on the experiences with XIML and structured according to the Cameleon Unifying Reference Framework (Balme et al. 2004). Among other models, UsiXML uses task, domain, context, abstract, and concrete user interface models.

© Springer International Publishing Switzerland 2015
A. Seffah, *Patterns of HCI Design and HCI Design of Patterns,*
Human-Computer Interaction Series, DOI 10.1007/978-3-319-15687-3_5

Building task models requires a great amount of expertise and knowledge especially when building a task model bfrom scratch. Not only this involves a lot of work and is error prone. Patterns can be a solution for such problems. In Breedvelt et al. 1997 task patterns are suggested. They capture a high level description of reoccurring activities. These activities can be performed with and without interactive applications.

This chapter supplements Chap. 3. It provides a specific approach of using the concept task patterns as a task modeling technique and as a tool to generate user interfaces from an HCI task models. A general pattern application framework is discussed and illustrated using a smart environment application. It abstracts from a specific model-based approach, a concrete pattern language, and a specific pattern notation in order to abstract as much as possible and make the framework applicable for different models.

5.2 Proposed Pattern Framework for Task Modeling

Figure 5.1 portrays the proposed framework for task modeling using task patterns. The application of patterns is into three main general phases.

In the first pattern *selection* phase, a designer works on a certain submodel and feels that a certain *user interface pattern* should be applied to the sub-model. It can also be possible that the designer identifies a certain problem in the sub-model and looks for a pattern that provides a solution to the problem. In both cases a pattern is chosen out of a *pattern repository*. It would be optimal if there would exist only one repository that contains the available patterns of the *pattern language*.

Within a pattern language, the patterns are hierarchically structured into patterns and sub-patterns. Each pattern in the pattern language is specified according to a specific *pattern notation*. It contains a model fragment that describes the pattern solution. This solution can be *generic* in order to be applicable in various contexts and to allow the pattern to be instantiated in multiple ways.

The generic parts of the selected pattern have to be adapted during the *pattern instantiation* phase. To be more precise the instantiation phase can be divided in two subphases, the adaptation of the pattern to the context of use. The generic part is adapted to the current sub-model under development. This has to be done in an interactive way. Later the instantiation can be performed. The whole process results in a *pattern instance* derived.

Finally, the interactively produced pattern instance has to be applied to the selected sub-model. This means that the sub-model is transformed by the pattern instance. The transformed sub-model has to be finally integrated in the context, the whole model. Corresponding links have to be updated. The whole phase is called pattern *integration* phase.

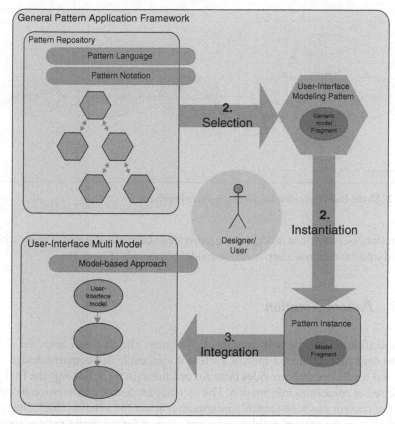

Fig. 5.1 The proposed pattern application framework. (Radeke 2007)

5.3 Task Modeling Patterns Notation

5.3.1 The Model-Based Approach We Used

The modelling approach we used was proposed in Wolff et al. 2005, and later adapted further in order to serve as modelling approach component within the framework implementation. Similar approaches of that of Fig. 5.1 were suggested by other publications as well (see, e.g., Stary 1999). According to this approach, the development of software starts with the envisaged task model that will be performed in the future via the user interface. A business object model describes properties of domain objects that are needed for the executing the tasks. Typical characteristics of user groups are specified within the user model. Information about platforms and general context information is specified by a domain model.

Based on these models, dialog model is specified that describes the navigational structure of the user interface in form of views and transitions between these views.

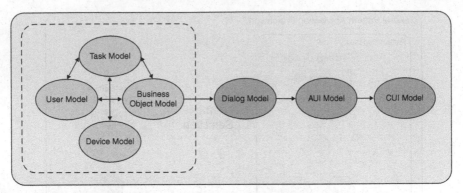

Fig. 5.2 Model-based approach for developing user interfaces

An abstract user interface model can be generated automatically that is interactively refined into the concrete user interface model afterwards (Fig. 5.2).

5.3.2   Pattern Notation

The specification of a pattern consists of two parts. The first part helps the developer to determine whether a specific pattern is applicable in a concrete design situation and the second part provides hints for solutions. In the following, the first part is referred as *contextual* information. The second part describes a solution but often does not contain machine-readable information about the solution. Including such information in the pattern enables computer support for the entire pattern application process. Such machine-readable information is referred to as *implementational* information in the following.

During a workshop at CHI 2003 (Conference on Human Factors in Computing Systems), the specification language Pattern Language Markup Language (PLML ; Forbrig et al. 2012) was developed. There was the goal to have a common language to express the specification of patterns. PLML contains common elements, like for instance the pattern name, the problem, and the solution, that can be found in most of the patterns suggested so far. UsiPXML structures its context information according to the format as suggested by PLML. The specification of the implementation is based on UsiXML (User Interface Extensible Markup Language, UsiXML 2014). The following figure gives an impression of the structure of the language (Fig. 5.3).

UsiXML is well suited for the specification of user interfaces. However, it is not generic. As patterns describe solutions in a *generic* way, this feature would be very helpful. The notation of UsiXML has been extended with pattern-specific components as outlined in the lower part of Fig. 5.3. Such extensions are structure attributes, variable declarations and assignments, and pattern references and interfaces. They will be discussed in the following by using an illustrative example. A more detailed description of the extensions can be found in Radeke 2007.

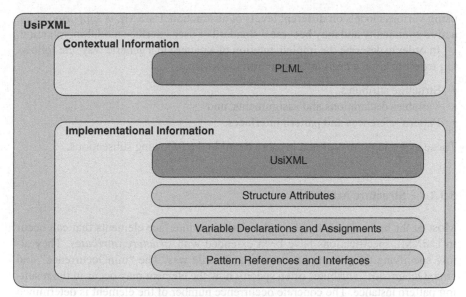

Fig. 5.3 Structure of the language UsiPXML

We will now address the question of describing the patterns in an appropriate way. Two problems have to be tackled. First, a pattern should provide information that supports the designer in selecting an adequate pattern. It is additionally stated in Molina and Hernández 2003 that a pattern has to be described in such a way that the result of its application is predictable. Thus, practitioners can realize quickly whether a pattern is suitable in a given context or not. Information that tackles this problem is referred to as contextual information in the following. Beside this contextual information, a pattern has to provide information that describes its solution in a machine-readable way in order to enable tool support for its application. In the following information of a pattern that described the solution in a machine-readable way is referred to as implementational information. UsiPXML strictly follows the structure of PLML and adds some more language elements that are presented separately below.

Although, PLML may be suitable to capture most of the patterns proposed so far, it does not tackle the problem of how to describe the solution itself in a machine-readable way in order to allow computer supported pattern application. Most of the patterns captured in pattern languages (e.g., Tidewell 1998; van Duyne et al. 2005; Welie 2012) are described in a textual or graphical form. In contrast to this, Sinnig (Sinnig 2004) developed a pattern notation for task patterns that contains, apart from the contextual information, details of the implementation which are described in a machine-readable way, called TPML (Task Pattern Markup Language). Analogous to common task modelling notations, TPML describes the task solution in a hierarchically structured XML-based notation. In the following, the UsiXML modelling notation will be extended in order to capture the information regarding the implementation of the pattern. UsiXML is capable to describe user-interface using various models on different levels of abstraction. UsiXML is supported by an active community and may become a standard of user-interface modelling notation.

In order to describe the implementation of a pattern in a generic way, the following extensions have been integrated into UsiXML:

- Structure attributes,
- Variables declarations and assignments, and
- Pattern references and pattern interfaces.

These extensions are outlined in more detail in the following subsections.

5.3.2.1   Structure Attributes

Most of the basic elements, like task or concrete interface elements that can occur in UsiXML specifications have been extended with *structure attributes*. They allow specifying the pattern structure in a flexible way. The "minOccurrence" and "maxOccurrence" attributes often specify how the element may occur in the resulting pattern instance. The concrete occurrence number of the element is determined during pattern instantiation by the designer. The "minOccurrence" and "maxOccurrence" attributes are optional. By default, an element is allowed to occur exactly one time.

minOccurrence	maxOccurrence	Meaning
0	1	*Elective* element. Element may occur once or not at all
1	unbound	*Recurring* element. Element may occur once or arbitrarily often
0	unbound	Elective and recurring element. Element may occur arbitrarily often or not at all
1	1	Element occurs exactly 1 time. (default)
1	5	Element may occur 1–5 times

Figures 5.4 and 5.6 demonstrate the usage of attributes by showing a fragment of a task pattern. The fragment contains the two tasks: "Root Task" and "Sub Task." The numbers in brackets indicate the values of the "minOccurrence" and "maxOccurrence" attributes. "Root Task" has to occur exactly once, whereas "Sub Task" can occur arbitrarily often. Figure 5.6 shows a task pattern at the top and a possible instance of that pattern at the button, where the task "Sub Task" occurs thrice.

Another structure attribute allows deactivating elements while setting its value to "false." The elements may be reactivated while setting the value back to "true." The attribute is used for activating and deactivating parts of the pattern. For instance, a designer may specify during pattern instantiation that the resulting solution is intended for a PDA. The "set" attribute may be used in this context to activate the

Fig. 5.4 Task "Sub Task" may occur arbitrarily often

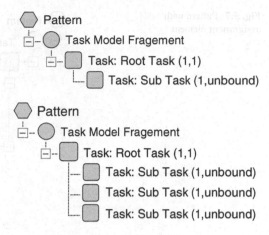

Fig. 5.5 Activated and deactivated task element

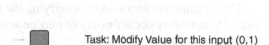

Fig. 5.6 Pattern with variable declarations

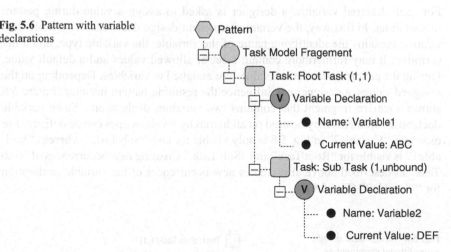

Fig. 5.7 Pattern with
assignment element

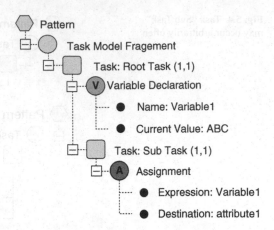

parts of the pattern that describe the PDA-specific solution, whereas the parts of the pattern that describe the desktop PC specific solution are deactivated. As shown in Fig. 5.7, deactivated elements are displayed in a gray color. Elements that are deactivated as well as their sub-elements are not integrated into the resulting pattern instance (Fig. 5.5).

The structure attributes allow specifying the pattern structure in a generic way since elements may occur flexibly or may be activated or deactivated depending on the context of pattern application.

5.3.2.2   Variable Declarations and Assignments

For each declared variable, a designer is asked to assign a value during pattern instantiation. In this way, the variables represent design decisions. A variable declaration contains the identifying name of the variable, the variable type, and a description. It may furthermore contain a set of allowed values and a default value. During the pattern instantiation, values are assigned to variables. Depending on the assigned values, a designer can influence the resulting pattern instance. Figure 5.8 shows a pattern fragment that contains two variables declarations. Since variable declaration elements may be used on all hierarchy levels, scopes can be defined. For example, "Variable2" in Fig. 5.8 is only visible for task "Sub Task," whereas "Variable1" is visible for "Root Task" and "Sub Task." Creating new occurrences of "Sub Task" as described above also creates new occurrences of the variable declaration for "Variable2" (Fig. 5.6).

Fig. 5.8 Assignment using
a conditional statement as
expression

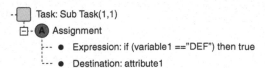

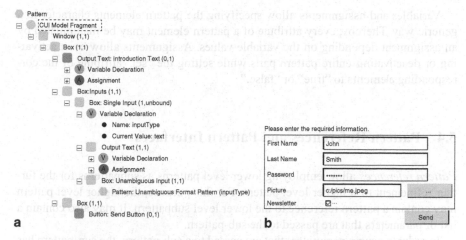

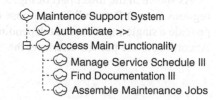

Fig. 5.9 UsiPXML structure (a) of the "Form Pattern" and a generated pattern instance (b)

Depending on the evaluation of variables, attributes of pattern elements can be changed. This is done by employing *assignment* elements within the pattern. The "destination" attribute allows specifying an attribute of the target element to which the expression value is assigned. The attribute "substitution form" specifies whether the value of the target attribute is replaced by the expression value or whether it is added to the original value of the attribute. In the following, an assignment is illustrated by an example (Fig. 5.7).

In the simplest case, the expression of an assignment element contains the name of a variable as shown in the example of Fig. 5.9. The expression has the content "Variable1. Evaluating such expression returns the value of the variable. In the example the expression result, which is the current value "ABC" of "variable1," replaces the destination attribute "attribute1" of the task element "Sub Task."

However, often it is helpful not to assign a variable value directly to an attribute as done in Fig. 5.9, but assign a specific value to an attribute depending on the variable value. For this purpose, the assignments may contain conditional statements as expressions as outlined in the example of Fig. 5.10, Fig. 5.8. Conditional statements can be specified using a notation similar to the Java programming language. The value of the expression in the example means that if the variable "variable1" has the current value "DEF," then return as expression result "true." The value "true" is later assigned to "attribute1."

Fig. 5.10 Initial task model

Variables and assignments allow specifying the pattern elements character in a generic way. Thereby, every attribute of a pattern element may be manipulated by an assignment depending on the variable values. Assignments allow even activating or deactivating entire pattern parts while setting the "set" attribute of the corresponding elements to "true" or "false."

5.4   Pattern References and Pattern Interfaces

Pattern references allow employing lower level patterns as subpatterns for the further refinement of a higher level pattern. For this purpose, the higher level pattern may contain a pattern reference to the lower level subpattern. It may also contain a list of parameters that are passed to the sub-pattern.

In order to access parameters that are passed to a sub-pattern, the sup-pattern has to define a *pattern interface*. The pattern interface contains a list of variable declarations, whereby each describes a single parameter. If the pattern is instantiated as stand alone, these parameters are handled like usual variables. Otherwise, if the pattern is employed as sub-pattern, each parameter receives the values that are passed to the sub-pattern via the pattern interface.

5.4.1   Example of a Pattern

The way of specifying task patterns with UsiPXML will be demonstrated by an example. Figure 5.9a shows the UsiPXML task structure of the "Form Pattern" that was discussed in Sinnig 2004. It is originally a UI pattern that can be employed in situation where the user has to enter a set of related values. Figure 5.9b shows a possible instance of a UI. However, a corresponding task model can be used to specify the features that have to be presented in the user interface.

The variable "Introduction Text" allows specifying an optional introduction text. In case the designer assigns "Please enter the required information" to that variable, the result looks like shown in Fig. 5.9b. The content of the variable is displayed on top of the form.

The element "Box: Single Input (0, unbound)" that can be found in the middle of Fig. 5.9a is allowed to occur arbitrarily often in the final instance. During instantiation, the designer has to determine the concrete number. The mentioned element occurs five times (each input) in the instance of Fig. 5.9b.

As shown in the lower part of Fig. 5.9b, the "Form Pattern" refers to the "Unambiguous Format Pattern." The purpose of the "Unambiguous Format Pattern" is to provide a single input element depending on the type of information that is entered. According to the pattern interface, the "inputType" is expected as parameter.

5.4.2 Application of Patterns

The UsiPXML pattern notation allows the usage of the patterns within tools. Such tools have been developed in order to implement a pattern-driven model-based approach. The tools are developed as so called plug-ins for the Eclipse (Eclipse 2014) environment.

They strictly follow the three steps of the pattern application process proposed by the framework:

1. Pattern selection,
2. Pattern instantiation, and
3. Pattern integration.

In order to find a pattern, a designer can browse the pattern hierarchy and retrieve contextual information. This allows him to select an appropriate pattern for the current modelling situation. The adaptation of the selected pattern is later supported by an "Instantiation Wizard." It supports to determine the structure of the pattern instance and to assign values to variables that occur within the pattern. The insertion of the resulting pattern instance into a target model is supported by an "Integration Wizard."

To get an impression of the support that those tools provide, let us have a look at a system that has to be developed in order to support maintenance work. It is the goal of the system to assist technicians in managing the maintenance jobs that arise. The entire case study is discussed in more detail in Radeke 2007.

It is assumed that the analysis of the domain resulted in an initial task model as outlined in Fig. 5.10. It specifies that an authentication of a user is necessary before the main functionality can be accessed. After a successful authentication, the tasks "Manage Service Schedule," "Find Documentation," and "Assemble Maintenance Jobs" can be performed concurrently.

At this stage, patterns can be employed for further refining the initial task model. The task "Authenticate" can be refined by the "Login Pattern" Sinnig 2004. This task pattern is applicable when users need to identify themselves in order to perform authorized operations. It contains the "Multi-Value Input Pattern" as shown in the following figure (Fig. 5.11).

Fig. 5.11 Login pattern

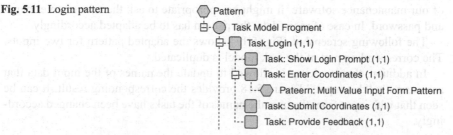

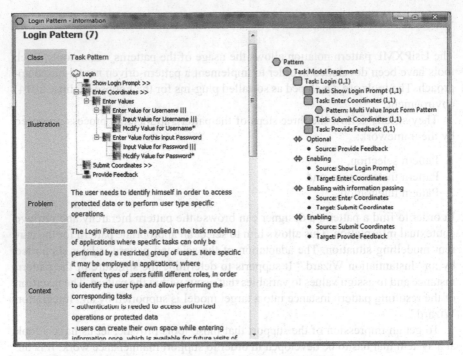

Fig. 5.12 First part of the description of the "Login Pattern" in the tool

For logging in, there has to be, as shown, a login prompt and later coordinates have to be entered. They have to be submitted, and finally feedback has to be given.

Within the tool, there is a possibility to have a look at the specification of each pattern. Figure 5.15 partly provides the "Login Pattern" description gives an impression of how users get support. It might be necessary to have a look at this specification before being able to apply the pattern (Fig. 5.12).

The "Login Pattern" employs the "Multi Value Input Form Pattern" a sub-pattern. The "Multi Value Input Form Pattern" can be used when the user has to provide a set of related values. In the context of the "Login Pattern," it is employed to specify which coordinates have to be provided to authenticate the user (Fig. 5.13).

One can see in the specification of the patter that there exists a task "Enter value for this input" that has to exist at least once in the pattern. However, this task can exist as often as the context of the application of the pattern asks for. For the example of our maintenance software, it might be appropriate to ask the user to enter name and password. In case of more data, the pattern has to be adapted accordingly.

The following screenshot (Fig. 5.17) shows the adapted pattern for two inputs. The corresponding part of the task model is duplicated.

In addition, the developer is allowed to update the names of the input data that are currently "this input." Figure 5.18 provides the corresponding result. It can be seen that with input from the user the names of the tasks have been changed accordingly.

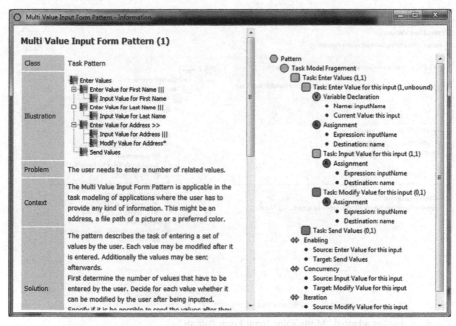

Fig. 5.13 First part of the description of the "Multi Value Input Form Pattern"

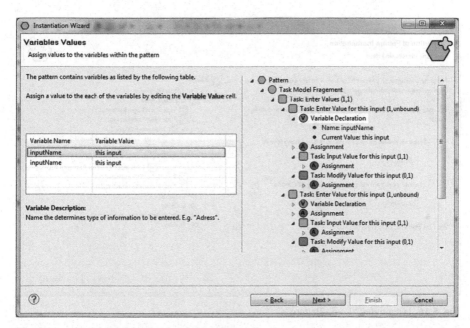

Fig. 5.14 Adapted "Multi Value Input Form Pattern"

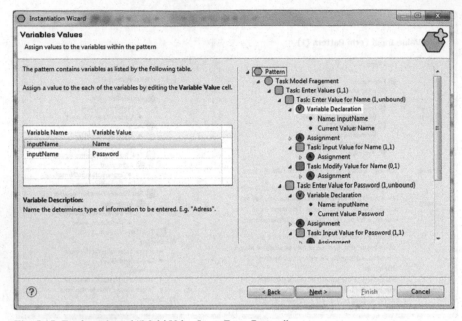

Fig. 5.15 Further adapted "Multi Value Input Form Pattern"

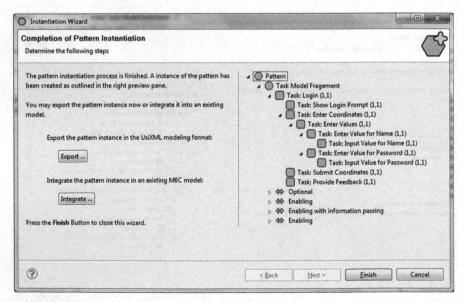

Fig. 5.16 Instantiated "Login Pattern"

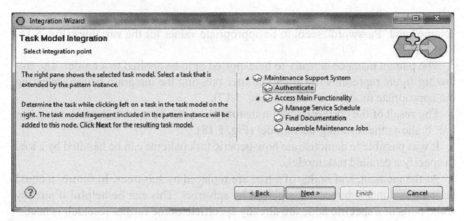

Fig. 5.17 Selected task for transformations

Fig. 5.18 Resulting task model

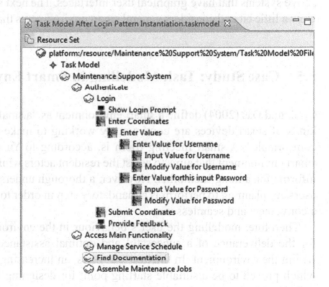

The resulting instantiated "Login Pattern" can be seen in Fig. 5.19. It includes an instantiated "Multi Value Input Form Pattern." This instance can, in our tool, now be exported for further usage in other tools or it can be used to transform a task model, which is the case in our example (Fig. 5.13). A task model has to be selected; and within a task model, a task has to be specified that is intended to be replaced by the task model of the instantiated pattern. Figure 5.20 demonstrates this situation for our example. The task "Authenticate" is selected for transformation. The task could be replaced. However, for our tool it was decided to have root of the subtree as subnode of the original task. The reasons were for demonstrational purposes only (Fig. 5.14).

Values can be changed according to the current context of use. Currently "Name" and "Password" seem to be appropriate values for the variables (Fig. 5.15, Fig. 5.16).

The pattern instance is ready to be exported or to be applied to a model. The following figure represents the situation after pressing the integrate button, selecting the appropriate model and subtask (Fig. 5.17).

The result of the corresponding transformation can be seen in the following figure. It shows the resulting task model (Fig. 5.18).

It was possible to demonstrate how generic task patterns can be handled by a tool to specify a detailed task model.

At the moment, leaf nodes of a tree are replaced by sub-trees. In future, it could be imagined that subtrees are replaced by sub-trees. This can be helpful if already some parts of a specific node are already specified. Some further research is necessary for such situations.

The considered task models were intended to support the development of interactive systems that have graphical user interfaces. The next section will broaden the view a little bit and considers general smart environments that have to be developed.

5.5   Case Study: Task Modelling in Smart Environments

Cook and Das (2004) define a smart environment as "a small world where different kinds of smart devices are continuously working to make inhabitants' lives more comfortable." A smart meeting room is, according to Yu and Nakamura 2010, a smart environment that aims to assist the resident actors while exchanging ideas and information among each other. However, a thorough understanding of the tasks the users are planning to perform is a mandatory step in order to make the room react in a convenient and seamless way.

Therefore, modelling the user's behaviour in the environment is recommended for the deliverance of a successful and optimal assistance to the resident actors within the environment. In the last few years, an increasing interest in task models which proved to be a suitable starting point for designing interactive applications is detectable.

However, in order to truly model the tasks executed in a given environment, the conditions and environmental settings intervening and affecting the way the tasks are performed have to be taken into account. For example, in a smart meeting room stationary and dynamic devices as well as some objects may be crucial for the execution of a given task in the environment. Thus, a simple task model isolated from the environmental constraints fails to express the exact way the tasks have to be executed in the environment. Therefore, the collaborative task modelling language (CTML) was developed by Wurdel et al. 2008. The following figure gives an impression of the models used within CTML (Fig. 5.19).

Table 5.1 presents a schematic sketch of a CTML cooperation model. Elements in the inner circle represent modelling entities (post fixed with "– 1") whereas dia-

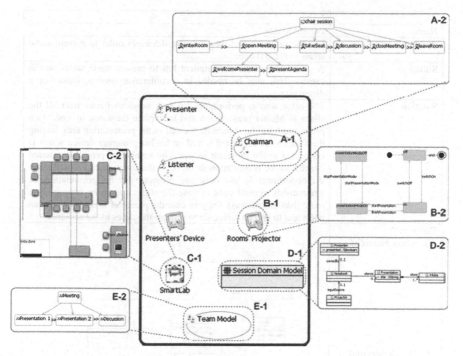

Fig. 5.19 CTML models for supporting meetings

grams outside of the inner circle show detailed specifications of the corresponding entities (post fixed width "-2"). The cooperation model specifies the relevant entities on an abstract level. Usually roles (e.g., A-1), devices (e.g., B-1), a location model (C-1), a domain model (D-1), and a team model (E-1) are necessary to be specified.

The potential actions a user is able to perform are determined by his role(s). More precisely, a role is associated with a collaborative task model (A-2).

Whereas, CTML seems to be able to successfully describe the scenarios taking place in a given smart environment, the building of the different included models (e.g., task model, device model, domain model…etc.) is a real burden for the developer. Moreover, the mutual dependencies existing between all the entities in a given environment increase the complexity of the modelling process, turning it to an error-prone and time-consuming activity.

The mentioned problems can be overcome by building a pattern language addressing this domain. It is noteworthy that the methodology that was employed to extract and define our patterns can also be used to define similar patterns for other types of smart environments.

As we already discussed, to have a comprehensive idea about the task performance in the environment, the task and all influencing surrounding factors have to be represented. Thus, we also consider the following entities: the devices assisting the user, the objects needed the specific location in which the user should be while performing the task, the user's characteristics, and finally the dependencies between

ID	1
Name	Present Slides
Problem	Use the projector and the presenter device in order to present some slides to the audience.
Situation	A given user in the environment has to present some slides on the canvas. This may be needed in a conference session, lecture or a discussion.
Solution	The actor who is performing this task needs to iterate over all the slides of his/her presentation and to explain them one by one. As a pre-request, he/she should be located in the presentation area, having the slides to be presented stored on his/her presenter device which is connected to the projector in use. The number of projectors needed depend on the presentation mode (e.g.: the smart room gives the user the opportunity to use only one projector for his presentation, or alternatively several ones in case the slides should be presented on more than one canvas). Only in case the presenter is deaf, he/she can use a text to speech converter to present the slides to the audience.

Diagram
  I. Task hierarchy
 	
  II. Environmental
        dependencies
 	
  III. Execution
         constraints
         visualization	

Adaptation variables	number of projectors, kind of user impairment
Referenced patterns	Deaf Output Accessibility

Table 5.1 Task pattern present slides

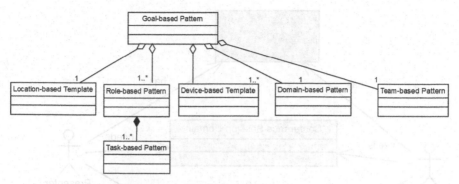

Fig. 5.20 Categories of patterns for smart meeting rooms

a given user's role and the roles to be played by the other actors in the environment. Thus, for every one of those intervening factors, a corresponding model has to be created and somehow linked to the task model embracing the tasks to be executed by a given actor in the environment.

In order to be able to extract useful reusable patterns, we started by identifying all common team-based goals (e.g., perform conference session) for which several actors may gather in a meeting room. Each of these goals can be realized through multiple different runs or scenarios. For example, to achieve the state "conference session performed" all presenters should be finished with their talks. However, whether there are impaired actors in the environment or not, as well as the exact number of presentations in the session may differ from one situation to another. Thus, we find it useful to create the so-called goal-based patterns that are abstracting from the detailed and precise context of execution. In other words, they provide a holistic model for the whole team-based goal, while the exact adaptation of this model to the developer's context of use is achieved during the pattern instantiation phase. Furthermore, by investigating those goals, a set of entity-based patterns are revealed. For example, some devices like a projector or a laptop are mandatory for various team-based goals, and consequently a device template capturing the dynamic behaviour of those devices can be considered as device patterns that can be reused several times in various situations. In addition, we defined role-based patterns, where a whole role to be played is represented using CTT and can also be adapted according to the characteristics of the actor performing the task, in addition to some other environmental factors. Those role-based patterns can be further decomposed to the so-called task patterns, which represent the lower level of patterns we have in our language. However, a new structure for the task patterns is suggested in order to maximize the benefit of those patterns.

The classification of our patterns is presented in Fig. 5.21. It consists of three distinguishable divisions. We will focus our discussion here on the task-based patterns that are related to the role-based patterns (Fig. 5.20).

A more detailed explanation of all patterns is provided in Zaki and Forbrig 2012. We argue for a broad definition of task patterns by specifying the environmental

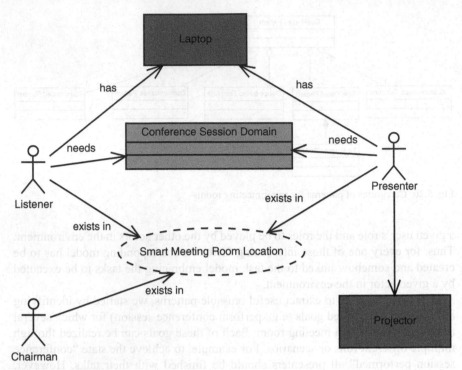

Fig. 5.21 Conference session goal-based pattern

preconditions and effects in the pattern structure. While Sinnig 2004 suggested the idea of having domain attributes to which the task template is adaptable; in Wurdel et al. 2008, there was the idea of using OCL constrains to specify the context of use. Actually, those approaches enable the adaptation of task patterns to various contexts like described in the previous paragraph.

However, the executions of every task within a given task pattern sometimes need a set of complex preconditions. The previous approaches were extended by a visual representation of the environmental and dependencies for executions. In Table 5.1, one of the task patterns "Present Slides Pattern" is depicted. The skeleton of the patterns is inspired by CTT Paterno and Meniconi 1997 and the solution provided by the pattern is textually described in the "solution" section, while in the "diagram" section a graphical representation of the solution is represented.

By having a closer look at the "Present Slides Pattern", one can notice that the solution is actually decomposed into three distinguishable parts. First of all, the task fragment to be loaded by the developer and integrated into his task model is provided. This task fragment specifies the tasks to be executed by the actor in the room. Then, a UML class diagram is used to identify the relevant entities for all the tasks represented in the task fragment. Finally, a formal representation of every individual task's execution constraints is available using UML activity diagram notation.

Actually, the execution of a given task may have two different types of constraints. We have the temporal constraints specifying the order of execution of this task with correspondence to the others, and we adopt the approach presented in Brüning et al. 2008 in order to have a valid transformation of temporal operators defined by CTT to activity diagrams notations.

The other sort of constraints is the one resulting from the environmental dependencies (e.g., device state, object existence, actor location...etc.). Preconditions and postconditions are provided by the activity diagrams notation. In that way, activity diagrams are able to visualize all the execution constraints related to the tasks to be performed. It is noteworthy that each of the solution's parts can be adapted according to the context of use. While decision nodes are used to adapt, both, task models and activity diagrams, the UML class diagram can be adapted using the cardinality associated to the objects. In the pattern example shown above, the case of having a deaf user in the room is considered. Thus, one of the attributes to which the pattern instance is adapted is the fact whether the actor suffers from any kind of hearing problems.

A last point to mention is that we define identically role-based patterns, which are task patterns abstracting from a complete repetitive role to be played in the environment.

Every entity that is sometimes relevant for the task execution has to be taken into account. By investigating CTML as an appropriate language for modelling collaborative environments, one can notice that an isolated model is needed for every entity type, and then those models are linked to the task model using dependencies.

The domain of smart meeting rooms reveals several models or templates, which can be reused. For instance, a device model capturing the dynamic behaviour of a projector is needed in most of the scenarios we discovered so far. Another example is the arrangement of the objects in the location (smart room) captured in the location model, and which can also be the same in various scenarios and while achieving several goals. Thus, as presented in Fig. 5.21 we develop a set of patterns for every environmental aspect to be considered. We compile the following patterns:

a. Device-based template: illustrates the dynamic behaviour of a device in the environment. We use state-chart diagrams to define those templates.
b. Domain-based pattern:captures the static attributes of all included entities in one of the defined team-based goals. UML class diagram notation is employed to represent those patterns.
c. Location-based template: defines a specific arrangement of objects and a precise description of zones within the environment.
d. Team-based pattern: presents the tasks to be executed by the group of users in cooperation (not every individual user). We build those patterns using task models.

A crucial point to mention is the fact that all of the above described patterns can be adapted according to some attributes that should be set by the developer.

If the goal for which the actors currently exist in the environment is one of the team-based goals we already expected, then we make it feasible for the developer to load a complete cooperation model (including all roles, device models, domain models, and location models), which then should be adapted according to the context of use in order to represent the exact encountered scenario. It is noteworthy that within our pattern language, those goal-based patterns after being adapted (adaptation attributes should have concrete values) provide the highest level of assistance, since the developer can load all the models needed to assimilate the scenario taking place in the environment.

Therefore, to effectively use our pattern language, the developer should start by iterating over our set of goal-based patterns. In other words, the developer starts by checking whether the scenario one is about to develop can be mapped to one of the goal-based patterns existing in the language. When this is the case, the pattern is loaded and the developer assigns concrete values to adapt the pattern as already described. Despite the fact, that we tried to identify all team-based goals for which a group of actors may gather in a smart meeting room, it is still possible to have some scenarios which are not covered by this level of patterns. In this case, the developer may be assisted by the entity-based patterns. Thus, she may load a complete model for one or more of the included entities (e.g., a device model for one of the existing devices). However, it is obvious that the assistance provided by those patterns is less than the assistance provided by the previous ones, as the developer still has to build the non-loaded models; and in addition, all the models should be linked to the task model. The developer may also take advantage of the existing role-based patterns. In case no complete matching roles are usable, the designer can still take benefit of the task patterns providing repetitive task fragments, which may be integrated within the developer's task model. In addition, those task patterns offer some information the developer may need to build the other environmental-related models. We illustrate one of our goal-based patterns in the example below.

For the sake of brevity, we only show one pattern application example. We present the "Conference Session Pattern" as an application example of a goal-based pattern in a scenario. First of all, let us consider the following conference session scenario taking place in a smart meeting room: "The chairman, Mr. Georges, enters the room, introduces the topic of the session, welcomes the audiences, and gives the floor to the first speaker. Before starting her talk, the presenter connects her presenter device to one of the projectors in the room. Later, she iterates over all the slides of her presentation, while explaining them to the listeners. Every listener is taking notes of the interesting information she gets from the talk. One of those listeners is actually deaf. Once this speaker is finished with her talk, the chairman asks the audiences for questions which should be answered by the talker.

The same process is repeated for three presenters, and at the end Mr. Georges concludes the ideas, thanks the presenters, and closes the session."

By investigating the above described scenario, the developer can easily notice that it is addressed by the "Conference Session Pattern," which is one of the team-based patterns available in our pattern language. Thus, the developer may model the previous scenario by loading this pattern and adapting it according to the exact situation described. Figure 5.4 illustrates this pattern before being configured and adapted to the developer's scenario (Fig. 5.21).

Every entity within the previous pattern is defined using a corresponding model. For example, the listener, presenter, and chairman roles are available using task

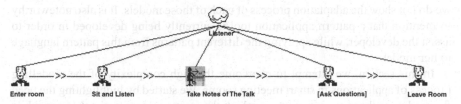

Fig. 5.22 Listener role

models. Also, the conference session domain is described using a UML class diagram. Actually, all of those entities are built out of some of the entity-based patterns available in the second category. Consequently, every goal-based pattern (e.g., Conference Session Pattern) is composed of a concatenation of entity-based patterns (e.g., Projector template, presenter role-based pattern, chairman role-based pattern, etc.) which actually enables us to achieve the idea of a pattern language for the domain. However, all those models are to be instantiated according to the scenario presented. Thus, an adaptation process for all these models is taking place and it results in a specific suitable configuration for the current situation. Figure 5.23 depicts the role listener for a normal user in the environment, while Fig. 5.24 depicts the role played by the only deaf user among the audiences. In Fig. 5.24, it is shown that the deaf user is using a conversion mechanism in order to be able to process the information provided by the speaker. Moreover, whenever this user needs to ask a question, she will provide the question in text format to a text-to-speech converter that is able to alter the modality of the information provided to usual speech and broadcast it in the room, so that the speaker can listen to the question and answer it. Thus, the instance resulting from the adaptation of the "conference session" goal-based pattern depicted in Fig. 5.22 will contain two different listener roles that are depicted in Fig. 5.23 and Fig. 5.24, and then everyone in the audience will be bound to one of those models. Similarly, all the other models are instantiated and that is how we achieve the final instance of our goal-based pattern. For the sake of brevity,

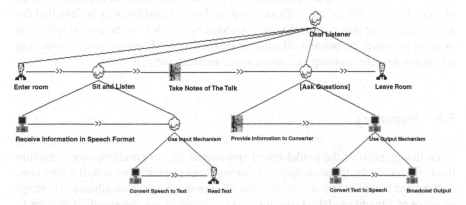

Fig. 5.23 Deaf listener role

we do not show the adaptation process of each of those models. It is also noteworthy to mention that a pattern application tool is currently being developed in order to assist the developer, while applying the different patterns from this pattern language to her model.

In this section, we attempt to overcome the high complexity of the modelling process of applications in smart meeting rooms. We started by highlighting the need for modelling those environments in which the main goal is to assist the user, while performing her daily life tasks. We discussed the various entities and factors which constrain the tasks' execution in the room, and thus should be considered.

We investigated one of the languages (CTML) that is designed to model collaborative environments, and enable the developer to represent and model all entities which are relevant for the task's execution. However, we explained that the dependencies existing between all those entities dramatically increase the burden on the developer who is supposed to build all those models, and goes afterwards through a verification process to guarantee the validity of the resulting model.

Therefore, in our work we suggested to build a pattern language addressing the domain of smart meeting rooms that can assist the user while building those models, and thus making this process of a better performing and less time-consuming. Our pattern language is composed of three distinguishable categories that we discussed.

We suggested the existence of a division containing patterns providing the highest level of assistance, but which are only convenient in case that the team goal is successfully expected. In other cases, we have the entity-based patterns where we offer the developer the possibility to load a complete model presenting one of the entities to be considered in her case. Finally, the last type of patterns that we have in our language and from which the developer can take benefit is the so-called task patterns. Those patterns enable the integration of task fragments acting as building blocks within the user's task model.

However, a new definition and understanding of the "task pattern" was also explained. In order to make our ideas more clear, we provided a pattern application example where a specific scenario was described and we illustrated the instantiation and application process of one of the goal-based patterns existing in our language. Our work is still missing the existence of a tool that facilitates the application of all of those patterns. We are currently developing this tool, and we truly believe that the idea of providing this pattern language assisted by the tool can be a successful step in order to deliver proper and effective assistance to the developer while modelling a learning scenario running in a given smart meeting room.

5.6   Summary

Even though most of the model-based approaches are supported by tools, creating the various models, transforming and linking them to each other is still a time consuming and complex activity. In addition, the approaches lack an advanced concept of reuse of already modelled solutions. In this chapter, we presented an attempt to overcome the high complexity of the modelling process of applications.

It was shown that patterns may be employed to avoid these disadvantages, since they provide an advanced concept of reuse by definition. After introducing the concept of pattern-driven and task-based development in general, concrete tool support was discussed.

It was demonstrated how the three pattern application steps:

1. Selection of an appropriated pattern in order to solve a given design problem,
2. Instantiating the pattern in order to achieve a concrete design solutions, and
3. Integrating the pattern instance in the existing models.

can be supported for task patterns.

Later, we highlighted the need for modelling environments in which the main goal is to assist the user while performing her daily life tasks. We discussed the various entities and factors which constrain the tasks' execution in the room, and thus should be considered.

However, we explained that the dependencies existing between all those entities increase dramatically the burden on the developer who is supposed to build all those models, and later goes through a verification process to guarantee the validity of the resulting model. Therefore, we suggested building a pattern language addressing the domain of smart meeting rooms and which can assist the user while building those models, and thus making this process better performing and less time consuming. We had a closer look at the so-called task patterns. Those patterns enable the integration of task fragments acting as building blocks within the user's task model. However, a new definition and understanding of the "task pattern" was also explained. In order to make our ideas more clear, we provided a pattern application example where a specific scenario was described, and we illustrated the instantiation and application process of one of the goal-based patterns existing in our language.

Our work is still missing the existence of a tool that facilitates the application of all of those patterns. We are currently developing this tool, and we truly believe that the idea of providing this pattern language assisted by the tool can be a successful step in order to deliver proper and effective assistance to the developer, while modelling scenarios running in a given smart meeting room.

References

Alexander C et al (1977) A pattern language. Oxford University Press, New York

Alexander C (1979) The timeless way of building. Oxford University Press, New York

Balme L, Demeure A, Barralon N, Coutaz J, Calvary G (2004) CAMELEON-RT: a software architecture reference model for distributed, migratable, and plastic user interfaces. In: Markopoulos Panos Eggen Berry Aarts Emile HL Crowley James L (eds.) EUSAI 2004– ambient intelligence—second european symposium November 8–11, Eindhoven, The Netherlands, pp. 291–302

Borchers J, Thomas J (2001) Patterns: what's in it for HCI? In: Proceedings of conference on human factors in computing (CHI) 2001. Seattle

Breedvelt I, Paternò F, Severiins C (1997) Reusable structures in task models. In: Proceedings of design, specification, verification of interactive systems '97. Springer Verlag, Granada, pp. 225–239

Breiner K, Seissler M, Meixner G, Forbrig P, Seffah A, Klöckner K (2011) PEICS: towards HCI patterns into engineering of interactive systems. In: Proceedings of the 1st international workshop on pattern-driven engineering of interactive computing systems (PEICS '10). ACM, New York, 1–3. doi=10.1145/1824749.1824750 (http://doi.acm.org/10.1145/1824749.1824750)

Brüning J, Dittmar A, Forbrig P, Reichart D (2008) Getting SW engineers on board: task modeling with activity diagrams. In: Gulliksen J et al (eds) Engineering interactive systems. Lecture Notes in Computer Science, vol 4940. Springer-Verlag, Berlin, pp. 175–192

Calvary G et al (2003) A unifying reference framework for multi-target user interfaces. Interact Comput 15(3):289–308

Cook D, Das S (2004) Smart environments: technology, protocols and applications, ISBN: 978-0-471-54448-7

Eclipse (2014) Eclipse—an open development platform. http://www.eclipse.org. Accessed Dec 2014

Forbrig P (2012) Interactions in smart environments and the importance of modelling, Romanian Journal of Human-Computer Interaction, vol 5, pp 1–12. (Special issue: Human Computer Interaction 2012 ISSN 1843–4460, http://rochi.utcluj.ro/rrioc/en/rochi2012.html)

Forbrig P, Wurdel M, Zaki M (2012) The roles of models and patterns in smart environments, EICS workshop—model-based interactive ubiquitous systems (MODIQUITOUS), Copenhagen

Forbrig P, Märtin Ch, Zaki M (2013) Special challenges for models and patterns in smart environments, human-computer interaction. Human-centred design approaches, methods, tools, and environments. LNCS 8004:340–349

Fincher S (2003) CHI 2003 workshop report—perspectives on HCI patterns: concepts and tools (introducing PLML). Interfaces, vol. 56, pp. 26–28

Janeiro J, Barbosa Simone DJ, Springer T, Schill A (2010) Semantically relating user interface design patterns. In: Proceedings of the 1st international workshop on pattern-driven engineering of interactive computing systems (PEICS '10). ACM, New York, pp. 40–43. doi=10.1145/1824749.1824759, http://doi.acm.org/10.1145/1824749.1824759

Johnson P, Diaper D, Long J (1985) Task analysis in interactive system design and evaluation. In: Johannsen J, Mancini C, Martensson L (eds) Analysis, design and evaluation of man-machine systems. Pergamon Press, Oxford

Johnson P, Wilson S, Markopoulos P, Pycock J (1993) ADEPT—Advanced Environment for Prototyping with Task Models. In: Ashlund, Stacey, Mullet, Kevin, Henderson, Austin, Hollnagel, Erik and White, Ted (eds.) Proceedings of the ACM CHI 93 Human Factors in Computing Systems Conference April 24–29, Amsterdam, The Netherlands. p. 56

Limbourg Q et al (2004) USIXML: a user interface desciption language for context-sensitive user interfaces. In: Proceedings of ACM AVI'2004 Workshop "Developing User Interfaces with XML: Advances on User Interface Description Languages". Gallipoli

Luyten K (2004) Dynamic user interfaces generation for mobile and embedded systems with model-based user interface development. PHD in Maastricht, Universiteit Maastricht

Mobile Design Pattern Galery (2013) http://www.mobiledesignpatterngallery.com/mobile-patterns.php. Accessed 19 July 2013

Mobile Patterns (2013) http://www.mobile-patterns.com/. Accessed 15 July 2013

Molina PJ, Hernández J (2003) Just-UI: using patterns as concepts for UI specification and code generation, CHI 2003 workshop. http://www.cs.kent.ac.uk/people/staff/saf/patterns/chi2003/submissions/pjmolinaCHI2003WS.pdf

Norman DA, Draper SW (1986) User centered system design: new perspectives on human-computer interaction, Hillsdale. Lawrence Erlbaum Associates, New Jersey

OCL (Object Constraint Language) (2014) http://www.omg.org/spec/OCL/. Accessed Dec 2014

Paternó F (2000) Model-based design and evaluation of interactive applications. Springer-Verlag, Berlin

Paterno F (2001) Task models in interactive software systems, handbook of software engineering & knowledge engineering. S. K. Chang, World Scientific Publishing Co

Paterno F, Meniconi C (1997) ConcurTaskTrees: a diagrammatic notation for specifying task models. IFIP TC 1: 362–369

Paternó F, Santoro C (2002) One model, many interfaces. In: Proceedings of CADUI 2002. Valenciennes, France

Puerta A, Eisenstein J (1999) Towards a general computational framework for model-based interface development systems. In: Proceedings of IUI99: International Conference on Intelligent User Interfaces. Los Angeles

Radeke F (2007) Pattern-driven model-based user-interface development, Diploma Thesis in the Department of Computer Science. University of Rostock, Rostock

Sinnig D (2004) The complicity of patterns and model-based UI development, Master's Thesis in the Department of Computer Science. Concordia University, Montreal

Stary C (1999) Toward the task-complete development of activity-oriented user interfaces. Int J Hum Comput Interact 11(2):153–182

TeresaXML (2012) XML languages of Teresa. http://giove.isti.cnr.it/tools/TERESA/. Accessed Nov 2012

Tidewell J (1998) Interaction design patterns: twelve theses, PLoP'98. Conference on pattern languages of programming. Illinois

Tidwell J (2005) Designing interfaces—patterns for effective interaction design. O'Reilly, Beijing

UI-Design Patterns (2013) http://ui-patterns.com/patterns. Accessed July 2013

UML (Unified Modeling Language) (2012) http://www.uml.org/. Accessed Dec 2012

UsiXML (2014) User interface extensible markup language. http://www.usixml.org. Accessed Dec 2014

van Duyne D Landay J Hong J (2005) The design of sites—patterns, principles and processes for crafting a customer-centered web experience, Addison Wesley, Boston

Welie M (2012) Patterns in interaction design. http://www.welie.com/. Accessed Nov 2012

Welie M, Trætteberg H (2000) Interaction patterns in user interfaces. In: Proceedings of Pattern Languages of Programs (PLoP 2000). Monticello, Illinois

Wurdel M, Radhakrishnan T, Sinnig D (2007) Patterns for task-and dialog-modeling, Springer, vol. 4550, pp. 1226–1235

Wurdel M, Sinnig D, Forbrig P (2008) CTML: domain and task modelling for collaborative environments. J.UCS 14:3188–3201

Wolff A, Forbrig P, Dittmar A, Reichard D (2005) Linking GUI elements to tasks—supporting an evolutionary design process. In: Proceedings of TAMODIA 2005. Gdansk, Poland

Wolff A, Forbrig P, Dittmar A, Reichard D (2005) Tool support for model-based generation of advanced user interfaces, MDDAUI. http://www.ceur-ws.org/Vol-159/paper2.pdf

XIML (2012) A universal language for user interfaces. http://www.ximl.org/. Accessed Oct 2012

Yahoo Design Pattern Library (2013) http://developer.yahoo.com/ypatterns/. Accessed 19 July 2013

Yu Z, Nakamura Y (2010) Smart meeting systems: a survey of State-of-the-Art and open issues. ACM Computing Surv 42(2):8

Zaki M, Forbrig P (2011) User-oriented accessibility patterns for smart environments. HCI (1) 2011:319–327

Zaki M, Forbrig P (2012) Towards the generation of assistive user interfaces for smart meeting rooms based on activity patterns. AmI 2012:288–295

Zaki M, Forbrig P (2013) A methodology for generating an assistive system for smart environments based on contextual activity patterns. In: Proceedings of the 5th ACM SIGCHI symposium on Engineering interactive computing systems (EICS '13). ACM, New York, 75–80

Zaki M, Forbrig P, Brüning J (2012) Towards contextual task patterns for smart meeting rooms. Second International Conference on Pervasice and Embedded Computing and Communication Systems (PECCS), Feb 24–26, 2012 Rome Italy. pp 162–169

Chapter 6
HCI Patterns in Multiplatform Mobile Applications Reengineering

Abstract With the advent of the Internet and mobile computing, more and more human–computer interaction (HCI) designers are asked to reengineer user interface (UI) for accommodating a diversity of users while taking into account variations in geographical regions, population, languages, and cultures. Developers are asked to implement the same UI with a variation of functionalities using diverse and continually changing development languages. The lack of methods that help developers with UI reengineering motivated us to explore patterns-oriented reengineering.

In this chapter, we demonstrate how patterns can drive the whole reengineering design process when dealing with the constraints of each computing platform. To illustrate our ideas, several examples will be described including how to adapt a Web navigation system to different sizes and models of abstract information structure (architecture) and to different contexts of use. We wish to ground our pattern-driven reengineering methodology as solidly as possible in empirical data and theoretical principles. In order to build the theoretical foundation of our framework, this chapter relies on a combination of proven facts, best-guess assumptions, and logic. In the long term, we will return to cover the individual issues in more detail and with more empirical and formal proof.

6.1 On the Needs for Reengineering

An inevitable fact is that user interfaces (UIs), like any software, change over time. Original design will have to be modified to account for changing user needs, advances in technology as well as shift to new interaction styles. Current trends in graphical user interface (GUI) design have been changing rapidly. The Web, as a vital medium for information transfer, has had an impact on UI design.

Furthermore, the introduction of new platforms and devices in particular mobile phones and personal digital assistant (PDA) has added an extra layer of com-

© Springer International Publishing Switzerland 2015   109
A. Seffah, *Patterns of HCI Design and HCI Design of Patterns,*
Human-Computer Interaction Series, DOI 10.1007/978-3-319-15687-3_6

plication to required UI system changes, from where the concept of multiple UIs emerges. In the migration of interactive systems to new platforms and architectures, many modifications have to be made to the UI. As an example, in the process of adapting the traditional desktop-GUI to other kinds of UIs such as Web or handheld UI or wearable computing, most of the UI code has to be modified. In this scenario, UI reengineering techniques can facilitate such transition. As illustrated in Fig. 6.1, reengineering methods can be applied, to result in a high-level model of the UI. This task-oriented model can then be used to help in the redesign of the UI.

The new technological context of UI development has made it necessary, for developers, to move to different tools and techniques that support both scripting and programming approaches. Writing code from scratch is no longer a viable solution, and many techniques concentrate on reuse. Furthermore, it is a critical necessity to bring an acceptable answer to the following question. How can an organization implement and validate N interfaces for M devices without writing N*M programs, training an army of developers in L languages and UI toolkits, and maintaining N*M architectural model for describing the same interface?

In this book, we will be introducing the use of patterns as a multiple user interface (MUI) reengineering tool. The use of patterns helps in the reuse of design solutions, and plays a significant role throughout the whole UI reengineering process. The fundamental aspect of our work in comparison with existing UI reengineering is that we take into account the vertical and horizontal usability issues. Vertical usability refers to the usability requirement specific to each platform while horizontal usability is concerned with the cross-platform usability issues of a MUI.

The remainder of this chapter is organized as follows: Sect. 6.2 will give an overview of the steps involved in UI reengineering. Section 6.3 will discuss the role that patterns can play in UI reengineering. Section 6.4 will provide three concrete examples where UI patterns are applied in the reengineering process. The first example entails the use of a specific pattern for the reengineering of text-based UI. The two other examples introduce the idea of web-based UI patterns in MUI development. Finally, Sect. 6.5 presents a perspective for a tool that supports the developers in using and selecting patterns for UI reengineering.

Fig. 6.1 Current and future context for user interface engineering

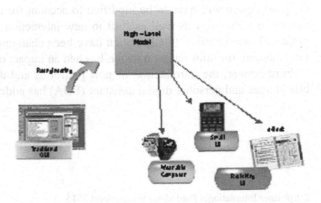

6.2 Steps in User Interface Reengineering

The UI reengineering process consists of three major steps:

- Reverse engineering where the challenge is to understand the interface code for building a high-level and declarative UI model. This UI model represents all the relevant aspects of a UI in some type of interface modeling language. Different high-level models have been suggested in the literature including object-oriented models, abstract UI specification, as well as general task model for the problem domain or environment-dependent task model. All these variety of models can be exploited to drive the interface development process (Bomsdorf and Szwillus 1998; El Kaim et al. 2001).
- Transformation that consists to redesign the UI model to accommodate new platform constraints and user needs.
- Forward Engineering in which we provide automatic support for the generation of a new UI. This operation consists to generate the complete or partial UI code using a specific programming language.

6.2.1   Reverse Engineering

Reverse Engineering is the process of analyzing software code with the objective of recovering its design and specification (Moore 1996b). In the reverse engineering of interactive systems, the ideal behavioral specification of the system is an abstract UI model with enough detail to allow appropriate UI techniques, in particular model-based approaches, to be chosen in the new interface domain (Moore 1996b). There are two main aspects of an interface that need to be analyzed during the reverse engineering process:

- The structural aspects which consist to identify the interface components and the relationships that can exist between them
- The behavioral aspects which describe the dynamic behavior of the interface including the dialogs and the user feedback

Merlo et al. (1993) introduce an intermediate representation language, called the *Abstract User Interface Description Language* (AUIDL). This language helps in the representation and description of UI structure and behavior. Since it is not necessary to understand all of an application's functionality to reengineer its UI, time and resources can be saved if only the significant parts of the system are investigated. Removing superfluous information from the code and higher-level representations can make the construction of an abstract model easier. Moore developed a technique for analyzing the UI by identifying the *user interface slice* (UIS) (Moore 1996a).

6.2.2   Transformation

The transformation process tries to first identify the problems of the old UI model, obtained during reverse engineering, and then attempts to come up with viable solutions that can help in the creation of a new UI model. The goal of the transformation process is to change the UI in order to meet the new requirements. This can include the computing platform capabilities and contrasts as well as the UI look and feel, and the dialog style. It is important to note that in the new UI model, some of the components of the old model can be reused if even their behaviors can be reengineered. Furthermore, input from human and their experiences is an essential part of the transformation phase (Moore 1996b; Lau and Stacsek 1999). As we will explain it, human experiences captured as UI design patterns can be used for driving and supporting the transformation process. Fundamentally speaking, a transformation is defined as follows:

T (GUI, P1) → {((Web UI, P2) or (Web UI, P3)) and (Web UI, P4)}

where P1, P2, P3, and P4 are patterns for navigation support. This transformation means simply that the equivalent of P1 pattern for Web UI is P2 or P3 and P4. Intuitively, a transformation can be as easy as "The equivalent of the GUI toolbar which provides a direct link to common features in GUI is a combo which includes the same features for a PDA. This transformation is motivated by the size of screens.

6.2.3   Forward Engineering

The last step of UI reengineering consists of the generation of a new interface. This new interface must provide all required services and tasks to the user, and must convey all information exchanged between the user and the system in an adequately designed manner. Several factors must be satisfied during forward engineering, which are indicative of the success of the UI reengineering process (Moore 1996b):

- The new UI has to be consistent with the reengineered UI, particularly in terms of functionality. We are not referring to *exact* functionality, but rather that the new UI should contain all original functionality even if enhancements or changes are made.
- The forward engineering phase should commence where the transformation phase is left off. In other words, the new UI abstract model should allow for the occurrence of forward engineering.
- Certain relationships exist between UI components and pieces of code. It is important to ensure the preservation of these relationships.

There are few tools and techniques suggested by researchers to support in the UI reengineering process; one of them called URGenT: User Interface ReGENeration Tool as described by Stroulia and Matichuk (1999). This tool records user interactions and then generates an appropriate GUI that can interact with the back-end of the legacy system.

6.3 Patterns in Reengineering

Current reengineering approaches exploit an explicit high-level UI model which is not always easily doable and time consuming. Here, we are exploring the UI design patterns as an alternative reengineering. Patterns can drive the reengineering process without the need to build and maintain explicitly a descriptive, abstract, and high-level model.

6.3.1 A Brief Overview on Patterns

The architect Alexander introduced design patterns in the early 1970s. He defined a pattern as follows: "Each pattern is a three-part rule, which expresses a relation between a certain context, a problem, and a solution." He went on to explain the nature of a pattern: "Each pattern describes a problem which occurs over and over again in our environment, and then describes the core of the solution to that problem, in such a way that you can use this solution a million times over." The concept of patterns became very popular in the software engineering community with the wide acceptance of the book *"Design Patterns: Elements of Reusable Object-Oriented Software"* (Gamma 1995). Since then, other categories of patterns, such as process patterns and activity patterns (Coplien 1995), have been defined. The goal of all these software-related patterns is to provide common solutions to recurring problems in various parts of the software development lifecycle.

During the last 3 years, the UI design community has been a forum for vigorous discussion on patterns for UI design. Many groups devoted themselves to the development of pattern languages for the UIs design and usability. Among the heterogeneous collections of pattern, "Common Ground," Experiences, and "Amsterdam" play a major role in this field and wield significant influence (Tidwell 1997; Coram and Lee 1998; Welie et al. 2000). It has been also reported that patterns are useful for a variety of reasons. They have the potential to support/drive the whole design process (Borchers 2000; Granlund and Lafrenière 1999; Javahery and Seffah 2002), and they are an alternative/complementary design tool to guidelines (Welie et al. 2000).

For UIs, design patterns can be seen as a medium to encapsulate user experiences and design practices. Pattern users, who are most often software developers unfamiliar with the new emerging platforms, need a thorough understanding of when the pattern applies (context), how it works, why it works (rationale), and how it should be implemented (Javahery and Seffah 2002; Welie et al. 2000).

6.3.2 The Various Role of Patterns in the UI Reengineering Process

In our approach to pattern-oriented UI reengineering, we distinguish between three categories of patterns:

- UI design patterns all deal with UI-specific concerns. They are product-oriented that capture best user experiences;
- Design patterns are more technical and applicable to the internal architecture of the system. Examples includes Abstract Factory and Command Action patterns. They can be used for implementing adaptation mechanisms;
- Reengineering and usability patterns are process-oriented. These patterns describe a proven, successful approach and/or series of actions for developing software. Reengineering patterns can come in many flavors, including but not limited to analysis patterns, reverse engineering patterns, transformation patterns, and forward patterns.

All these patterns are descriptions of a general solution to a common problem or issue from which a detailed solution to a specific problem may be determined. In our work, we mainly investigated the first category. For example, the Web convenient toolbar pattern helps the user reach the most commonly used pages/screens quickly regardless of where the user has navigated. It can provide direct access to frequently used pages such as what are New, Search, Contact Us, Home Page, and Site Map. Figure 6.2 illustrates the descriptive notation we used (Javahery and Seffah 2002).

What make patterns an interesting reengineering tool is the fact that the same pattern can be implemented differently for a Web browser and a PDA. For a PDA, the convenient toolbar pattern can be implemented as a combo box using the Wireless Markup Language (WML). For a Web browser, it is implemented as a toolbar using embedded scripts or a Java applet in HTML. Pattern descriptions should provide advice to pattern users in terms of selecting the suitable implementations for their context.

The concept of applying patterns in reengineering has been explored by a number of individuals (Ismail and Keller 1999; Ducasse et al. 2000; Beedle 1997). However, there has been little work done in the area of UI reengineering with patterns. Design patterns have been applied in the forward engineering phase of reengineering to further refine design models (Ismail and Keller 1999). Furthermore, the actual concept of a *reengineering pattern* was discussed by Ducasse et al. (2000). Their definition was that a reengineering patterns "describes how to go from an existing legacy solution to a new refactored solution," and essentially, they deal with process patterns specific to reengineering.

Figure 6.3 describes the process of pattern-oriented reengineering that we are introducing. UI design patterns are mainly used during the transformation phase. Let us take the example of a text-based legacy system. To make the interface user friendly and to adapt it to newer technologies, we need to change the design of the UI. This could entail the construction of a GUI. Applying a proper usability pattern in transforming the old design to the new GUI can make the process of design

Pattern_Name: **Convenient Toolbar Pattern**	
type:	**Navigation Support Pattern**
Context_Use	**User:**Expert **Task:** Assist user to reach the most useful and frequently visited pages at any time through the Web site.
Workplace:	Web applications
Usability_Problem:	The user can easily find most commonly used pages regardless of the current state of the artifact. The user can reach these convenient pages promptly.
Usability_Factor:	**Factor:**Efficiency, Safety **Criteria:** Consistency, Minimal Action, Minimal Memory, User Guidance, Helpfulness
Example:	⊕OCLC Home ⊙ Search ⊕Site Map ○What's New ⊙Feedback OCLC ONLINE COMPUTER ◀ home ▶
Design_Solution:	Group the most convenient action links, such as home, site map, help and etc. Use meaningful metaphors and accurate phrases as lables Place it consistently throughout the Web site
Other Language Attributes:	Design_Principle Related Usability_Patterns Reading

Fig. 6.2 A description of the convenient toolbar pattern

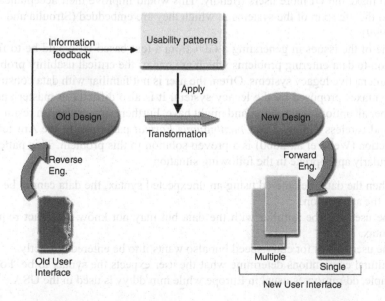

Fig. 6.3 Role of patterns in UI reengineering

easier, and will result in less usability errors. In addition, since usability patterns are context-oriented, their use will assure that the best solution has been applied.

In our approach to pattern-driven reengineering, patterns should be considered as early on as during the reverse engineering phase, and then describe their role during the other phases of the reengineering process. Information gathered during the reverse engineering phase could help the software engineer to make a decision about which usability pattern is appropriate for design. Information such as domain knowledge and UI system architecture can be used to assess the appropriateness of a pattern. Knowing the capability of the system and usability problems will help the software developer in deciding which pattern to use. Furthermore during the forward step, since the context of use is included in pattern descriptions, the designer can easily select appropriate pattern implementation according to the desired context. There is no need to provide the code explicitly, as part of the pattern descriptions. We provide different strategies for implementing the patterns for different context of use.

6.4   Examples of UI Reengineering with Patterns

6.4.1   Migration from Text-Based to GUI for Legacy Interactive Systems

In this first example, patterns are applied to redesign the interface of an interactive legacy system. This design entails replacing a text-based interface with a perspective to make the UI more users friendly. This would improve their acceptance and extend the life span of the systems in which they are embedded (Stroulia and Stacsek 1999).

One of the issues in generating a GUI from a text-based UI would be to find a solution to data entering problems which are one of the critical usability problems with interactive legacy systems. Often, the user is not familiar with data constraints and syntaxes proposed by the legacy system. It is also difficult to master and remember all options that a command might have. Furthermore, errors can result from fast and careless typing. The *Unambiguous Format* pattern from the Amsterdam Collection (Welie et al. 2000) is a proven solution to this problem. This pattern is particularly appropriate in the following situation:

- When the data are entered using an unexpected syntax, the data cannot be used by the application.
- The user may be familiar with the data but may not know the exact required syntax.
- The user strives for entry speed but also wants it to be entered correctly.
- Cultural conventions determine what the user expects the syntax to be. For example, dd/mm/yy is usual in Europe while mm/dd/yy is used in the USA.

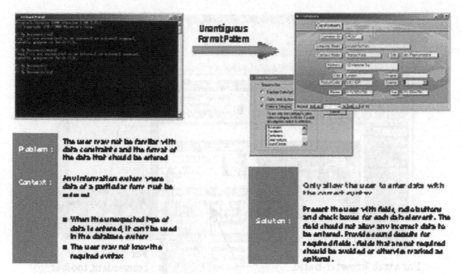

Fig. 6.4 Pattern in legacy UI reengineering

As shown in Fig. 6.4, these forces will result in a design that will prevent the user from entering any incorrect syntax. The solution for this problem can be implemented via the use of radio buttons, check boxes, drop-down menus, and field parameters. Additionally, explaining the syntax to the user with an example, providing concrete defaults for the required fields, and marking optional fields, are supplementary options in the description of this pattern.

6.4.2   Reengineering a Web-Based Interface for Small Devices

Most often, Web applications are designed first for a desktop with a Web browser. It is common to see the following reminder on some Web sites "This Website is better viewed or optimized with/for Internet Explorer or Netscape Communicator." With the rapid shifting toward mobile computing, these Web sites need to be customized and migrated to different devices with different capabilities. In this context, when designing a big versus small screen, we need to rethink the strategies for displaying information. For example, an airline reservation system may display choosing a flight and buying the ticket on two separate screens for a small PDA. This separation is not required for a large screen that unifies the choosing and buying into a single screen. Also, the PDA interface may eliminate images or it may show them in black-and-white. Similarly, text may be abbreviated on a small display, though it should be possible to retrieve the full text through a standardized command. For all these situations, patterns can facilitate the reengineering while ensuring that all these constraints will be taken into account.

Figure 6.5 illustrates an example with the CNN site. Even though the basic functionality and information provided are the same for all three platforms (desktop,

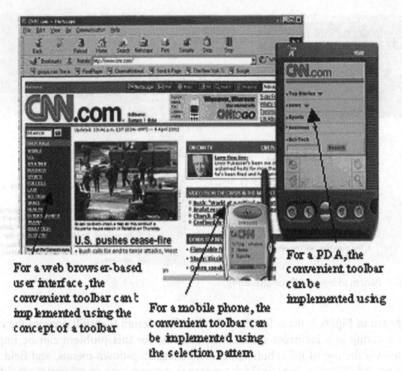

For a web browser-based user interface, the convenient toolbar can't implemented using the concept of a toolbar

For a mobile phone, the convenient toolbar can be implemented using the selection pattern

For a PDA, the convenient toolbar can be implemented using

Fig. 6.5 Usability patterns in a MUI framework

mobile phone, and PDA), it has been adapted according to the context of use and the limitations of each platform. In this design, different navigation support patterns have been used in the three designs. They provide the same solution for the same problem, but they are implemented in different ways.

For example, as previously explained in Sect. 6.3.2, the convenient toolbar pattern can help the user to search for the most frequented and important information on a Web site. For the PDA, the convenient toolbar can be implemented using the *Combo Box* to solve the limitation of space. Finally, for the mobile phone, the navigation system is limited to a few buttons and it has a small monocolor screen. Popular Web sites like CNN have been adapted to these constraints by using a design solution similar to that described in the *Selection Pattern* (Welie et al. 2000). For this pattern, the user is provided with a list of all possible links that can be chosen.

6.4.3 Reengineering Navigation Systems to different Architecture Sizes

Web sites are generally a dynamic system where the size and the structure of content can vary over a period of time. It can start very small and grow very fast. The volume of information can be reduced to accommodate the capabilities and constraints of large diversity of users and variety of technology. The UIs are continually

Table 6.1 Number of menu levels and pages as a function of architecture size

Number of pages	Size range measured in terms of number of pages	Label	Examples
17	1–100	Small	Personal pages
273	100–1000	Medium	Medium size companies
4396	1000–10,000	Large	Large organizations
69,905	10,000–100,000	Very large	Global information sites: CNN
1,118,481	100,000–4,000,000	Extra large	Worldwide portals: Yahoo

designed, redesign, and reengineered. In particular, the original navigation system has to be adapted or customized. An empirical study we conducted shows us that a good navigation system for a small Web site is not necessary suitable for a very large Web site architecture (Engelberg and Seffah 2002). A navigation system has to be reevaluated and possibly replaced for different sizes and models of abstract information structure (Table 6.1).

For example, when reengineering a very large portal like Yahoo for mobile phones, the navigation patterns have to be replaced by other more appropriate for small or medium size. This is because only a view of the whole Web site will be available for PDA and mobile phones users. Users are also interested to have an access to some specific pages such latest news, sport, movies, etc. Table 6.2 outlines the appropriateness of several design patterns adapted to certain attributes of the context of use and in particular to the size of architecture and physical constraints of the devices. This table is the result of the empirical analysis we did.

This list is far from exhaustive, but helps to communicate the flavor and abstraction level of design patterns for navigation that we are targeting. Due to space limitations, we can only provide the title and a brief description, rather than the full description format as described by Borchers (2001). The contents and structure of the list will be elaborated in future publications. In the following lists, we have found it useful to distinguish between model-based (top-down), data-based (bottom-up), and hybrid navigation patterns (combination model and data-based).

The following are some of the popular model-based navigation patterns:

- M.1—Bread crumbs pattern: Navigation trail from home page down to current page; see Amsterdam collection
- M.2—Contextual (temporary) horizontal menu at top (called up by a higher-level menu or a link)
- M.3—Contextual (temporary) vertical menu at right in content zone (called up by a higher-level menu or a link)
- M.4—Information portal: Broad first and second level on home page. Same principle as the Amsterdam collection's "Directory" pattern
- M.5—Permanent horizontal menu at top
- M.6—Permanent vertical menu at left
- M.7—Progressive filtering (see Amsterdam collection)

Table 6.2 Design patterns as a function of architecture size

Size	Best approach for navigation	Design patterns
Small (2 levels)	Model (menu) based approach: Simple 1-and 2-level main menus	M5, M6, M8
Medium (4 levels)	Model (menu) based approach: Simple 1-and 2-level menus calling up contextual (temporary) menus for the deeper levels Alphabetical index	M2, M3, M9, M10, M12 D1.1
Large (6 levels)	Model-based approaches adapted to deep menus Possibly hybrid approach (depending on efficiency of search agent): Keyword search (or other data-based navigation) to target followed by menu-based navigation within target Within the target, use a navigation patterns consistent with the size of the target (*See small or medium*) Data-based (bottom-up) approaches (depending on efficiency)	M1, M4, M7, M9, M11, M13, M14 (H1) D1.1, D1.2, D1.3, D2
Very and extra large (8+levels)	Hybrid approach: Keyword search (or other data-based navigation) to target followed by menu-based navigation within target Within the target, use a navigation patterns consistent with the size of the target (See small, medium or large) Data-based (bottom-up) approaches Model-based approaches adapted to deep menus	H1 D1.2, D1.3, D2 M1, (M14)

- M.8—Shallow menus (1 or 2 levels in same menu)
- M.9—Simple universal: Shallow left-hand main menu for top levels, usually permanent. After running out of top menu levels, use a series of sequential one-level contextual menus in content zone
- M.10—Split navigation (see Amsterdam collection)
- M.11—Sub-sites: Shallow main menu or broad portal leading to smaller sub-sites with simple navigation architectures
- The following list includes data-based (bottom-up) navigation patterns:
- D.1—User-driven
  - D.1.1—Alphabetical index;
  - D.1.2—Key-word search: D.1.2.1 Global vs. D.1.2.2 Contextual;
  - D.1.3—Key-word search: D.1.3.1 Simple vs. D.1.3.2 Iterative (embedded).
- D.2—Intelligent agents.

The following potentially useful patterns are uncommon in Internet sites, but known in other applications:

- M.12—Container navigation: Different levels of menu displayed simultaneously in separate zones (e.g., Outlook Express or Netscape Mail)
- M.13—Deeply embedded menus (e.g., file manager menu).

The following are some new and experimental design patterns that we are exploring:

- H.1—Hybrid approach: Keyword search to access target, followed by menu-based navigation within target;
- M.14—Refreshed shallow vertical menus (see slide presentation).

6.5 Key Issues and Contributions

This chapter introduced the idea of utilizing usability patterns as an approach for UI reengineering. Some work in the area of reengineering patterns has commenced, although there is much more that needs to be explored, especially in UI redesign. Patterns for UI reengineering can effectively fill the existing gap in present methods. These patterns capture best design practices, and can play a role throughout the complete reengineering process. The application of patterns has a number of advantages. First, they can make the process of reengineering shorter since, for the most common usability problems, there already exists a pattern solution. Second, they reduce the cost of the reengineering process. Third, possible usability errors are reduced since most of the patterns have already been tested by other systems. Finally, usability patterns help the comprehension of the system for future maintenance.

In particular, we demonstrate how pattern can be used to reengineer Web site navigation systems that adapt to different sizes and models of information structure (architecture). One of our most important conclusions is that in large architectures, model-based navigation patterns are good for navigating within the target, but relatively poor for navigation to the target.

We plan to investigate some of the three following research issues in the near future:

- Define more data points (empirical data) for the patterns applicability and appropriateness
- Validate and compare design patterns with usability tests, particularly for new and experimental patterns
- Using XML as language for documenting and implementing patterns

References

Beedle M (1997) Pattern based reengineering. Object magazine

Bomsdorf B, Szwillus G (1998) From task to dialogue: task-based user interface design. SIGCHI Bull 30:4

Borchers JO (2000) A pattern approach to interaction design, proceedings of the DIS 2000 international conference on designing interactive systems, pp 369–378, ACM Press, New York, 16–19 Aug 2000

Borchers JO (2001) A pattern approach to interaction design. Wiley, New York

Coplien JO, Schmidt DC (1995) Pattern language of program design. Addison Wesley

Coram T, Lee J (1998) A pattern language for user interface design. <http://www.maplefish.com/todd/papers/experiences>. Accessed 15 April 2013

Demeyer S, Ducasse S, Nierstrasz O (2000) A pattern language for reverse engineering. EuroPLoP conference 189–208

El Kaim W, Burgard O Muller P-A (2001) MDA compliant product line methodology, technology and tool for automatic generation and deployment of web information systems. In: Proceedings of the 14th international conference on software engineering and its applications, Paris

Engelberg D, Seffah A (2002) A design patterns for the navigation of large information architectures. 11th annual usability professional association conference. Orlando (Florida), USA

Gamma E, Helm R, Johnson R, Vlissides J (1995) Design patterns: elements of reusable object-oriented software. Addison Wesley.

Granlund A, Lafreniere D (1999) PSA: A pattern-supported approach to the user interface design process, Scottsdale, Arizona, July

Ismail K, Rudolf KK (1999) Transformations for pattern-based forward engineering. Universite de Montreal. <http://www.iro.umontreal.ca/~labgelo/Publications/Papers/sts99.pdf>. Accessed 15 April 2013

Javahery H, Seffah A (2002) A model for usability pattern-oriented design. In: Proceedings of TAMODIA 2002, Bucharest, Romania, pp 104–110

Lau T, Stacsek J (1999) A contextual inquiry-based technique of the strudel web site maintenance. Department of computer science, University of Washington

Merlo E, Girard J, Kontogiannis K, Panangaden P, Mori RD (1993) Reverse engineering of user interfaces. In: Working conference on reverse engineering, pp 171–179, Baltimore, MD

Moore M. (1996a) Representation issues for reengineering interactive systems. ACM Comput Surv 28(4es):199

Moore M (1996b) Reverse engineering user interfaces: a technique. ACM Comput Surv 199–es

Stroulia, KE, Matichuk B (1999) Legacy interface migration: a task-centered approach. 8th International Conference on Human-Computer Interaction, Munich, Germany, 22–27 Aug 1999

Tidwell J (1997) Common Ground: A Pattern language for human-computer interface design. <http://www.mit.edu/~jtidwell/common_ground.html>. Accessed 15 April 2015

van Welie M, van der Veer GVC (2000) Patterns as tools for user interface design. International workshop on tools for working with guidelines, Biarritz, France, Oct 7–8

Chapter 7
Generative Patterns for Cross-Platform User Interfaces: The Case of the Master-Detail Pattern

Abstract To become valuable, such design patterns should encode the structure of a solution and its associated forces, rather than cataloguing just a solution, often for a specific platform. We introduce the generative pattern as a way of both documenting and implementing the human–computer interaction (HCI) patterns. A generative pattern not only tells us the rules for implementing a user interface (UI) design is considered as a generic solution to a problem at different levels of abstraction (in the way that a UI could be modeled), but also shows us how to transform these expressions into programmable codes for the diverse computing platforms, while being compliant with the style guide rules that may prevail for these platforms. As a case study, the master-detail (M-D) pattern, one popular and frequently used HCI design pattern, is developed: this displays a master list of items and the details for any selected item. While this MD pattern is documented in very different, possibly inconsistent, ways across various computing platforms, the M-D generative pattern consolidates these particular implementations into a high-level pattern description based on design options that are independent of any platform, thus making this pattern "cross-platform." A framework provides developers and designers with a high level UI process to implement this pattern in using different instances and its application in some designated languages. Some examples of applying an M-D generative pattern are explained as well as a particular implementation for the Android platform.

7.1 Introduction

A human–computer interaction (HCI) pattern is not considered as a finished user interface (UI) design that can be programmed straightforwardly. The importance of implementing design patterns has been pointed out since its inception (Alexander 1977). Here, by implementation we mean designing an effective support for

© Springer International Publishing Switzerland 2015   123
A. Seffah, *Patterns of HCI Design and HCI Design of Patterns*,
Human-Computer Interaction Series, DOI 10.1007/978-3-319-15687-3_7

applying design patterns and transforming this intention into a code. Each time the problem has to be addressed, the pattern application and transformation are applied, thus repeating each time yet another application-specific concrete implementation. Each such implementation often remains specific to one single context of use, i.e., one single user or category of users conducting an interactive task on one dedicated computing platform in a designated location, thus reducing the reusability of this concrete implementation for another context of use. If any dimension of the context of use changes, for instance a new user, a new platform, or a new location, a new transformation has to be applied that is not necessarily available for this new context.

Since the emergence of new devices offering a multitude of interaction styles and allowing every user access to information and services from everywhere and at any time, cross-context patterns are required. Therefore, we hereby define *cross-context patterns* as a general repeatable solution to a commonly occurring task to be conducted in various contexts of use, possibly with different users, platforms, and locations.

Similarly, we hereby define *cross-platform patterns* as a general repeatable solution to a commonly occurring task to be conducted on various computing platforms, independent of user and locations. Consequently, the question arises how to structure and implement such a design pattern on a large myriad of platforms. The goal is to give the opportunity of HCI designers and UI software developers to "switch" patterns when engineering an application for diverse platforms. Because different design patterns may offer different advantages and suffer from different drawbacks depending on the platform, even if they are intended to support the same interactive task of the pattern, another design pattern could become more suitable for a system as it evolves. Or a different behavior observed for the same task that could not be realized by the original patterns might be needed later. However, we cannot switch design patterns using the same implementation, as long as these application-specific implementations are derived from design patterns.

Platform capabilities and constraints largely influence the way a cross-platform pattern could be implemented on a target platform: the programming or markup language expressiveness, the operating system, the underlying development toolkit, the constraints imposed by the platform itself such as screen resolution, interaction style, and interaction devices.

Rendering a cross-platform pattern could be achieved in two ways: (i) *by code generation*, when UIs are implemented in using a set of instructions of any programming language, whatever programming paradigm it follows, and/or a set of assertions of this language; (ii) by *interpretation*, when the UI is described by a declarative language or a user interface description language (UIDL) to be interpreted at run time by a rendering engine. Typical examples of rendering by code generation are: direct coding in a programming language such as C, Java, Visual Basic, model-to-code transformation in model-driven engineering such as in JustUI (Molina 2004), code generation techniques such as generative programming, template filling such as Velocity. Typical examples of rendering by interpretation are declarative languages such as Hypertext Markup Language (HTML),

EXtensible Markup Language (XML), any UIDL or integrated environment like systems, applications & products in data processing (SAP) or Oracle that produces their UI internally.

The remainder of this chapter is structured as follows: Sect. 7.2 reviews various definitions of the M-D pattern found in the literature using classifications and illustrations. Based on the shortcomings and requirements identified in this literature, Sect. 7.3 revisits the definition of the master-detail (M-D) pattern to transform it into a cross-platform pattern as intended. The following sections then respectively examine this pattern more closely at the various levels of abstraction of the Cameleon Reference Framework (CRF): Sect. 7.4 details the UI development life cycle of the M-D pattern by instantiating it at the task and domain, abstract, concrete and final UI levels respectively, Sect. 7.5 explains how to generate a UIDL-document to facilitate its implementation on cross-platform context and illustrates this framework on a case study of a "car rental" task; Sect. 7.6 concludes the chapter by discussing the contributions of our approach comparing it with respect to related work and by presenting some future avenues of this work.

7.2 Related Work

In order to substantiate this research, we decided to focus its discussion on the M-D pattern, also known as master-slave or director-detail pattern (Pastor and Molina 2007). This pattern has been selected for the following reasons: it starts from a domain model, thus offering a data-oriented perspective and a conceptual starting point; it is widely used both in the literature and in practice, by designers, developers, private ones, and software vendors; it is largely considered in systematic development of interactive information systems; previous work do not examine the cross-platform dimension of this pattern in the light of UI implementation and usability concerns; this pattern can be defined as a unified class or can be interpreted such as an aggregation in relationship between two different classes.

This section is divided into five sub-sections regarding five major dimensions of the M/D pattern: the definitions discussed in the literature, its classification in collection patterns, its generative form, its current engineering implementation based on illustrations, and the motivations to present this pattern into a cross-platform one.

7.2.1 Master-Detail Pattern—An Operational Definition

The M-D pattern is typically used in a single scenario where several tasks are performed at the same time, while maintaining the details synchronized related to its master (Pastor and Molina 2007). An M-D pattern is applied, like any pattern, to reflect on possible changes to a technical space or situation (Nilsson 2009). By relying on the context, patterns can prevent repetitive errors in a cross-platform environment.

That also allows understanding better possible impacts of new technologies, the screen resolution being probably one of the most constraining one. This pattern should be prescriptive to promoting creation of new instances in order to help designers in its implementation. The presentation of the M-D pattern for a wide variety of screen types defines how and which elements are suitable. The pattern can then be used to capture essential problems of different "sizes" in using different customizations. Therefore, the using of patterns for documenting design knowledge allows dividing "a large problem area into a structured set of manageable problems (Nilsson 2009)."

In HCI, a *master-detail interface* displays a master list of items, called *master area*, and the details for any selected item, called the *detail area*. A master area can be a form, a list or a tree of items, and a detail area can be a form, a list or a tree of items typically placed as close as possible to the master area (e.g., below or next to it) in order to satisfy the usability guideline: "Semantically, related information should be placed close to each other to reflect this link, while unrelated information should be placed far from each other." Selecting an item from the master area causes the details of that item to be populated in the detail area. A master-detail relationship is a one-to-many type relationship, among which typical examples are: a set of purchase orders and a set of line items belonging to each purchase order, an expense report with a set of expense line items or a department with a list of employees belonging to it. An application can use this master-detail relationship to enable users to navigate through the purchase order data and see the detail data for line items only related to the master purchase order selected.

Figure 7.1 graphically depicts a master-detail by showing how to display information in soccer regarding teams that plays in a league. Let us assume that LeagueList is a collection of leagues. Each league has a name and a collection of divisions, and each division has a name and a collection of teams. Each team has a team name. The divisions ListBox automatically tracks selections in the leagues ListBox and displays the corresponding data. The teams ListBox tracks selections in the other two ListBox controls.

Figure 7.1 also shows that the M-D pattern could be applied recursively (this is sometimes called master-detail-MoreDetail pattern):

Fig. 7.1 An example of a user interface (UI) implementation of the master-detail (M-D) pattern on desktop view

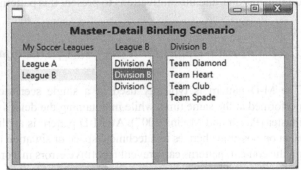

1. The three ListBox controls bind to the same source. You set the path property of the binding to specify which level of data you want the ListBox to display
2. You must set the IsSynchronizedWithCurrentItem property to true on the List-Box controls of the selection you are tracking. Setting this property ensures that the selected item is always set as theCurrentItem. Alternatively, if the ListBox gets it data from a CollectionViewSource, it synchronizes selection and currency automatically.

7.2.2   The M-D Pattern Usage in Pattern Collections

Multiple user interfaces (MUIs) have to adapt to any variation of the cross-platform context. Using a pattern approach allows us to design UIs by a set of models (the model-based UI development) (Seffah and Forbrig 2002) and to provide high abstraction elements before coding the software. Several HCI pattern collections were introduced in the literature since Alexander (1977). "Using patterns to clearly and succinctly describe particular workplaces, in order to understand possible impacts of new technologies." (Bayle et al. 1998)

UI patterns are found more descriptive than generative in most pattern collections (Table 7.1): *descriptive patterns* are aimed at maximizing their descriptivity (i.e., the level with which they have described in the collection) and their genericity (i.e., the scope in which they are applicable; Vanderdonckt and Montero 2010). To become descriptive, a pattern should solve a trade-off: contain enough information to foster its descriptivity, but not too much in order not to constrain its genericity. A *generative pattern* is aimed at maximizing its expressivity (i.e., the capability with which they are expressed in a rigorous way) and their generativity (i.e., the level

Table 7.1 Classification of patterns collection according to the four properties: descriptivity, genericity, expressivity, generativity (From " "=no information, +=low, ++=medium, to+++=high)

Classification of patterns collection				
Pattern collection	Descriptivity		Genericity	
	Descriptivity	Genericity	Expressivity	Generativity
Pattern catalogue				
Tidwell (2010)	+++	+++	+	+
van Welie and van der Veer (2003)	+++	+++	+	
van Duyne et al. (2006)	+++	++	++	
Management patterns				
Brochers (2000)	+++	+++		
Pemberton and Griffiths (1999)	++	++	++	
Coram and Lee (2011)	+++	+++	++	
Pattern-based design tool				
Molina (2002)	+++	++	+++	+++
Henninger (2001)	++	++	++	

Table 7.2 Description of master-detail in pattern collections (From " "=no information,+=low,++=medium, to+++=high)

Master-detail pattern in pattern collections									
General description						Management	Pattern-based design tool	Usability	
Gang of four (Gamma et al. 1994)	Tidwell (2010)	van Welie and van der Veer (2003)	van Duyne et al. (2006)	Bro-chers (2000)	Pem-berton (1999)	Molina (2002)	Hen-ninger (2003)	Lor-anger et al. (2002)	Johnson (2003)
+	+	+	++			+++	++	+	+

with which they could lead to a final user interface (FUI), manually or (semi-)automatically. To become generative, a pattern should solve another trade-off: express enough information to foster its expressivity, but not too much or not too informally in order to foster their generativity.

Table 7.1 compares some famous pattern collections according to the aforementioned four properties classified as: "+" if the specification of the language is limited but we have some elements and directives with example to describe UI patterns. "++" if the patterns are described with a specific language for one context and "+++" if their description involving two or more languages for several contexts of use (user, platform or environment). An empty field means that not enough information belonging to this property is available in the publicly accessible literature to assess it.

Table 7.2 reveals that most pattern collections cover the M-D pattern, but with a limited genericity. Some other collections do not contain the M-D pattern explicitly, but refers to it in a different way. For instance, van Welie and van der Veer (2003) presents the "tab UI element" as a possible master area in an M-D pattern and another UI element called "overview by detail" as a detail area in this pattern. Its description focuses on a single implementation language and usability explanation. Moreover, Loranger et al. (2002) and Johnson (2003) cover this usability explanation. Globally speaking, the definition of patterns found in these collections are too often oriented towards one single context of use, for instance a particular user, a single computing platform, or a specific environment. They do not cover the three aspects together and they do not cover variations within these aspects.

7.2.3   The Master-Detail as a Generative Pattern

JUST-UI, an object-oriented (OO) framework for generating UI from object-oriented models, was probably the first to introduce a generative pattern, for instance for the M-D (Molina et al. 2002). JUST-UI automatically generates interactive application from a series of conceptual models, such as the presentation model (Fig. 7.2), built

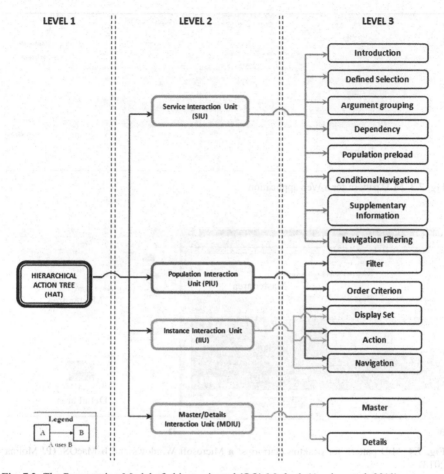

Fig. 7.2 The Presentation Model of object-oriented (OO)-Method. (Aquino et al. 2010)

upon conceptual patterns. The presentation model, also used in OO-Method, is decomposed into three levels (Fig. 7.2):

- Level 1: *Hierarchical action tree* (HAT). HAT is also called system access structure. This level solves the user–system interaction issue.
- Level 2: *Interaction units* (IUs). Each element composing the IUs represents a possible scenario through which users can perform tasks. This middle level is composed of four different types of Interaction Units.
- Level 3: *Elementary patterns* (EPs). This last level is defined by a large set of basic elements, also named building blocks, from which a variety of scenarios (IUs) are founded.

The M-D pattern starts at level 2 as a combination of a population interaction unit and an instance interaction unit, which are then automatically generated as a web

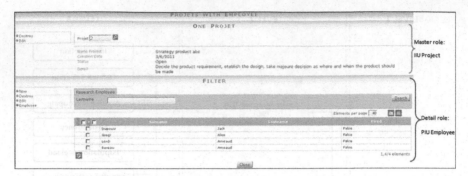

Fig. 7.3 M-D pattern for a Web application

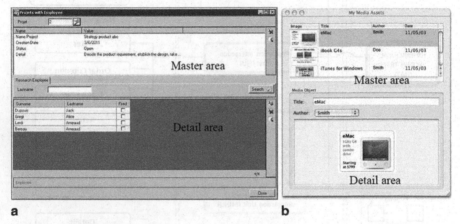

a b

Fig. 7.4 M-D pattern for desktop platforms: **a** Microsoft Windows and **b** MacOS. (PJ Molina 2013)

application (Fig. 7.3), a desktop application for MS Windows (Fig. 7.4a) and for MacOs (Fig. 7.4b).

7.2.4 Previous Work on M-D Pattern

HCI design patterns have proven their potential as a solution to guide developers in capturing knowledge at a high level of abstraction while facilitating the design of MUIs. But their scattered information is sometimes too complex to understand for some developers, especially when different platform style guides and software manuals address the pattern in different, possibly inconsistent, terms. Figure 7.5 reproduces the instructions to follow for implementing the M-D pattern in Objective-C, the programming language used by Apple for OS X and iOS operating systems for mobile platforms. While Fig. 7.6 does the same job for desktop, but for

Fig. 7.5 A guidance of M-D pattern implementation based on Objective-C

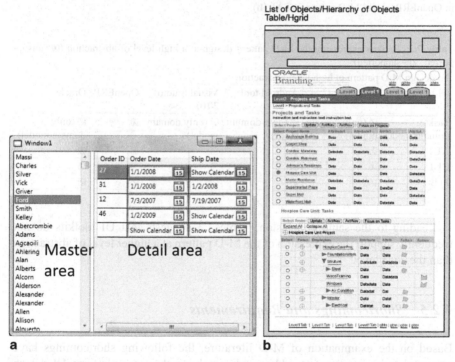

Fig. 7.6 M-D pattern with an expanded List of Detail part on Oracle instance (**a**) and a list on Windows view (**b**)

Oracle (Fig. 7.6a) and MS Windows again (Fig. 7.6b) and Fig. 7.7 for OpenERP (Fig. 7.7a) and SAP (Fig. 7.7b), which are however two desktop-based Entreprise Resource Planning systems.

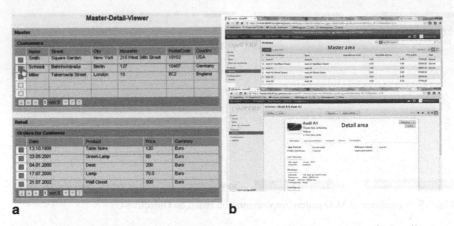

a   **b**

Fig. 7.7 A list of elements to present the master pattern and a single presentation for Detail pattern in OpenERP (**a**) and M-D pattern in SAP (**b**)

Table 7.3 Toolkits expressing the M-D pattern design at a high level of abstraction ($\boxtimes$=unsupported, $\boxtimes$=supported)

To design M-D pattern in high level abstraction					
UI toolkit	Objective-C	Android tool	Visual Studio 2010	OpenERP	Oracle
Task & domain model	☑ (only domain model)	☑ (only domain model)	☑ (only domain model)	☒	☑ (only domain model)
AUI	☒	☒	☒	☒	☒
CUI	☒	☒	☒	☒	☒
FUI	☑	☑	☑	☑	☑

Leading to the same conclusion, Table 7.3 suggests that UI toolkits do not frequently support the expression of the M-D pattern at a higher level of abstraction than the code level.

7.2.5   Shortcomings and Requirements

Based on the examination of M-D literature, the following shortcomings have appeared to be important to address when solving the cross-platform UI design problem:

S1. **Lack of expression consistency.** Information related to the pattern description and its applicability is fragmented across different attributes. A list of factors or criteria is necessary to validate a pattern.

S2. **Partial pattern representation**. The current works about patterns are constrained to one or some levels of the UI development life cycle. When they do it, the entire process is not completely addressed.

S3. **Limitation of technological space.** Most UI patterns available are specific to one platform or at least provides an example for one platform, often for the Web and desktop.

S4. **Lack of usability approach.** Tools to support pattern assisted design and development exist but the way they handle usability knowledge is limited, if not explicitly incorporated.

S5. **Lack of implementation information**. Only some tools offer effective instructions on how to guide the pattern application and implementation.

In order to address the aforementioned shortcomings, the following requirements are elicited:

R1. Revisiting the M-D pattern definition with up-to-date information
R2. Integrate the M-D pattern in the whole UI development process
R3. Consolidate methods and techniques in using a guidance system
R4. Design M-D pattern within usability concerns explicitly incorporated
R5. Structure an M-D pattern based on Dijkstra's principle of separation of concerns (Dijkstra 1959)

In order to satisfy these requirements, the following section revisits the M-D description with a focus on expressivity and generativity, as opposed to descriptivity and genericity. The usability concern is a large scope. It needs more application and technic. We will just use it in the guidance system.

7.3   Revisiting the M-D Pattern Description

During a period of steady technological growth, a large variety and availability of devices and hardware/software platforms are being developed. The ideal situation for users is to have access to information and services on the device that they are using in a different context or environment. Usability concerns should be integrated to UI patterns (Folmer and Bosch 2003). M-D patterns are therefore augmented in this work by ergonomic criteria (Scapin and Bastien 1997) such as user guidance, or consistency, or error management which are addressed when applying the pattern. Table 7.4 provides an enriched pattern definition based on the template introduced by the Gang-of-Four (Bayle et al. 1998), such as template attributed found in Wendler et al. (2013). Information from Bayle et al. (1998), van Welie et al. (2002), and Kruschitz (2009) about the M-D patterns are also included. Elements of the consistent template (Engel et al. 2013) are:

- **Pattern Name:** How is the pattern called?
- **Also Known As:** What are the other names for this pattern?
- **Classification:** Is the pattern creational, structural, or behavioral?
- **Motivation or Problem:** What is an example scenario for applying this pattern?
- **Intent or Solution:** What problem does this pattern solve?
- **Restriction:** What restriction does this pattern require? What are its constraints?

Table 7.4 Master-detail pattern description

Pattern name	Master/details
Also known as	Master/slave, director/details
Classification	Structural/object centric
Problem	The scenario, in which the user has to search in a list and select an item to have more details, is frequent. A set of information units linked or not by a relationship have to be presented to users. At the end these have a scenario that the master interaction unit determines information of details interaction unit will show
Solution	Perform a composed presentation in which master and detail data are shown in a synchronized way. In the master unit, its object is to guide and trigger the update in the details unit. Detail unit presentation is provided while master unit presentation is changing
Restriction	The constraint is to have synchronized information between the master information units and detail information units
Forces	This pattern is used in numerous situation, context. The scenario of this pattern allows simplifying the user's task. Indeed, navigation is decreased for getting specific information. Moreover, information is maintained synchronized between the master and details units
Weakness	The size of screen can discourage the presentation of this pattern. Less information can be shown at the same time on a screen. The details need to have a great navigation and to follow some usability guidelines in order to respect users' requirements and to have a graceful presentation
Rationale	Provide a presentation to reduce several navigations and to simplify the user task. Users need to interact with several objects aggregated or not. The scenario offered by M-D pattern allows us to get detailed information aligned with its master component. Moreover, the purpose of this pattern is to make explicit information related to an instance
Context of use	All types of users can use this pattern. All environments can get this pattern and adapt it. For instance, we can use this pattern to show the cases Project/Employees or Invoice/Lines. All kinds of platforms can adapt this pattern in line with usability studies
Applicability	The M-D pattern is used when we need to interact with several objects aggregated
Structure	In the case of an aggregated relationship, the master unit is the head element of the details unit
Participants	One or two instances with an aggregated relationship
Collaborations	Objects can operate though their aggregated relationship or attributes.
Consequences	Need to use usability elements for adapting this pattern on different platform. Knowledge about these devices is required
Implementation	The issue about using a unity class or aggregated classes is necessary before implementing this pattern. The M-D pattern uses a list of model objects which can be presented in the table list pattern. Each selected object is presented in the display pattern. Therefore, the user navigates through a list with synchronize information
Known uses	Commercial system can use this pattern to show the case invoice/line
Related patterns	Object presentation, population unit, instance interaction unit, display form, table list pattern

- **Forces:** What are advantages and forces to use this pattern?
- **Weakness:** What are disadvantages or limits to use this pattern?
- **Rationale:** Why does this pattern work? What is the history behind the pattern?
- **Applicability or Content:** When does this pattern apply?
- **Context of use:** What are the category of user, environment, and platform that this pattern can be applied?
- **Structure:** What are the class hierarchy diagrams for the objects in this pattern?
- **Participants:** What are the objects that participate in this pattern?
- **Collaborations:** How do these objects interoperate?
- **Consequences:** What are the trade-offs of using this pattern?
- **Implementation:** Which techniques or issues arise in applying this pattern?
- **Known Uses:** What are some examples of real systems using this pattern?
- **Related Patterns:** What other patterns from this pattern collection are related to this pattern?

A complete description is necessary to address all parts of the pattern and to show its application:

- Provide a comprehensive and descriptive solution involving the three parameters of the context of the problem (user, platforms, and environment) by integrating usability knowledge
- Reuse general/standard solution reducing errors and research a complete solution in using an abstract solution in order to implement them in a straightforward way
- Visual explicit view of ergonomic design before implementing.

We can see that the implementation attribute is often missing. That requires more details of the pattern application in several programming languages. The pseudo-code aims to facilitate its implementation in different programming languages while bringing better understanding for developers. In this pseudo-code, the master pattern is encapsulated in a table view listing each object and gets the detail of the object.

Pseudo-code of M-D Pattern:

```
do
    insert master record
      for object_1 in tableView_Master
        get
            detailed record (object_1, "details_1" )
        //set foreign key from master record
        loop until end of detailed records
        for object_2 in tableView_Master
            get
          detail record (object_2, "details_2" )
        ...
        ...
    loop until end of master records
```

As we can also see on the current shortcomings in the previous section, the major element to take into account in the pattern implementation is the cross-platform context and to improve the software lifecycle development integrating the development of usability studies.

7.4   Integrate the M-D Pattern in the Whole UI Development Process

This section presents one possible way of incorporating the M-D pattern usage into the UI development process based on a UIDL that supports the four levels of abstraction of the CRF. Other XML-compliant frameworks are available such as Object Management Group's (OMG's) framework (Computation Independent Model (CIM), platform-independent model (PIM), platform-specific model (PSM)) for developing multitarget UIs. Our choice is motivated by its simplicity of hierarchical structure of each abstract model and its transition of progression levels along the development lifecycle on a variety of devices.

7.4.1   Task Model

A *task model* is a description of tasks that a user will be able to accomplish in interaction with the system. This description is a hierarchical decomposition of a global task, with constraints expressed on and between the subtasks. The USer interface eXtensible Markup Language (UsiXML) task model relies on ConcurTaskTree (CTT) notation (Paterno 1999): a hierarchical task structure, with temporary relationships specified between sibling tasks.

Since the M-D pattern is based on a domain model, it needs to be augmented with tasks so as to produce a corresponding task model. Depending on it, the domain model is interpreted, two task models could result from this process:

- A unity instance expressed as the master element and its object domain attributes could compose the details element (Fig. 7.8). In this task model, an object or a collection of objects is edited by browsing all the attributes belonging to the class object and by invoking typical management methods, such as those found in the create, read or retrieve, update, delete, and search (CRUDS) pattern.
- An aggregation representation between two domain objects (Fig. 7.9). In this task model, all object attributes are edited at once or one by one, all object methods are invoked at once or one by one on demand

7.4.2   Domain Model

The domain model presents the important entities of the particular application domain together with their attributes, methods, and relationship (Sinnig et al. 2003).

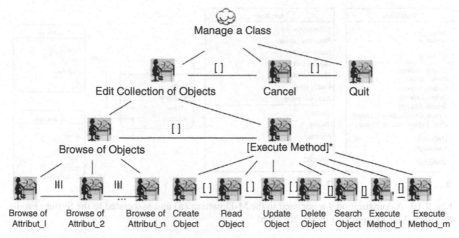

Fig. 7.8 M-D pattern defined by a unity class

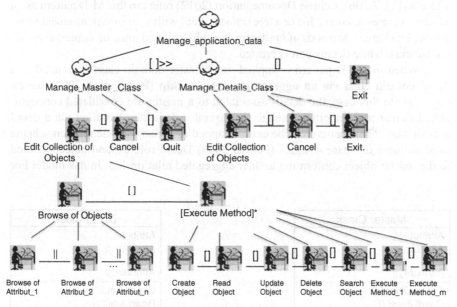

Fig. 7.9 M- pattern defined by an aggregation relationship

Various notations could be used for this purpose, such as the entity-relationship-attribute (ERA) notation, the OO notation, or more frequent and up-to-date the unified modeling language (UML). Two cases could occur:

1. When the M-D pattern is applied on **a single domain class**. In this case, the domain case merely consists of its usual attributes and methods (Fig. 7.10). Applying the M-D pattern therefore consists of displaying a list of objects belonging to this domain class and displaying its attributes and methods on demand. For instance, the Mac Developer Library (2012) uses this method where the root is the collection of these objects (Fig. 7.10a). Note that the master domain class could

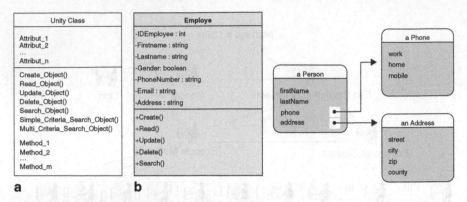

Fig. 7.10 A domain model associated to the M-D pattern (**a**) and associated to the System Environment (Mac Developer Library 2012) (**b**)

refer to several detail areas that are related to some different areas, such as phone or address (Fig. 7.10b). Eclipse Documentation (2012) refers to this M-D pattern as an M-D block presented as a list or a tree (master area) with a set of synchronized properties (detail area). Methods of master unit are abstract and must be implemented by the subclass while details unit is created.

2. When the M-D pattern is applied on a master domain class associated to a detail domain class **via an aggregation relationship** (Pedro et al. 2002) see on Fig. 7.11. In this case, the details associated to a master are considered conceptually different and important enough to warrant a dedicated handling via a detail area display. "This pattern can be easily mapped to a many-to-one relation schema used within a database design." (Perrins 2008) Detail role expand objects related to the master object conforming to their aggregated relationship. In this model For

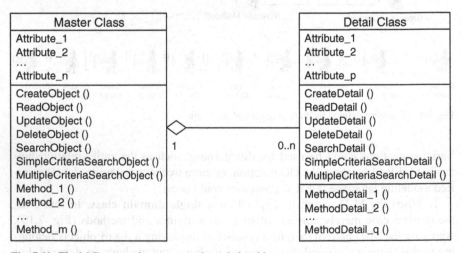

Fig. 7.11 The M-D pattern in an aggregation relationship

example, the Employee class contains a sub-group Address, which could in turn be decomposed into attributes contained in a separate class: zip code, street, etc. This concept could be mapped in an aggregation relationship between two distinct entities if the cardinality of the relation from master class to details class is 0…n. In the Employee object, Address is considered as a fundamental attribute. Therefore, a mapping from its domain model into two external specific objects could not possible with a 0…n relationship.

7.4.3   Abstract User Interface Model

The abstract user interface (AUI) model specifies a UI independent of any interaction modality (we do not know yet whether this UI will be graphical, tactile, gestural, vocal, or multimodal in the future) and any technological space (we do not know which computing platform will be the target). The AUI model is the counterpart of the PIM) used in model driven engineering (MDE). An AUI consists of a recursive definition of abstract interaction units, each unit could be of input, output, input/output, selection, or trigger, each of them coming with their own event listener. For instance Fig. 7.12 reproduces a possible AUI for the Employee class of Fig. 7.10b, as edited in UsiAbstract, an Eclipse plug-in for editing AUI models.

7.4.4   Concrete User Interface

The concrete user interface (CUI) model specifies a UI independent of any technological space, but for a given interaction modality. The CUI model is the counterpart of the PSM in MDE. The benefits consist mainly in improved and expanded definitions of the description of UI elements. The CUI depends on the type of platform and media available. This model allows both the specification of the presentation and the behavior of a UI with elements that can be concretely perceived by end

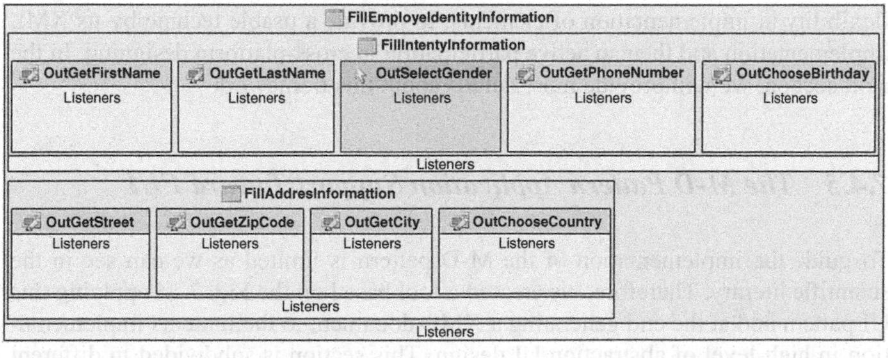

Fig. 7.12 The M-D pattern leading to a AUI model

Fig. 7.13 A concrete user interface (CUI) model of tabbed list presentation for M-D pattern according to van Welie et al. (2000)

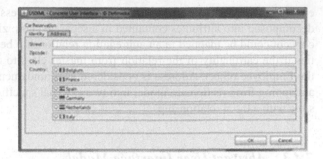

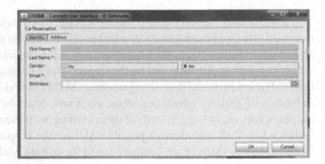

users. That means to define widgets layout and interface navigation independent of any computing platform.

Figures 7.12 and 7.13 present merely one possible AUI and CUI respectively for applying an M-D pattern independent of any technological space. We could continue with several final UIs that could cover different contexts of use. But our goal is to show many high level UI models. We want to define different models to specify how sub-tasks of a given task are assembled together for cross-platform environments. Therefore, we began with the presentation model from Fig. 7.2 and we modified its level 3 to adapt with our sub-task presentations of objects. The result in the Fig. 7.14 shows different models of possible dynamic presentations from AUI models to FUI models. The contribution of this framework is to offer a great flexibility in implementation of elements, to provide a usable technic by its XML implementation and then an active participation in cross-platform designing. In the next section, we will provide more details about this framework.

7.4.5 The M-D Pattern Application Support Toward FUI

To guide the implementation of the M-D pattern is limited as we can see in the scientific literary. Therefore, we created a tool based on the Fig. 7.14 applying this UI pattern and at the end generating a XML-document to facilitate its implementation in high level of abstraction UI design. This section is subdivided in different

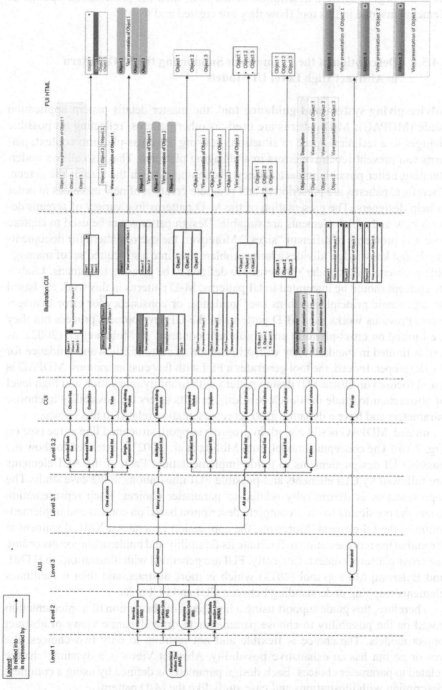

Fig. 7.14 The design M-D patterns in abstract user interface (AUI), CUI, and final user interface (FUI) customization

sections: beginning by a description of the tool, then the presentation options of elements inserted in this tool (how they are created and why).

7.4.5.1 Description of the Framework Supporting the M-D Pattern in Abstract High Level UI Models

Advice-giving system and guidance tool, the master details pattern application guide (MDPAG): M-D patterns are used, as other patterns, reflecting on possible changes to a technical space or situation. In using the cross-platform context, patterns can prevent repetitive errors in a changing platform. That also allows understanding better possible impacts of new technologies such the size of the screen. Therefore, patterns are prescriptive and promote creation of new instances in order to help designers. The presentation of the M-D patterns in a variety of screens defines how and which elements are suitable. Design patterns can be used to capture essential problems of different "sizes." Moreover, the use of pattern for documenting design knowledge "divides a large problem area into a structured set of manageable problems." Alexander's patterns are defined to be pleasant to humans. Usability concept should be integrated to UI patterns. M-D patterns in this work are based on ergonomic principles such as user guidance, or consistency, or error management. Previous works used M-D patterns in the UI development process but they are limited on cross-platform and ergonomic contexts. In Molina et al. (2002), its tool is limited in standard view with a limitation of customization and guidance for the developer. Indeed, the tool generates a FUI with few customizations. MDPAG is a tool focused on abstract UI design pattern with usability integration and high level of abstraction to guide the developer/designers. Its offers the possibility to choose parameters and have a dynamic abstract representation related to this choice.

Indeed, MDPAG is still a work in progress support, structured like a tree (see on Fig. 7.14). The conceptual model from Molina et al. (2002) is extended to show the possible UI design elements to guide implementation. Each of the AUI elements are followed by CUI elements and possible FUI illustrations in the case study. The representation is dynamically related to parameter choices. Each representation offers the possibility to see a complete description based on context and implementation of the UI element. Moreover, the application generates a XML document at the end of the representation to facilitate its flexibility and implementation according the cross-platform context. Currently, FUI are generated with illustrations in HTML and Balsamiq Morkup tool (2014) which is more abstract, and then it facilitates elements mapping understanding between CUI and FUI units.

Therefore, this guide support using a high level of abstraction of implementation based on the possibility to choose parameters to draw dynamic views of abstract object models. The choice is flexible and not restraint to only two choices like yes or no but has an exhaustive possibility. Abstract Views is a dynamic change related to parameter choices. Each design parameter is defined by using a complete description with illustrations and case study like the M-D pattern.

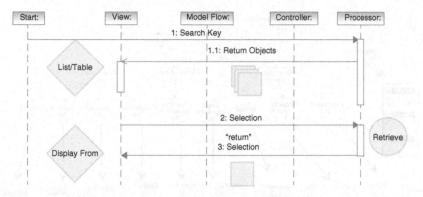

Fig. 7.15 An example of M-D pattern presentation. (Perrins 2008)

7.4.5.2 Possible Presentation Options Toward FUI Model

The M-D pattern presentations have some usability restrictions. Indeed, they need to have a correct layout to present information in order to perform a task. The scenario of tasks for this pattern needs to get synchronized information between the master and details units. The layout of some devices can limit their presentation. Consistency and usability are essential characteristics for presentations. In this section, we can find different presentations of the master unit. In Fig. 7.15, you can see a suggestion of presentation using List or Table of objects in starting point. When an item is selected, its details are presented in the display form pattern. We have two ways: one column list or multicolumn list. In the first case, master unit can be shown by a simple list, a drop-down list or a fish-eye menu. In the multicolumn table, attributes of the master unit are presented by prioritized criteria: the most frequent, critical or mandatory.

To build MDPAG, we need to draw different presentation options for the M-D patterns. The Fig. 7.16, different presentation specifies how objects of a given task are assembled together. Instances can be presented in direct mode or progressive presentation. In the first format, each object is shown one by one. It is a list that includes all attributes and methods in one view for each object. The vertical and horizontal scroll can be heavy for the users. In the progressive mode, methods and attributes can be selected for each object.

The Fig. 7.17 suggests a presentation of an instance in the M-D pattern case for desktop view. The attributes and methods of objects are presented by specific criteria: the most importance, recurrence of use, and critical characteristic. Therefore, attributes and methods are characterized by multiple criteria: simple/repetitive, elementary/decomposable, and optional/mandatory. Attributes can have the label presentation or optional checkbox. For methods, we can find the traditional CRUD Method in the unit. Other methods are obviously possible. Each method can have a specific view: a textual, graphical or both presentations on their button.

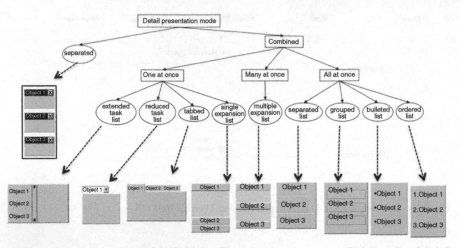

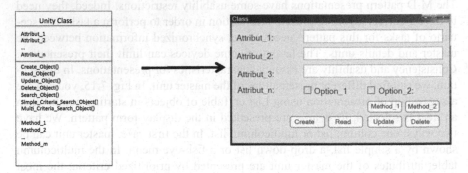

Fig. 7.16 Object presentation in M-D pattern

Fig. 7.17 Instance presentation of M-D pattern in desktop view

In the design option presentation of the M-D pattern, we explain the possible representation of objects. In Fig. 7.17a unity class is represented in specific desktop window. Attributes can be edited by fields or in using checkboxes. Methods are action buttons.

This standard representation can be completed by graphical or/and textual option for buttons. Standard buttons for common methods such as add, create, or delete an item can use frequent icons with extra information. User experiences allow us to act quickly and to reduce stress. On mobile platform, a list view is preferred. That allows a great structure and improves the usability. Another usability guideline specifies to use the button in correct and understandable context. The button cannot appear in confuse situation.

In Fig. 7.18, we can observe two same situations: we want to add a new contact. In the figure on the left, we can see this situation on Android 1.1. That does not respect usability guidelines described above. On the right, we can observe a

Fig. 7.18 Graphical presentation of class methods on Android OS. (Android 2012)

list view of Android 1.5 using both graphical presentations: textual and graphical. Usability graphic is better to understand the meaning of the application.

The technique of M-D information used in progressive or direct display, are presented in a specific public support online to guide developers/designers in using the question of, how subtasks of a given task could assemble together. By a set dynamic choice, different subtask presentations in AUI, CUI and FUI models are displayed. The next section presents the application of M-D pattern in a specific tool with a case study: the renting car.

7.5 The M-D Pattern Application Support

These options are presented in the tree (cf. Fig. 7.14) and applied in a specific support called MDPAG. The translation from the Task/Domain model, AUI, CUI, and FUI are based on study case. For example with the renting car study case, the CUI of the M-D pattern is illustrated in Fig. 7.19. The CUI of the M-D pattern is presented with the following selection of parameters: The master interaction unit is reified into object-combined presentation in AUI model. Its objects are shown one at once in using a tabbed list. In CUI, its representation in using tab object is illustrated in the guide support and in a FUI instance. The detail interaction unit is shown in each object of the tab list of its master in using AUI presentation based on all at once with a separated list. In its CUI model, objects are represented by a separated choice element.

These generated dynamic applications are validated by different guidelines (Fig. 7.20). We can observe what guidelines are validated for each illustration. At the end of the preview illustration and selected parameters, the end user can also generate a XML-document related to dynamic choice for the implementation. Other illustration of the application, based on other operating system and platform integrated in this support, is presented in the following section.

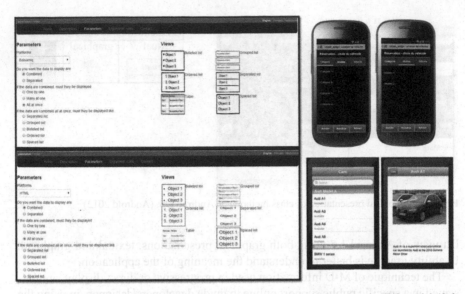

Fig. 7.19 A tool of guidance for M-D pattern implementation with Balsamiq FUI model (*left above*), with HTML FUI model (*left below*), final CUI model (*right above*), FUI model (*right below*)

Ergonomic rules

Rule	Extended task list	Reduced task list	Tabbed list	Single expansion list	Multiple expansion list	Separated list	Grouped list	Bulleted list	Ordered list	Spaced list	Table	Pop up
Elements of a window have to be align	⊘	⊘	⊘	⊘	⊘	⊘	⊘	⊘	⊘	⊘	⊘	⊘
Minimize scrolling.	⊘	⊘	⊘	⊘	⊘	⊘	⊘	⊘	⊘	⊘	⊘	⊘
A text should not be written entirely in capital letters	⊘	⊘	⊘	⊘	⊘	⊘	⊘	⊘	⊘	⊘	⊘	⊘
Put symbol (puce) for a better structure and visibility	✖	✖	✖	✖	✖	✖	✖	⊘	⊘	✖	✖	✖

Fig. 7.20 Renting car application validated with ergonomic guidelines in MDPAG

7.5.1   Support for M-D Pattern Application

The application is developed in order to adapt the M-D pattern in mobile devices. We decided to focus on the Android-based mobile systems. The motivations are the free accessibility of Android-Framework and its code language, Java that is a widespread programming language known by all developers.

The usability concern is the screen size limitations of general mobile devices. Therefore, a minimal set of information is available at any time. A possible situation is to minimize the accessible information set thanks to an adequate use of "reducing" and "expanding" controls of the list, so that the user keeps the focus on the part of the application that he is using (see on Fig. 7.21 on the right).

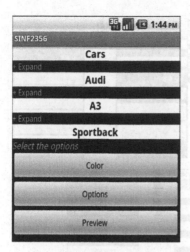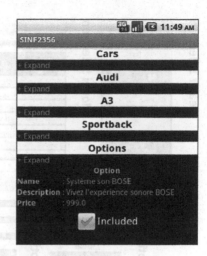

Fig. 7.21 M-D pattern in Android system

"Cars" is the class "title." All attributes of this class are included in details presentation by using a combined way. In this way, three detail views are possible of attributes: one at once, many at once, or all at once. It is a basic possible presentation and using of M-D pattern combined with the population pattern and other auxiliary popular patterns such as filters, order criterions, selection, and display sets. All used patterns in Mandroid are presented. All attributes of Mandroid are viewed many at once or all at once. That depends on auxiliary patterns used.

In the Fig. 7.22, the relevant patterns are the master-detail and the order ones. This model selection allows sorting alphabetically the brands and, secondly, when a brand is selected, the details (i.e., the next step of the car configuration) appear. Then, the user has to select a model of car represented by a standard button of the Android System. Basically, this step is implemented the same way as the previous one, using master-detail and ordering, but it also contains the Filter pattern. Once the model is selected, the resulting detail concerns the selection of the body style of the car. This step uses a nested M-D pattern.

Next, the user can specify the options and the color that he wants. So, we only focus on the "Options" one. Typically, the detail of this button is a list of options, which, once again, use the M-D pattern. When an option is selected, a screen allowing the user to select it appears. To get back to the options list, the "+ Expand" link can be clicked. This link is present each time the M-D pattern is used in order to get back to the master. Finally, a preview of the car is available.

On a technical point of view, the filling of the application is done automatically thanks to our XML parser compatible with Android. Thanks to the developed tool, the data is fetched from a XML-file and then presented on the user interface. This strategy enables us to update the data about cars and even add new models and/or brands (without having to recompile the application). The idea behind the algorithm is the following: each time we meet a node in the XML-file we check its value and create the corresponding elements with the attributes specified in the XML-file. Example: a node with value "model" causes the creation of a master element. Every

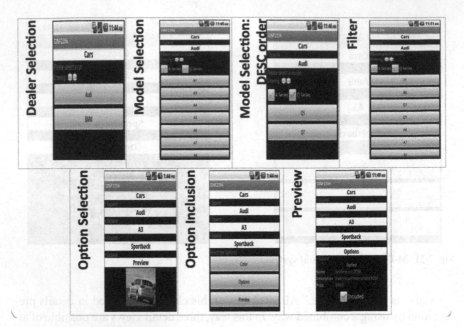

Fig. 7.22 Mandroid application

node that follows and whose value is different from "model" concerns the model previously created (we go through the XML-file line by line). Then, depending on the values of the next nodes, masters and details elements are created and added to previous elements. If the value is equal to "ordering" or "filter", the corresponding patterns are initialized on the population of the appropriate master. This XML parser helped us to maintain our application clean, well structured, to enforce the quality of the user interface and to efficiently work in a team.

Another illustration of application is the Fig. 7.7 in the Oracle instance, the master is also the table of objects. When an object in the master table is selected from the single select column, the details section below draws with label/data layout of object details. Multiple selections of objects are not allowed in the master objects table. If multiple selections are functionally required and there are drill down actions for the objects, then the actions will have to be performed in separate pages, such as an object template. To access full object details, the user must select the master object from the single select column, then select the "Advance Update" button in the detail section. Details are represented as a single object (label/data layout) based on the selection of a master object.

7.5.2 *M-D Pattern Presentation for Tabbed List Presentation in Mobile Application*

The combination of the two interactions units (master and details) is shown in two tabs on the mobile view (cf. Fig. 7.23). We take our example with the employee

Fig. 7.23 M/D pattern using a tabbed list presentation of mobile platform

class in aggregated relationship with project class. In our instance, we have in the master role: the interface interaction unit of project class. In the Detail role is the population interaction unit of the employee class. The detail role means to show only the employee from the selected project in the master part. It is the same with the mobile view, the second tab shows all employees from the project in the first tab. Therefore, we can say that a dependence part is defined.

A navigation bar on the top is not visually correct because the title is reproduced twice as we can observe on the right of this figure. Moreover, it is not in line with the specific guideline: Indicate the position of the user only once. Without a navigation bar, the user cannot come back to the menu. The solution can be to integrate this in the bottom menu bar which defines the action patterns. The problem with this solution is that it reduces the options of action set and information quantity.

7.5.3   M-D Pattern in Grouped, Ordered, or Structured List Presentation

The majority of the tools and M-D pattern presentation is defined by grouped, ordered, and structured element presentation in its master part and by a large information content in its details part. For instance, in the systems, applications, and products in data processing (SAP) FUI (cf. Fig. 7.7), the two tables in the master-detail viewer is be filled with data records that are saved in the context of the view controller. The (upper) Master table displays a row for each customer, containing his or her name and address. The (lower) Detail table displays the order records for the currently selected customer. They are presented in order of date (old date to new date). Another illustration, on Oracle system (cf. Fig. 7.6) represents the hierarchy of objects; and single object details (from list.). Master is a hierarchic of objects. When one of the objects in the tree is selected, the details section draws with selected objects details. Depending on the detail contents for each item in the Tree, it is possible to show a different master/detail template depending on what object type is selected. For instance, if the master tree is a hierarchy of banks, branches, and accounts, and the user selects an account. Single Object Details are represented as a single object (label/data layout) based on the selection of a master.

7.6   Contributions of the Chapter

Several problems of implementing software design patterns have been pointed out, for example, ordinary object-oriented style implementations reduce the traceability of design patterns and the reusability of the implementation of design patterns. Our approach is one of the solutions for these problems.

In this chapter, we proposed a technique for describing and implementing a generative UI design pattern in general that improves reusability and effective applicability of the HCI design pattern. It instantiates this general definition for a cross-platform pattern for a specific case such the M-D pattern. For structuring and coding, the proposed technique relies on the concept of generative patterns and a set of rules for implementations. These rules can be encapsulated in several programming languages or UI development tools such as task modelers and UIDLs. More particularly, the M-D cross-platform pattern is systematically described according to the formalisms and notations recommended by W3C for model-based UI design. We describe this implementation for two platforms, i.e., a web application and a mobile application, and compare it to other languages and cross-platform environments.

The major contributions of this research are the following:

- A definition of the general concept of generative UI pattern is provided that expresses various aspects to consider when applying the pattern for multiple contexts of use
- An instantiation of this general concept as cross-platform UI pattern for applying it for multiple computing platforms
- An exemplification of a cross-platform UI pattern based on the M-D pattern that is then subsequently detailed at the different levels of abstraction recommended by the CRF (Calvary 2003)
- An abstraction of design options found in various computing platforms into a cross-platform M-D pattern, thus offering a wide range of options at once.
- An implementation environment of this cross-platform pattern for two platforms: iOs and Androïd.

The proposed meta-model of M-D pattern is structured into four levels of abstraction to foster portability and reusability. It supports user interfaces that are or have to be easily customizable. Another contribution of this work is a systematic review and analysis of the recent scientific literature regarding M-D pattern description and implementation. We revisited its description and implementation for better understanding, to facilitate its integration and to demonstrate how the proposed method works. Indeed, current tools offer the possibility to generate FUI in standard representation in involving the context of uses and some usability guidelines. But they are limited in the customization of design UI patterns. Our support MDPAG offers the observation of possible design options of the M-D pattern on different platforms at different high abstraction levels. The case study focuses on heterogeneous context and design M-D pattern presentation in an attempt to validate the outcomes. We show, for example how the M-D pattern could be represented at the bottom level of UI development process (such as task model) independent of platform implementation. Then, different abstract models of M-D based on a real life case are dynamically generated in integrating usability concerns. At the end, the developer can generate a XML document to facilitate the pattern implementation.

Between discussions and the case study presented here, the advantages and disadvantages of these definitions and methods have been highlighted. The main advantage of these methods is the ability to identify the origin of the M-D pattern and to revisit it including the current innovation, cross-platform environment. "Experience" and "usability" are both defined in its meta-model, illustrations, and applications. The main disadvantage is the measure of performance and reliability of these methods. Developers understand the definition and capability of these methods but it needs more quantifying evaluations. Therefore, the future works are to evaluate them in long term by integrating more parameters based on the context of uses and usability points. In addition to the user and developer experiments, another future work is to quantify the gain of times of its implementation on cross-platforms.

Acknowledgments The authors would like to thank the computer science master student Tristan Dorange for his participation in the study to build the framework MDPAG. We also acknowledge the support of this work by the DESTINE (Design & Evaluation Studio For Intent-Based Ergonomic Web Sites) project, funded by DGO6 of Walloon Region, under convention #315577 in «WIST» Wallonie Information Science & Technology research program

References

Alexander C (1977) A pattern language. Oxford University Press, New York

Android Developers (2012) https://developer.android.com/guide/topics/ui/index.html. Accessed 15 April 2015

Aquino N, Vanderdonckt J, Condori-Fernández N, Dieste Ó, Pastor Ó (2010) Usability evaluation of multi-device/platform user interfaces generated by model-driven engineering. In: Proceeding of ESEM'2010. ACM, New York, Article #30

Balsamiq Morkup Support (2014) http://balsamiq.com/

Bayle E, Bellamy R, Casaday G, Erickson T, Fincher S, Grinter B (1998) Putting it all together: towards a pattern language for interaction design. SIGCHI Bull 30(1):17–24

Brochers JO (2000) A pattern approach to interaction design. In: Proceedings of ACM conference on disiging interactive systems DIS 2000. ACM, New York, pp 369–378

Calvary G, Coutaz J, Thevenin D, Limbourg Q, Bouillon L, Vanderdonckt J (2003) A unifying reference framework for multi-target user interfaces. Interact Comput 15(3):289–308

Coram T, Lee J (2011) Experiences-a pattern language for user interface design. http://www.maplefish.com/todd/papers/Experiences.html

Dijkstra EW (1959) Numerische Mathematik. In Numerische Mathematik 1(1):269–271. doi:10.1007/bf01386390

Eclipse Documentation (2012) Master/Details block. http://help.eclipse.org/juno/index.jsp?topic=%2Forg.eclipse.platform.doc.isv%2Fguide%2Fforms_master_details.htm

Engel J, Märtin C, Herdin C, Forbrig P (2013) Formal pattern specifications to facilitate semi-automated user interface generation. In: Kurosu M (ed) Proceedings of HCI International'2013. Springer, Heidelberg, pp 300–309 (LNCS, vol 8004)

Folmer E, Bosch J (2003) Usability patterns in software architecture. In: Proceeding of workshop on SE-HCI. Citeseer, Greece, pp 61–68

Gamma E, Helm R, Jonhson R, Vlissides J (1994) Patterns: elements of reusable object-oriented software. Addison-Wesley, New York

Henninger S (2001) An organizational learning method for applying usability guidelines and patterns. Engineering for human-computer interaction, 8th IFIP international conference, EHCI 2001. Toronto, Canada, May 11–13, 2001, Revised Papers. Lecture notes in computer science 2254, Springer 2001

Henninger S, Keshk M, Kinworthy R (2003) Capturing and disseminating usability patterns with semantic web technology. CHI 2003 workshop

Johnson J (2003) Web bloopers, 60 Common Web design mistakes and how to avoid them. Morgan Kaufman, San Francisco

Kruschitz C (2009) XPLML—a HCI pattern formalizing and unifying approach. In: 27th international conference on human factors in computing systems, CHI 2009, extended abstracts volume. Boston, MA, USA, April 4–9, 2009

Loranger H, Schade A, Nielsen J (2002) Website tools and applications with Flash. http://media.nngroup.com/media/reports/free/Website_Tools_and_Applications_with_Flash.pdf Accessed on April 15, 2015

Mac Developer Library (2012) Cocoa bindings programming topics, creating a master-detail interface. https://developer.apple.com/library/mac/#documentation/Cocoa/Conceptual/CocoaBindings/Tasks/masterdetail.html

Molina PJ (2004) User interface generation with OlivaNova model execution system. Proceeding of IUI'2004. ACM, New York, pp 358–359

Molina PJ (2013) Conceptual User Interfaces Pattern, Master/Detail Interaction Unit http://pjmolina.com/cuip/node-MasterDetailIU

Molina P, Meliá S, Pastor O (2002) Just-UI: a user interface specification model. Proceeding of CADUI 2002. Kluwer Academics, Dordrecht

Nilsson EG (2009) Design patterns for user interface for mobile applications. Adv Eng Softw 40(12):1318–1328 (Oxford)

Pastor O, Molina J-C (2007) Model-driven architecture in practice. Springer, Berlin

Paterno F (1999) Model-based design and evaluation of interactive applications. Springer, Berlin

Pemberton L, Griffiths R (1999) The Brighton usability pattern collection. http://www.it.bton.ac.uk/Research/patterns/home.html

Perrins M (2008) The 12 Patterns for User Interface Design. http://mattperrins.wordpress.com/2008/12/21/the-12-patterns-for-user-interface-design/

Scapin DL, Bastien JMC (1997) Ergonomic criteria for evaluating the ergonomic quality of interactive systems. Behav Inf Technol 16(4/5):220–231

Seffah A, Forbrig P (2002) Multiple user interfaces: towards a task-driven and patterns-oriented design model. Interactive systems. Design, specification, and verification, 9th international workshop, DSV-IS 2002, Rostock Germany, June 12–14, 2002. Lecture notes in computer science 2545, Springer 2002

Sinnig D, Forbrig P, Seffah A (2003) Patterns in model-based development, INTERACT 03 workshop software and usability cross-pollination: the role of usability patterns, September 2003

Tidwell J (2010) Designing interfaces, patterns for effective interaction design, 2nd edn. O'Reilly Media Inc, USA

van Duyne J, Landay J, Hong J (2006) The design of sites, patterns for creating winning websites, 2nd edn. Prentice Hall International, New Jersey

van Welie M, van der Veer GC (2003) Pattern languages in interaction design: structure and organization. In: M Rauterberg, M Menozzi, J Wesson (eds) Proceedings of INTERACT'03, 1–5
September, Zurich, Switzerland. IOS Press, Amsterdam, pp 527–534

van Welie M, van der Veer GC, Eliens A (2000) Patterns as tools for user interface design. Proceeding of international workshop on tools for working with guidelines TFWWG'2000. Springer,
Berlin, pp 313–324

van Welie M, Mullet K, McInerney P (2002) Patterns in practice: a workshop for UI designers.
ACM Conference on Human Factors in Computing Systems (CHI) Extended Abstracts. Mine-
apolis, USA, April 20–24, pp 908–909

Vanderdonckt J, Montero F (2010) Generative pattern-based design of user interfaces, Proceeding of 1st international workshop on pattern-driven engineering of interactive computing
PEICS'2010. ACM, New York

Wendler S, Ammon D, Philippow I, Streitferdt D (2013) A factor model capturing requirements for
generative user interface patterns. In: Proceeding of patterns 2013, fifth international conferences on pervasive patterns and applications. May 27–June 1, 2013, Valencia, Spain

Chapter 8
POMA: Pattern-Oriented and Model-Driven Architecture

Abstract The proposed pattern-oriented and model-driven architecture (POMA) architecture illustrates how several individual models can be combined at different levels of abstraction into heterogeneous structures, which can then be used as building blocks in the development of interactive systems. This chapter presents the key concepts, an overview, justifications, and specifications of the proposed POMA architecture, a detailed description of architectural levels and categories of patterns used in the proposed POMA architecture, and a detailed description of five levels and categories of models used by POMA. First, we describe the model categorization as well as the key concepts of POMA. We detail POMA while comparing its architecture with N-tiers architectures, pattern-oriented design and architecture (POD), and model-driven architecture (MDA). We describe the architectural levels and categories of patterns including pattern composition rules (i.e., the relationships between pattern considered in this architecture). We describe the pattern mapping rules that enable one to obtain the final models of the proposed architecture. Finally, we define model transformation rules which apply for each type of model, [POMA.PIM] (Platform Independent Model) or [POMA.PSM] (Platform Specific Model). These rules build a relationship between models of each category, i.e., models [POMA.PIM] and [POMA.PSM].

8.1 Key Concepts of POMA

The five key concepts of POMA are:

- Architectural levels and categories of patterns (details in Sect. 8.5)
- Models ([POMA.PIM and [POMA.PSM]) (details in Sect. 8.6)
- Pattern composition rules (details in Sect. 8.5.2)
- Pattern mapping rules: PIM to PSM (details in Sect. 8.5.3)
- Model transformation rules: PIM to PIM and/or PSM to PSM (details in Sect. 8.6.6)
- Code generation rules (this level of POMA is not included in first edition) Figure 8.1 shows the five concepts of POMA and their relationships.

© Springer International Publishing Switzerland 2015   155
A. Seffah, *Patterns of HCI Design and HCI Design of Patterns,*
Human-Computer Interaction Series, DOI 10.1007/978-3-319-15687-3_8

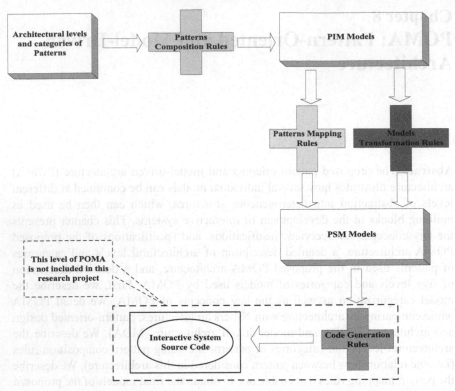

Fig. 8.1 Key concepts of POMA

At this stage, it is interesting to revise some important definitions of each concept used in POMA architecture which is given below.

Architecture "The software architecture of a program or computing system is the structure or structures of the system, which comprise software components, the externally visible properties of those components, and the relationships among them" (Bass et al. 2003).

Pattern "Each pattern describes a problem that occurs constantly in the environment, and describes the heart of the solution to the problem in such a way that this solution may be used millions of times, but will never do it twice the same way" (Alexander et al. 1977).

Model A model is a formal description of key aspects of an interactive system from a specific viewpoint.

Composition Composition refers to the process and rules for creating design platform independent models (PIM) by combining patterns using composition rules.

Mapping Mapping is the process of creating a design specific model for each platform (PSM) from PIM while using rules for mapping (only PIM to PSM).

Transformation The transformation of models is the process of creating a model from another model using transformation rules (only PIM to PIM and/or PSM to PSM).

8.2   POMA Overview

The proposed POMA architecture (Fig. 8.2) for interactive systems development is an architecture comprising five architectural levels of models using six categories of patterns of software architecture (Taleb et al. 2009). The POMA architecture (Fig. 8.2) includes:

- Six architectural levels and categories of patterns;
- Ten models, five of which are [POMA.PIM] and five others [POMA.PSM];
- Four types of relations used in POMA architecture, which are:

  1. Composition: used to combine different patterns to produce a [POMA.PIM] by applying the composition rules.
  2. Mapping: used to build a [POMA.PIM], which becomes a [POMA.PSM] by applying the mapping rules ([POMA.PIM] ⇨ [POMA.PSM]).
  3. Transformation: used to establish the relationship between two models ([POMA.PIM] ⇨ [POMA.PIM]) and/or ([POMA.PSM] ⇨ [POMA.PSM]) by applying the transformation rules.
  4. Generation: used to generate the source code of the whole interactive system by applying the generation code rules.

The direction in which to read the POMA architecture in (Fig. 8.2) is as follows:

- Vertically, concerns the composition of the patterns to produce ten PIM and PSM models;
- Horizontally, concerns the composition and mapping of the patterns to produce five PIM and five PSM models, and the generation of the source code for the whole interactive system.

8.3   POMA Justifications

The justifications for POMA are as follows:

1. The N-tiers architectures such as Model-View-Controller (MVC) which is 3-tiers architecture, J2EE which is a 5-tier architecture, and Zachman which is a multi-tiered architecture allow POMA architecture to inherit the concept of architectural levels.
2. The Pattern-Oriented Design (POD) architecture based on composition techniques such as behavioral and structural techniques of patterns, allows POMA architecture to inherit the concept of these composition techniques.

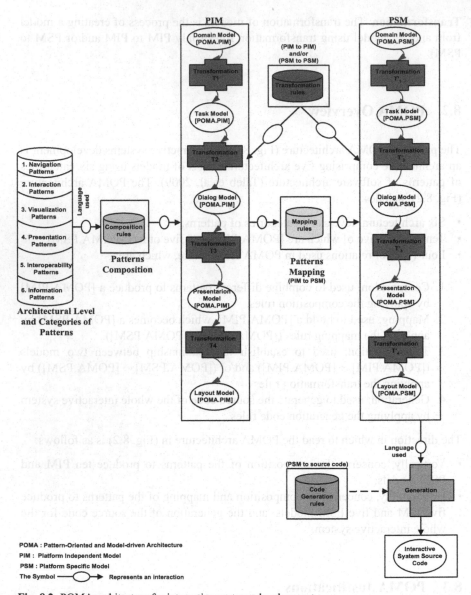

POMA : Pattern-Oriented and Model-driven Architecture
PIM :   Platform Independent Model
PSM :   Platform Specific Model
The Symbol ——◯——▶ Represents an interaction

Fig. 8.2 POMA architecture for interactive systems development

3. The PSA architecture based on the categories of patterns allows POMA architecture to inherit the concept of this categorization of patterns.
4. The MDA architecture based on types of models such as PIM and PSM, and their transformation and mapping, allows POMA architecture to inherit the concept of models (PIM and PSM) and the concepts of model transformation and mapping.

8.4 POMA Specifications and Representation

In this research project, two notations have been adopted: eXtensible Markup Language (XML) and Unified Markup Language (UML) for representing the POMA architecture.

8.4.1 The eXtensible Markup Language (XML) Notation

XML notation is used to specify and formalize the language for POMA called PO-MAML (Pattern-Oriented Modeling Architecture Markup Language) for modeling patterns and models of the proposed POMA architecture.

Indeed, there has been a surge recently in initiatives toward modeling and engineering interactive systems based on model-driven architecture (MDA) using XML.

XML is a meta-language that provides directions for expressing the syntax of markup languages. Instances of these markup languages are hierarchically structured documents that typically consist of content encapsulated within markup and grammatical instructions on how to process it. The term "document" has a special meaning in XML. A document is a standalone object of representation that acts as a container for processable information. An XML document could, for example, be a physical file on a hard disk or a stream of bytes over a network. Elements and attributes form the most commonly used constructs of an XML document. A given document can conform to the XML specification in two ways. It can be well formed by allowing further constraints. There are a number of ancillary technologies that strengthen the XML framework. XML Infoset is a description of the information available in a (well-formed) XML document. XML DTD and XML Schema are languages that provide a grammar for structural and data type constraints on the syntax and content of the elements and attributes in XML documents. This allows for verification of formalism or validity in a given document. Namespaces in XML are a mechanism for uniquely identifying elements and attributes of XML documents specific to a markup language, making it possible to create heterogeneous documents that unambiguously mix elements and attributes from multiple different XML documents. Xlink provides the bidirectional linking capabilities necessary for hypertext. XSLT is a style sheet language for transforming XML documents into other formats.

All models are expressed in some notation language. The evolution of notation languages for modeling interactive systems in the last decade has taken place in three orthogonal directions: abstraction; partition (of concerns); standardization. Abstraction has made it possible to define models without getting into the details of implementation or the underlying computing environment. Partition (of concerns) permits describing and dealing with semantically different aspects of the interaction in a changing environment. Standardization has brought some order to the growing complexity of isolated notations that do not always communicate with one another and thereby threaten interoperability among systems. Standardization has also encouraged industry involvement. After embracing a variety of notations and languages over the years for modeling interactive systems, XML has become a popular language in the research community and among practitioners.

8.4.2 The Unified Modeling Language (UML) Notation

During the development of interactive systems, the specification of the interactive system and the interaction design are often performed in parallel, and therefore must be coordinated. A common notation that can be used and understood by both developers and interface designers would foster integration. This is of particular importance since the interface must eventually be integrated into the rest of the interactive system. UML is a standard language for specifying, visualizing, constructing, and documenting the components of the different types of systems, in particular, interactive systems.

Since its beginnings in 1998, UML has gradually evolved to become an industry standard. UML notation according to Gamma et al. (1995):

- Is visual modeling which uses the standard graphical notation of patterns;
- Is a communication tool for various patterns;
- Manages the complexity of composed patterns;
- Defines software architecture;
- Enables and supports reuse;
- Improves the pace at which interactive systems are developed;
- Eases the integration of interfaces with preexisting modules;
- Decreases interactive system development costs.

UML consists of a set of notations developed to specify and design object-oriented software. UML is made up of a family of notations and models. Among them, class and object diagrams for static domain modeling and use cases and sequence diagrams and activity diagrams are used for documenting functional requirements. In addition, the system's behavior can be specified using sequence, collaboration, state, and activity diagrams.

8.5 Architectural Levels and Categories of Patterns, Composition, and Mapping Rules

Many noteworthy patterns related to content architecture, navigation support (control) and the physical and logical structures of common pages have been established. Recently, we conducted a literature survey in 2002 that informed us that there are at least five categories of design patterns for Web applications engineering. Together, these patterns provide an integrative solution to the challenges.

8.5.1 Architectural Levels and Categories of Patterns

This section illustrates how the existing categories of patterns can be used as building blocks in the context of the proposed six architectural levels.

This research project has identified at least six architectural levels and six categories of patterns that can be used to create pattern-oriented interactive system architecture. Table 8.1 illustrates these six levels of POMA architecture for an interactive system, including the corresponding categories of patterns, and gives examples of patterns in each category.

Each of these six categories of patterns is discussed hereunder, and examples are provided.

8.5.1.1 Information Patterns

An information pattern, also called an information architectural pattern (Fig. 8.3), expresses a fundamental structural organization or schema of information. It provides a set of predefined subsystems (information spaces or chunks), specifies their responsibilities, and includes rules and guidelines for organizing the relationships between them.

An information pattern is everything that happens in a single information space or chunk. With another pattern, the content of a system is organized in a sequence in which all the information spaces or chunks are arranged as peers, and every space or chunk is accessible by all the others. This is very common on simple sites where there are only a few standard topics, such as: Home, About Us, Contact Us, and Products. Information which naturally flows as a narrative, a time line, or in a logical order is ideal for sequential treatment. An index structure is like the flat

Table 8.1 Architectural levels, categories of patterns and examples

Architectural level and category of patterns	Examples of patterns
Information	Reference model pattern
This category of patterns describes different	Data column pattern
conceptual models and architectures for organiz-	Cascaded table pattern
ing the underlying content across multiple pages,	Relational graph pattern
servers, and computers. Such patterns provide	Proxy tuple pattern
solutions to questions such as which information	Expression pattern
can or should be presented on which device. This	Schudler pattern
category of patterns is described in Heer and	Operator pattern
Agrawala (2006)	Renderer pattern
	Production rule pattern
	Camera pattern
	Linear pattern
	Hierarchical pattern
	Circular pattern
	Composite pattern
	Hub-and-spoke

Table 8.1 (continued)

Architectural level and category of patterns	Examples of patterns
Interoperability This category of patterns describes decoupling the layers of an interactive system, in particular, between the content, the dialog, and the views or presentation layers. These patterns are generally extensions of the Gamma design patterns, such as MVC (Model, View, and Controller) observer and command action patterns. Communication and interoperability patterns are useful for facilitating the mapping of a design between platforms	Adapter pattern
	Bridge pattern
	Builder pattern
	Decorator pattern
	Façade pattern
	Factory pattern
	Method pattern
	Mediator pattern
	Memento pattern
	Prototype pattern
	Proxy pattern
	Singleton pattern
	State pattern
	Strategy pattern
	Visitor pattern
Visualization This category of patterns describes different visual representations and metaphors for grouping and displaying information in cognitively accessible chunks. They mainly define the format and content of the visualization, i.e., the graphical scene, and as such, relate primarily to data and mapping transforms	Favorite collection pattern
	Bookmark pattern
	Frequently visited page pattern
	Navigation space map pattern
Navigation This category of patterns describes proven techniques for navigating within and/or between a set of pages and chunks of information. This list of patterns is far from exhaustive, but helps to communicate the flavor and abstraction level of design patterns for navigation	Shortcut pattern
	Breadcrumb pattern
	Index browsing pattern
	Contextual (temporary) horizontal menu at top pattern
	Contextual (temporary) vertical menu at right pattern
	Information portal pattern
	Permanent horizontal menu at top pattern
	Permanent vertical menu at left pattern
	Progressive filtering pattern
	Shallow menus pattern
	Simple universal pattern
	Split navigation pattern
	Sub-sites pattern
	User-driven pattern
	Alphabetical index pattern
	Key-word search pattern
	Intelligent agents pattern
	Container navigation pattern
	Deeply embedded menus pattern
	Hybrid approach pattern
	Refreshed shallow vertical menus pattern

Table 8.1 (continued)

Architectural level and category of patterns	Examples of patterns
Interaction This category of patterns describes the interaction mechanisms that can be used to achieve tasks and the visual effects they have on the scene; as such, they relate primarily to graphical and rendering transforms	Search pattern
	Executive summary pattern
	Action button pattern
	Guided tour pattern
	Paging pattern
	Pull-down button pattern
	Slideshow pattern
	Stepping pattern
	Wizard pattern
Presentation This category of patterns describes solutions for how the contents or the related services are visually organized into working surfaces, the effective layout of multiple information spaces, and the relationship between them. These patterns define the physical and logical layout suitable for specific interactive systems	Carrousel pattern
	Table filter pattern
	Detail on demand pattern
	Collector pattern
	In place replacement pattern
	List builder pattern
	List entry view pattern
	Overview by detail pattern
	Part selector pattern
	Tabs pattern
	Table sorter pattern
	Thumbnail pattern
	View pattern
	List pattern
	Table pattern
	Map pattern
	Graph pattern
	Home page pattern

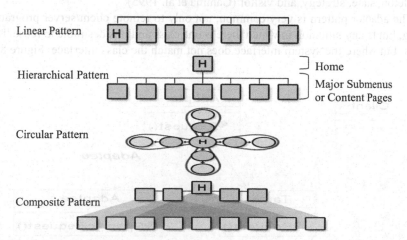

Fig. 8.3 Examples of information patterns

structure, with an additional list of contents. An index is often organized in such a way as to make its content easier to find. For example, a list of files in a Web directory (the index page), an index of people's names ordered by last name. Dictionaries and phone books are both very large indices.

The hub-and-spoke pattern is useful for multiple distinct linear workflows. A good example would be an email system where the user returns to his inbox from several points, e.g., after reading a message, after sending a message, or after adding a new contact. A multidimensional hierarchy is one in which there are many ways to browse the same content. In a way, several hierarchies may coexist, overlaid on the same content. The structure of the content can appear to be different, depending on the user's task (search, browse). A typical example would be a site like Amazon, which lets one browse books by genre or by title, and also allows search by keyword. Each of these hierarchies corresponds to a property of the content, and each can be useful, depending on the user's situation. A strict hierarchy is a specialization of a multidimensional hierarchy, and describes a system where a lower-level page can only be accessed via its parent.

8.5.1.2 Interoperability patterns

Interoperability patterns are useful for decoupling the organization of these different categories of patterns, for the way information is presented to the user, and for the user who interacts with the information content. Patterns in this category generally describe the capability of different programs to exchange data, via a common set of exchange formats, to read and write under the same file formats, and to use the same protocols.

Gamma et al. (1995) offer a large catalog of patterns for dealing with such problems. Examples of patterns applicable to interactive systems include adapter, bridge, builder, decorator, factory method, mediator, memento, prototype, proxy, singleton, state, strategy, and visitor (Gamma et al. 1995).

The adapter pattern is very common, not only to remote client/server programming, but to any situation in which there is one class and it is desirable to reuse that class, but where the system interface does not match the class interface. Figure 8.4

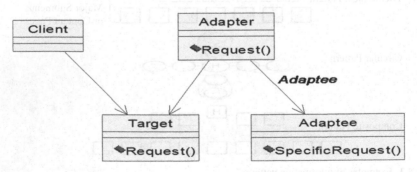

Fig. 8.4 Adapter pattern

illustrates how an adapter works. In this figure, the client wants to invoke the method *Request()* in the target interface. Since the adaptee class has no *Request()* method, it is the job of the adapter to convert the request to an available matching method. Here, the adapter converts the method *Request()* call into the adaptee method *specificRequest()* call. The adapter performs this conversion for each method that needs adapting. This is also known as *wrappering*.

8.5.1.3 Visualization Patterns

Information visualization patterns allow users to browse information spaces and focus quickly on items of interest. Visualization patterns can help to avoid an information overload, a fundamental issue to tackle, especially for large databases, Web sites, and portals, as they can access millions of documents. The designer must consider how best to map the contents into a visual representation which conveys information to the user while facilitating exploration of the content. In addition, the designer must undertake dynamic actions to limit the amount of information the user receives, while at the same time keeping the user informed about the content as a whole. Several information visualization patterns generally combine in such a way that the underlying content can be organized into distinct conceptual spaces or working surfaces which are semantically linked to one another.

For example, depending on the purpose of the site, users can access several kinds of "pages", such as articles, URLs, and products. They typically collect several of these items for a specific task, such as comparing, buying, going to a page, or sending a page to others. Users must be able to visualize their "collection".

The following are some of the information visualization patterns for displaying such collections: favorite, bookmark, frequently visited page, preferences, and navigable spaces map. This category of patterns provides a map to a large amount of content which can be too large to be presented reasonably in a single view. The content can be organized into distinct conceptual spaces or working surfaces which are semantically linked, so that it is natural and meaningful to go from one to another. The map in Fig. 8.5 is an example of this category of patterns.

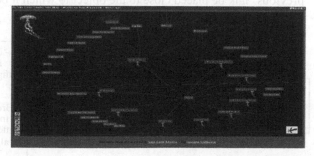

Fig. 8.5 The navigation spaces map pattern implemented using tree hyperbolic, a sophisticated visualization technique

8.5.1.4   Navigation Patterns

Navigation patterns help the user move easily and in a straightforward manner between information chunks and their representations. They can obviously reduce the user's memory load (Nielsen 1999) and (Lynch and Horton 1999). See Engelberg and Seffah (2002) and Garrido et al. (1997) for an exhaustive list of navigation patterns.

The linear navigation pattern is suitable when a user wants a simple way to navigate from one page to the next in a linear fashion, i.e., move through a sequence of pages.

The index browsing pattern is similar to the linear navigation pattern and allows a user to navigate directly from one item to the next and back. The ordering can be based on a ranking. For every item presented to the user, a navigation widget allows the user to choose the next or previous item in the list. The ordering criterion should be visible (and be user-configurable). To support orientation, the current item number and total number of items should be clearly visible. A breadcrumb (Fig. 8.6) is a widely used pattern which helps users to know where they are in a hierarchical structure and to navigate back up to higher levels in the hierarchy. It shows the hierarchical path from the top level to the current page and makes each step clickable.

8.5.1.5   Interaction Patterns

This category of interaction patterns provides basic information on interaction style, mainly on how to use controls such as buttons, lists of items, menus, and dialog boxes. This category of patterns is employed whenever users need to take an important action that is relevant in the current context of the page being viewed. Users must be made aware of the importance of the action in relation to other actions on the page or site.

To view/act on a linear-ordered set of items, the stepping pattern (Fig. 8.7) allows users to go to the next and previous task or object by clicking on the "next" or "previous" links. The "next" link takes the users to the next item in the sequence, while the "previous" link takes them a step back. It is recommended that a "next" or "previous" link be placed close to the object to which it belongs, preferably above

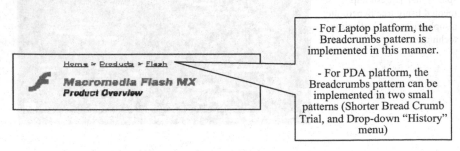

Fig. 8.6 Breadcrumb pattern (Extracted from Swish Zone Website)

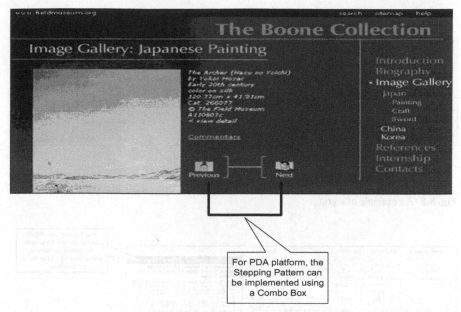

Fig. 8.7 Stepping pattern (Extracted from Field Museum Website)

the object so that users do not have to scroll to it. One must make sure the next/
previous links are always placed in the same location, so that users clicking through
a list do not have to move the mouse pointer. The convention, at least in Western
cultures, is to place the "previous" link on the left and the "next" link on the right.

8.5.1.6 Presentation Patterns

The authors of technical documents discovered long before interactive systems
were invented, that users appreciate short "chunks" of information (Horton 1994).
Patterns in this category, called presentation patterns, also suggest different ways
for displaying chunks of information and ways for grouping them in pages. Presentation patterns also define the look and feel of interactive systems, while at the same
time defining the physical and logical layout suitable for specific systems, such
as home pages, lists, and tables. For example, how long does it take to determine
whether or not a document contains relevant information? This question is a critical
design issue, in particular for resource-constrained (small) devices.

Patterns in this category use a grid, which is a technique taken from print design,
but which is easily applicable to interactive system design as well. In its strictest
form, a grid is literally a grid of X by Y pixels. The elements on the page are then
placed on the cell borderlines and aligned overall on horizontal and vertical lines.
A grid is a consistent system in which to place objects. In the literature on print
design, there are many variations of grids, most of them based on modular and

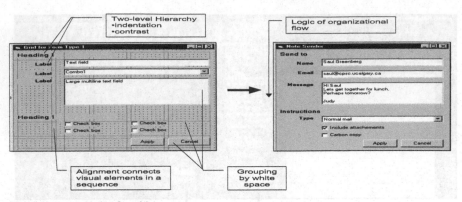

Fig. 8.8 An example of a grid

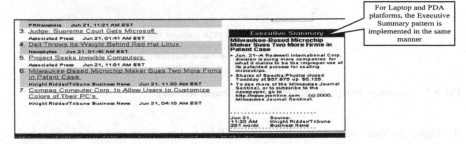

Fig. 8.9 Example of structural patterns: executive summary pattern (Extracted from CBC Website)

column grids. Often, a mix of both types of grids will be used. An example of a grid in Fig. 8.8 is used to create several dialog box patterns.

An example of these types of patterns is the executive summary pattern. The executive summary pattern gives users a preview of the underlying information before they spend time downloading, browsing, and reading large amounts of information (Fig. 8.9).

8.5.2 Patterns Composition

A platform-independent pattern-oriented design exploits several relationships between patterns. We use the relationships defined in Chap 3, including:

- **Similar**. Two patterns (X, Y) are similar or equivalent, if and only if, X and Y can be replaced by each other in a certain composition.
- **Competitor**. Two patterns (X, Y) are competitors if X and Y cannot be used at the same time for designing the same artifact relationship that applies to two patterns of the same pattern category. Two patterns are competitors if and only if they are similar and interchangeable.

- **Superordinate**. A pattern X is a superordinate of pattern Y, which means that pattern Y is used as a building block to create pattern X.
- **Subordinate**. (X, Y) are subordinate if and only if X is embeddable in Y. Y is also called a superordinate of X.
- **Neighboring**. Two patterns (X, Y) are neighboring if X and Y belong to the same pattern category.

The following figure portrays the UML diagram of the patterns at an architectural level.

The class diagram in Fig. 8.11 represents the class structure of the five models and the pattern structure that represent POMA components. Figure 8.11 shows the basic class structure of the POMAML structure notation (see Appendix III for XML source code). For the sake of simplicity, only concrete classes and their public attributes and methods are displayed.

POMAML is an acronym for Pattern-Oriented and Model-driven Architecture Markup Language and is graphically XML structure displayed in Fig. 8.12 described in the Fig. 8.10 and Fig. 8.11. In other words, Fig. 8.12 is a form or structure of XML notation that is used to represent patterns used in Fig. 8.10 and Fig. 8.11. POMAML XML notation for tasks and feature patterns were developed.

The POMAML schema (Fig. 8.12) consists of the classic elements of patterns like name, problem, context, solution and rational. However, these attributes are primarily used only to select an appropriate pattern. The implementation of the pattern has been formalized in the "body". At this point, one should distinguish between Task and TaskTemplates. Tasks are further decomposed into SubTasks and contain no variable parts. Thus they can be adopted 1:1 without further adaptation. On the contrary, TaskTemplates are hierarchically structured as well, but also contain variable definitions and variables and must therefore be adapted first.

8.5.3 Patterns Mapping

Another component in POMA architecture is the concept of *pattern mapping* (Sect 8.1 for the definition). Using a desktop system as a starting point, it is possible to redesign the PSM model for other platforms. The original set of patterns used in the system is mapped or replaced in order to redesign and re-implement the system and, in particular, the user interface (UI) for mobile or Personal Digital Assistant (PDA) systems. Since patterns hold information about design solutions and context of use, platform capabilities and constraints are implicitly addressed in the transformed patterns.

Figure 8.13 illustrates different mappings of the *Quick Access pattern* for three different platforms. This navigation design pattern helps the user reach specific pages, which reflect important interactive system content, from any location on the site. For a news interactive system, direct and quick access to central interfaces such as *Top Stories*, *News*, *Sports*, and *Business* can be provided. A web browser, for example, on a desktop, is implemented as an *index browsing toolbar*. For a PDA,

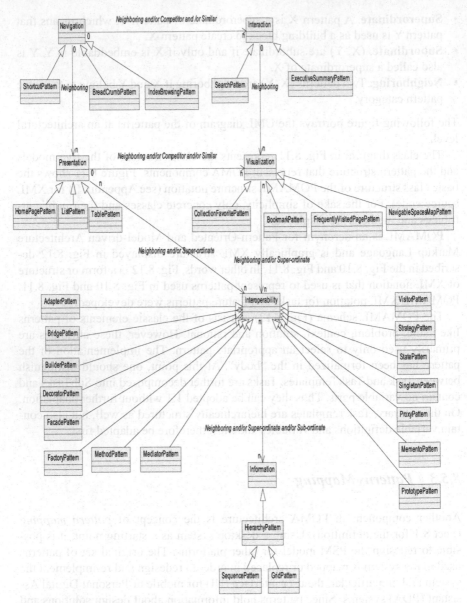

Fig. 8.10 UML class diagram of architectural level and categories of patterns of POMA for interactive system

the Quick Access pattern can be implemented as a *combo box*. For a mobile phone, the Quick Access pattern is implemented as a *selection*. Pattern descriptions should provide advice to pattern users for selecting the most suitable implementation for a given platform.

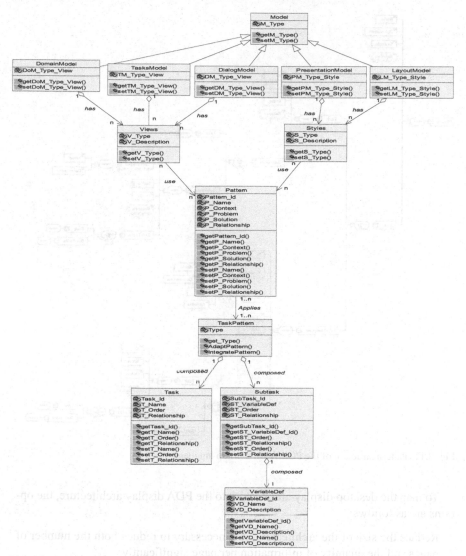

Fig. 8.11 Class structure of POMA's models and patterns

To illustrate pattern mapping, a description is given here of the effect of screen size on selection and use of patterns. Different platforms use different screen sizes, and these different screen sizes afford different types and variants of patterns. The problem to resolve when mapping a pattern-oriented design (POD) is how the change in screen size between two platforms affects redesign at the pattern level. The amount of information that can be displayed on a given platform screen is determined by a combination of area and the number of pixels. The total difference in information capacity between platforms will be somewhere between these two measures: 20 times the area and 10 times the pixels.

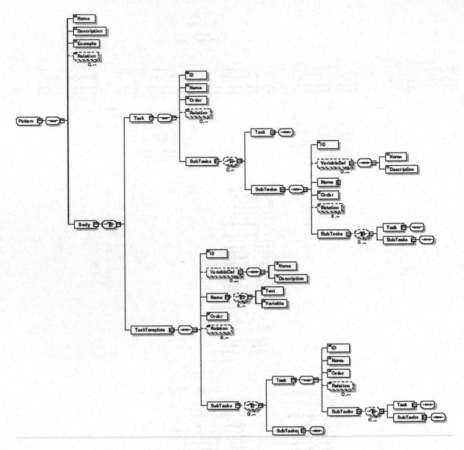

Fig. 8.12 Pattern structure of the POMAML markup language

To map the desktop display architecture to the PDA display architecture, the options are as follows:

1. Reduce the size of the architecture; it is necessary to reduce both the number of pages and the quantity of information per page significantly.
2. Hold the architecture size constant (i.e., topics or pages); it is necessary to significantly reduce the quantity of information per page (by a factor of about 10–20).
3. Retain all the information in the desktop architecture; it is necessary to significantly increase the size of the architecture, since the PDA can hold less information per page.

The mapping choice will depend on the size of the architecture and the value of the information:

- For small desktop architectures, the design strategy can be weighted either toward reducing information, if the information is not important, or toward increasing the number of pages if the information is important;

Fig. 8.13 The web convenient toolbar pattern implementations and look and feels for different platforms (Extracted from the CNN Website)

- For medium and large desktop architectures, it is necessary to weight the design strategy heavily toward reducing the quantity of information, otherwise the architecture size and number of levels would rapidly explode out of control.

Finally, one can consider mapping patterns and graphical objects in the context of the amount of change that must be applied to the desktop design or architecture to fit it into a PDA format. The following is the list of suggested mapping rules:

1. **Identical:** No change to the original design. For example, drop-down menus pattern can usually be copied from a desktop to a PDA without any design changes.
2. **Scalable:** Changes to the size of the original design or to the number of items in the original design. For example, a long horizontal menu pattern can be adapted to a PDA by reducing the number of menu elements.
3. **Multiple:** Repeating the original design, either simultaneously or sequentially. For example, a single long menu can be transformed into a series of shorter menus.
4. **Fundamental:** Change the nature of the original design. For example, permanent left-hand vertical menu patterns are useful on desktop displays, but are not practical on most PDAs. In mapping to a PDA, a left-hand menu pattern normally needs to be replaced with an alternative, such as a drop-down menu.

These mapping rules can be used by designers in the selection of patterns, especially when different patterns apply for one platform but not for another, when the cost of adapting or purchasing a pattern is high, or when the applicability of a pattern (knowing how and when to apply a pattern) is questionable.

   This list of four mapping rules is especially relevant to the automation of cross-platform design mapping, since the designs that are easiest to map are those that require the least mapping. The category of patterns therefore identifies where human intervention will be needed for design decisions in the mapping process. In addition, when building a desktop design for which a PDA version is also planned, the category of patterns indicates which patterns to use in the desktop design to allow easy mapping to the PDA design.

   Figure 8.14 illustrates some of the navigation design patterns used in the home page of a desktop-based system. Once these patterns are identified in the desktop-based system, they can be mapped or replaced by others in a PDA version.

   Figure 8.15 demonstrates the redesigned interface of the CBC site for migrating to a PDA platform. The permanent horizontal menu pattern at the top (P5) in the original desktop UI were repositioned to a shorter horizontal menu pattern (P5s). In order to accommodate this change on the small PDA screen, the three different horizontal menus had to be shortened, and only important navigation items were used. The keyword search pattern (P13) remains as a keyword search. The permanent vertical menu on the left pattern (P6) was redesigned to a drop-down menu pattern (P15). The drop-down menu pattern in the PDA design also includes the menu headings, "What's on today?" and "Online features" from the temporary vertical menu pattern (P3) in the original desktop design. Finally, the information portal pattern (P4), which is the first item that captures the user's attention, was redesigned as a smaller information portal pattern (P4s).

   What has just been illustrated in this section and the examples in Fig. 8.13, Fig. 8.14 and Fig. 8.15 can be characterized in the form of composed and mapped pattern-oriented design architecture (Fig. 8.16).

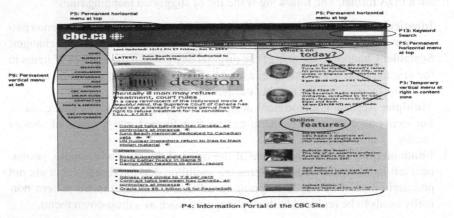

Fig. 8.14 Examples of patterns (Extracted from the CBC News Website)

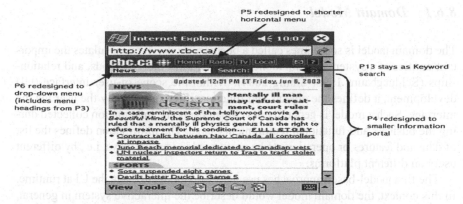

Fig. 8.15 Migration of the CBC site to a PDA platform using pattern mapping (Extracted from the CBC News Website)

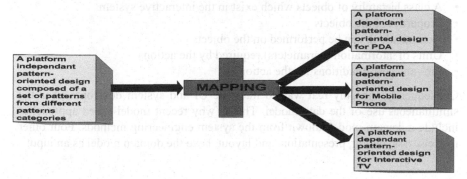

Fig. 8.16 Pattern-oriented composition and mapping design architecture

8.6   Model Categorizations

A categorization of models is proposed here. Examples of models are also presented to illustrate the need to map and/or to transform several types of models, to provide solutions to problems on the six architectural levels. This section describes how these models can be used at six levels of the proposed POMA architecture to create a model-driven architecture for interactive systems.

The focus is on a subset of the proposed models by this research project and consists of:

- A domain model
- A task model
- A dialog model
- A presentation model
- A layout model

8.6.1   Domain Model

The domain model is sometimes called a business model. It encapsulates the important entities of a system domain along with their attributes, methods, and relationships (Schlungbaum 1996; Sinnig 2004). Within the scope of user interface (UI) development, it defines the objects and functionalities accessed by the user via the interface. Such a model is generally developed using the information collected during the business and functional requirements stage. The information defines the list of data and features or operations to be performed in various ways, i.e., by different users on different platforms.

The first model-based approaches use a domain model to drive the UI at runtime. In this context, the domain model would describe the interactive system in general, and include some specific information for the UI. For example, the domain model (Schlungbaum 1996) would include:

- A class hierarchy of objects which exist in the interactive system
- Properties of the objects
- Actions which can be performed on the objects
- Units of information (parameters) required by the actions
- Pre- and post-conditions for the actions

Consequently, the only real way to integrate UI and system development is the simultaneous use of the data model. This is why recent model-based approaches include a domain model known from the system engineering methods. Four other models: task, dialog, presentation, and layout, have the domain model as an input.

8.6.2   Task Model

The task model makes it possible to describe how tasks can be performed to reach the user's goals when using an interactive system (Paternò 2000). Using this model, designers can develop integrated descriptions of the system from a functional and interactive point of view. Task models are typically tasks and subtasks hierarchically decomposed into atomic actions (Souchon et al. 2002). In other words, the task model is the set of tasks that users need to perform with the interactive system. In addition, the relationships between tasks are described with the execution order or dependencies between peer tasks. The tasks may contain attributes about their importance, their duration of execution, and their frequency of use.

For purposes here, the following definition is applied:

A task is a goal, along with the ordered set of subtasks and actions that would satisfy it in the appropriate context (Schlungbaum 1996).

This definition highlights the intertwining nature of tasks and goals. Actions are required to satisfy goals. Furthermore, the definition allows the decomposition of tasks into subtasks, with some ordering among the subtasks and actions. In order to support this definition, one needs to add the definitions for goal, action, and artefact.

A goal is an intention to perform the task which is the state of an artefact based on Schlungbaum (1996);

An action is any act which has the effect of changing or maintaining the state of an artefact based on Schlungbaum (1996);

An artefact is an object which is essential for a task. Without this object, the task cannot be performed; the state of this artefact is usually changed in the course of the performance of a task. Artefacts are real things which exist in the context of task performance. In business, artefacts are modeled as objects and represented in the business model. This implies a close relationship between the task model and the business model.

These definitions derive the information that needs to be represented in a task model. According to Schlungbaum (1996), the description of a task includes:

- A goal
- A non-empty set of actions or other tasks which are necessary to achieve the goal
- A plan of how to select actions or tasks
- A model of an artifact, which is influenced by the task

Consequently, the development of the task model and the domain model is inter-related. One of the goals of model-based approaches is to support user-centered interface design. Therefore, they must enable the UI designer to create the various task models. Three other models (dialog, presentation, and layout) have the domain and task models as inputs.

8.6.3 Dialog Model

Dialog model enables one to provide dialog styles to perform tasks and to provide proven techniques for the dialog. The dialog model defines the navigational structure of the UI. It is a more specific model and can be derived mostly from the more abstract task and domain models.

A dialog model is used to describe the human-computer interaction. It specifies when the end user can invoke commands, functions, and interaction media, when the end user can select or specify inputs, and when the computer can query the end user and present information (Puerta 1997; Sinnig 2004). The dialog model describes the sequencing of input tokens, output tokens, and the way in which they are interleaved. It describes the syntactical structure of human-computer interaction. The input and output tokens are lexical elements. Therefore, and in particular, this model specifies the user commands, interaction techniques, interface responses, and command sequences permitted by the interface during user sessions. Two other models, presentation and layout, have the domain, task, and dialog models as inputs.

8.6.4 Presentation Model

The presentation model describes the visual appearance of the UI (Schlungbaum 1996). This model exists at two levels of abstraction: the abstract and the concrete. In practice, they define the appearance and the form of presentation of a system within an interactive system providing solutions on how the contents or related services can be visually organized into working surfaces, the effective layout of multiple information spaces and the relationship between them. Moreover, they define the physical and logical layout suitable for specific interactive systems such as home pages, lists, and tables.

A presentation model describes the constructs that can appear on an end user's display, their layout characteristics, and the visual dependencies among them. The displays of most systems consist of a static part and a dynamic part. The static part includes the presentation of the standard widgets like buttons, menus, and list boxes. Typically, the static part remains fixed during the runtime of the interactive system, except for state changes like enable/disable, visible/invisible. The dynamic part displays system-dependent data, which typically change during runtime (e.g., the system generates output information, while the end user constructs system-specific data).

The former provides an abstract view of a generic interface, which represents corresponding task and dialog models. Another model, layout, has the domain, task, dialog, and presentation models as inputs.

8.6.5 Layout Model

A layout model constitutes a concrete instance for an interface. It consists of a series of UI components which defines the visual layout of a UI and the detailed dialogs for a specific platform and context of use. There may be many concrete instances of a layout model which can be derived from presentation and dialog models.

The layout model makes it possible to provide conceptual models and architectures for organizing the underlying content across multiple pages, servers, databases, and computers. It is concerned with the look and feel of interactive systems and with the construction of a general drawing area (e.g., a canvas widget), and all the outputs inside a canvas must be programmed using a general-purpose programming language and a low-level graphical library.

8.6.6 Transformation Rules

Model transformation is the process of converting one or more models—called source models—to an output model—the target model—of the same system. Transformations may combine elements of different source models in order to build a target model. Transformation rules apply to all the types of models listed above.

The following steps make up the list of transformation rules suggested in IN-TERACT (1999) and are considered as part of POMA architecture.

1. Maintain tracking structures of all class instances where needed
2. Maintain tracking structures for association populations where needed
3. Support state machine semantics

4. Enforce event ordering
5. Preserve action atomicity
6. Provide a transformation for all analysis elements, including:

- Domain, domain service
- Class, attribute, association, inheritance, associative class, class service
- State, event, transition, superstate, substate
- All action-modeling elements

The transformations between models (Si Alhir 2003) provide a path which enables the automated implementation of a system to be derived from the various models defined for it.

8.7 Key Issues and Contributions

This chapter has focused on an architectural model that combines two key approaches: model-driven and pattern-oriented.

1. Architectural levels and categories of patterns have been described (navigation patterns, interaction patterns, visualization patterns, presentation patterns, interoperability patterns, and information patterns) as well as the different relationships between patterns. Their relationships are used to combine using the composition rules described in Sect. 8.5.2 such as similar, competitor, superordinate, subordinate, and neighboring to create a platform independent model (PIM) and to map several types of patterns to create a platform-specific model (PSM) design using mapping rules described in Sect. 8.5.3 such as identical, scalable, multiple, and fundamental for interactive systems, as well as to generate specific implementations suitable to different platforms from the same pattern-oriented design;
2. Five categories of models (domain model, task model, dialog model, presentation model and layout model) to address some of the challenging problems such as: (a) decoupling the various aspects of interactive systems such as business logic, user interface, navigation, and information architecture; (b) isolating platform-specific problems from the concerns common to all interactive systems.

References

Alexander C, Ishikawa S, Silverstein M, Jacobson M, Fiskdahl-King I, S. Angel. (1977) A pattern language. Oxford University Press. New York
Bass L, Clements P, Kazman R (2003) Software architecture in practice, 2nd Edn. Addison-Wesley Boston, USA

Engelberg D, Seffah A (2002) A design patterns for the navigation of large information architectures. 11th annual usability professional association conference. Orlando (Florida). USA

Gamma E, Helm R, Johnson R, Vlissides J (1995) Design patterns: elements of reusable object-oriented software. Addison Wesley, USA

Garrido A, Rossi G, Schwabe D (1997) Pattern Systems for Hypermedia. Pattern Language of Programming Conference

Heer J, Agrawala M (2006) Software design patterns for information visualization. IEEE Transact Visual Comp Graphics (TVCG) 12(5):853–860

Lynch PJ, Horton S (1999) Web style guide: basic design principles for creating web sites. Yale University Press, New Haven

Nielsen J (1999) Designing web usability. The practice of simplicity. New Ridersm, San Francisco

Paternò F (2000) Model-based design and evaluation of interactive applications. 208 pages. ISBN 1-85233-155-0. Springer, Germany

Puerta A (1997) A model-based interface development environment. IEEE Software 14:41–47. http://www.arpuerta.com/pdf/ieee97.pdf. (0740–7459/97)

Schlungbaum E (1996) Model-based user interface software tools—current state of declarative models. Graphics, Visualization and Usability Center Georgia Institute of Technology, Georgia. (Technical Report 96-30)

Si Alhir S (2003) Understanding the model-driven architecture (MDA). Methods Tools 11(3):17–24. http://www.methodsandtools.com/PDF/Dmt0303.pdf

Sinnig D (2004) The complicity of patterns and model-based UI development (p 148). Concordia University, Montreal. (Master of Computer Science)

Souchon N, Quentin L, Jean V (2002) Task modelling in multiple contexts of use. In Proceedings of DSV-IS 2002. pp 77–95. Rostock. Germany

Taleb M, Seffah A, Abran A (2009) 'Interactive Systems Engineering: A Pattern-Oriented and Model-Driven Architecture', The 2009 International Conference on Software Engineering Research and Practice (SERP'09), July 13–16, 2009, CSREA Press, pp 636–642, Las Vegas, Nevada, USA

Chapter 9
Patterns in Web-Based Information Systems

Abstract Day-to-day experiences suggest that it is not enough to approach Web-application engineering armed with Web guidelines and user manuals on how to use the underlying technologies, such as Java and Simple Object Access Protocol (SOAP). Many of the Web designer and user problems tend to recur in various projects. Web designers often try to reinvent design solutions from scratch. Developers must be able to use proven design solutions emerging from the best design practices to solve common problems. Without this, the designer will not properly apply Web guidelines, or take full benefit of the power of Web technology, resulting in poor performance, poor scalability, and poor usability of the developed applications. In this chapter, we introduce different types of Web design patterns as a vehicle for capturing and disseminating good designs while detailing a motivating example on how Web design patterns can be combined to create a home page. Our investigations are based on several years of Web applications development, ethnographic interviews with Web developers, as well as suggestions from others. Such suggestions include reported best practices for using patterns as a bridge over the gaps between the design practices and software tools. Our experiences also highlighted that in order to render the patterns understandable by novice designers and software engineers who are unfamiliar with Web engineering, patterns should be represented to developers using a flexible structure, to make it easy for the pattern authors, reviewers, and users.

9.1 Introduction

A complex Web site is the place where all the elements of a company, such as graphic identity, customer service, products, services, and structure, come together in one place. Interacting with a Web site conveys much more than the graphic brand identity of the company—it is all about the user experience of moving through the site and interacting with all of its various parts. Web design must incorporate what people do on the site rather than simply how it looks. More consideration toward the user's experience and interactions with the website are necessary, such as how the site is perceived, learned, and mastered. This includes ease-of-use and, most importantly, the needs that the site should fulfill with respect to services and information.

© Springer International Publishing Switzerland 2015   181
A. Seffah, *Patterns of HCI Design and HCI Design of Patterns*,
Human-Computer Interaction Series, DOI 10.1007/978-3-319-15687-3_9

The design of the website should focus on the behavior of users. Consequently, we must analyze and understand users, and provide designs based on user experiences and persona.

For some complex Web sites such as e-commerce, online banking, and educational systems, as well as Web sites for a specific set of users such as scientists, usability is recognized as a key element of the site's success and acceptance by its end users. The bad news is that most of such sites employ horribly misguided methodologies that do not assess real usability. A good methodological framework should address the following concern: More and more, Web sites are designed for an international audience and for universal usability. In this context, a universal design approach should be adopted to accommodate the vast majority of the global population. This entails addressing challenges of technology variety, user diversity, and gaps in user knowledge in ways only beginning to be acknowledged by educational, corporate, and government agencies (Shneiderman 2000).

Web applications are moving away from the paradigm of an online-type brochure with a static presentation to highly interactive web-based software systems. With the advent of Web scripting languages and document object models, the user has been given more sophisticated techniques to interact with server-side services and information. In addition, the convergence of the internet and mobile device technologies has led to the emergence of a new generation of web applications. One of the major characteristics of these new applications is that they allow a user to interact with services using different kinds of computers and devices, with particularities in interaction style. These devices include the traditional office desktop, laptop, palmtop, personal digital assistant (PDA) with and without keyboard, mobile telephone, and interactive television.

In this new technological context, we can distinguish four kinds of interactive Web applications with four different styles of user interfaces:

Traditional Web applications that are based on the Web browser. Most popular Web applications are Web sites, corporate intranet environments, portals, and e-commerce applications;

Embeddable Web services. Examples of basic services can include open uniform resource locator (URL) from FrontPage Explorer, browse through links in a portable document format (PDF) file using Adobe Acrobat and send mails from most Microsoft productive tools;

Web applications that offer an optimized and specialized user interface to a set of Internet features. An example of such applications is e-mail that provides an example of the interplay between specialized applications and toned-down web applications. It is often possible to access your email through a Simple Mail Transfer Protocol (SMTP) client provided as an accessory to the browser (such as Outlook in Microsoft Internet Explorer and Messenger in Netscape Communicator). The same applies to Network News Transfer Protocol (NNTP) clients that enable a user to access Usenet newsgroups on the Internet;

Resource constrained Web applications for small and mobile devices that cannot support the full range of Web application features, because of the lack of screen space or low bandwidth. These applications include mobile telephone-embedded Internet applications (read e-mail, browse mobile portal sites, etc.).

This mosaic of applications has led to the emergence of Web engineering as a subdiscipline of software engineering for creating high-quality Web interactive systems. Web engineering is governed by its own set of fundamental principles, even if it borrows many of the software engineering methodologies and theories, and emphasizes similar technical and management activities. There are subtle differences in the way these activities are conducted, but an overriding philosophy dictating a disciplined approach to the development of the system is identical. As an example, we can adapt and refine pattern-assisted engineering to the development of Web applications.

Our objective can be stated as follows: To facilitate the engineering of Web applications while improving the usability and quality of the developed applications; by composing different kinds of patterns such as architectural, navigational, and interaction patterns to create a high level and reusable design with the goal to support the generation of application code. A subobjective of our research is to define a systematic methodology, supported by a Web CASE tool, to glue the patterns together.

9.2   Design Challenges of Web Applications

The following are some of the challenges associated with web design that we are addressing:

First, in an attempt to segment the different aspects of Web application architecture and isolate platform specifics from remaining issues, the vast majority of current industry Web applications have adopted a layered approach. As with other multitiered schemes such as client-server architecture, a common information repository is at the core of the architecture. The repository is accessed strictly through this layer, which in addition to the functions listed, also provides decoupling of the data from the device specific interfaces. In this way, device application developers need to only worry about the standardized middleware interface rather than having to concern themselves with the multitude of application programming interfaces (APIs) put forth by database repository manufacturers. Segmenting the architecture and reducing coupling to stringent specifications allows the designer to quickly understand how changes made to a particular component effects the remaining system. That is because achieving these goals requires a consistent approach to applying both cognitive and social factors to UI design, and that would require independent developers to coordinate their activities. Unfortunately, conspiring at this level may be beyond the abilities of the industry.

Second, web applications are efficient at managing heterogeneous environments. This point is critical, as more and more Web applications will need to interact with very different platforms and devices. This diversity results in computing devices that exhibit drastically different capabilities. For example, PDAs use a pen based input mechanism and have average screen sizes in the range of 3 inches. On the other hand, the typical PC uses a full size keyboard, a mouse, and has an average screen size of 17 inches. Coping with such drastic variations implies much more than mere layout changes. Pen-based input mechanism are slower than traditional keyboards and thus are inappropriate for applications such as word processing that require intensive user input. Similarly the small screens available on many PDAs only provide coarse graphic capabilities and thus would be ill suited for photo editing applications.

Another challenge is that heterogeneity in the computing platform ranging from traditional desktop to mobile phone via PDA is the source of a further complication in Web applications engineering. Certain form factors are better suited to particular contexts. For example, walking down the street, one user may use her mobile telephone's Internet browser to lookup a stock quote. However, it is highly unlikely that this same user reviews the latest changes made to a document using the same device. Rather, it would seem more logical and definitely more practical to use a full size computer for this task. It would therefore seem that the context of use is determined by a combination of internal and external factors. The internal factors primarily relate to the user's attention while performing a task. In some cases, the user may be entirely focused, while at other times greatly distracted by other concurrent tasks. An example of this latter point is when a user—while driving a car—operates a PDA to reference a telephone number. External factors are determined to a large extent by the device's physical characteristics. It is not possible to make use of a traditional PC as one walks down the street—a practice quite common with a mobile telephone. The challenge for a system architect is thus to match the design of a particular device's UI with the set of constraints imposed by the corresponding context of use.

Finally, many system manufacturers and researchers have issued design guidelines to Web-application designers (Lynch and Horton 1999). Recently, Palm Inc. has put forth design guidelines to address the navigation issues, widget selection, and use of specialized input mechanisms such as handwriting recognition. (Macintosh 1992; Microsoft 1995; IBM 2015; Sun Microsystems 2001) have also published their own usability guidelines to assist developers with programming applications targeted at the Pocket PC/Windows CE platform. However, these guidelines are different from one platform or device to another. When designing a multidevice Web application, this can be a source of many inconsistencies. The Java "look-and-feel" developed by Sun is a set of cross-platform guidelines that can fix such problems. However, cross-platform guidelines do not take into account the particularities of a specific device, in particular the platform constraints and capabilities. This can be a source of problems for a user using different kinds of devices to interact with the server side services and information of a Web application. Furthermore, for a novice designer or a software engineer who is not familiar with this mosaic of guidelines, it is hard to remember all design guidelines, let alone using them effectively. It is sometimes difficult to make the trade-offs among these principles when they come into conflict; we often have to figure out the best solution by guessing, or by resorting to other means.

9.3 Web Design Principles

Patterns also are not enough to design usable and useful Web applications. They need to be used in junction with high-level design. For example, the design of the previous home page, we also used the following rules:

- *Organize the page for scanning.* The homepage is organized to be help users scan down the page, trying to find the area that will serve their current goal. Links are the action items on a homepage, and when you start each link with a relevant word, you make it easier for scanning eyes to differentiate it from other links on the page. A common violation of this guideline is to start all links with the company name, which adds little value and impairs users ability to quickly find what they need;
- *Provide clear affordance of links.* Navigation elements, in particular, links must provide clear affordance. Their appearance should help users understand them. The mouse pointer change provided by web browsers, to indicate that the element pointed at a link is not sufficient. The designer can use differences in size to establish a hierarchy between links, but HyperText Markup Language (HTML) text has poor graphic quality and doesn't allow much visual characterization. Differentiation between navigation elements and information is indeed the main affordance problem to be solved;
- *Strive to avoid users making errors.* We should provide alternative links so that the user can recover from the error quickly and easily, communicate in the user's vocabulary, use Web server, which allows you to customize the error messages. If an error occurs, tell users what the error is, why it occurred, what they can do to fix it.

The same design approach can be applied to the following patterns of pages that we generally use to design a Web site:

1. Central page (one or more)—Central page of your site from which all, other pages can be reached (directly or indirectly). The home page is a specialization of such page. For a large Web site, we can have more than one central page (e.g. university, department, research group, personal web sites).
2. Navigation pages for directing the user to the proper area of your site for the information they are seeking.
3. Content pages provide the information users are seeking when they visit your site. They may also contain navigational links to give users a sense of location within the site and allow them to progress to more information or return to a previous page.
4. Input page (transaction forms, search, feedback) is to collect information from users or establish a dialog with the user.
5. Utilities pages (bookmarks, extra things, help, archive, configuration, etc.).

One of the major problems we found is that mastering and applying type patterns and a large collection of patterns require in-depth knowledge of both the problems and forces at play, and most importantly must ultimately put forth battle-tested solutions. As such, it is inconceivable that pattern hierarchies will evolve strictly from theoretical considerations. Practical research and industry feedback are crucial in determining how successful a pattern-oriented design framework is at solving real-world problems. It is therefore essential to build an "academia–industry bridge" by establishing formal communication channels between industrial specialists in human–computer interaction (HCI) patterns, software design patterns, information architecture patterns as well as software pattern researchers. Such collaboration will lead to a common terminology which is essential for making the large diversity of patterns accessible to common Web designers.

9.4 Case Study: A Detailed Discussion

9.4.1 Overview

This section presents a case study that describes the design of a functional user interface simplified prototype of an "Environmental Management Interactive System" (IFEN), illustrating and clarifying the core ideas of the Pattern-Oriented and Model-Driven Architecture (POMA) approach and its practical relevance.

This environmental management interactive system permits requirement analysis of the environment, its evolution, its economic and social dimensions, and proposes indicators of performance. The main objectives of environmental management are the treatment and distribution of water, improving air quality, monitoring noise, the treatment of waste, the health of fauna and flora, land use, preserving coastal and marine environments, and managing natural and technological risks (IFEN).

A simplified prototype of the "Environmental Management Interactive System" is developed here. The interactive system and corresponding models will not be tailored to different platforms. This prototype illustrates how patterns are used to establish the various models, as well as, the transformation of one model into another while respecting the pattern composition rules described in the Chap. 8 in Sect. 8.5.2, the pattern mapping rules described in Sect. 8.5.3 and the transformation rules described in Sect. 8.6.6.

This case study presents a general overview of the Platform-Independent Model (PIM) and Platform-Specific Model (PSM) models of the "Environmental Management Interactive System" by applying pattern composition steps and mapping rules, as well as transformation rules for the five models. The details of this illustrative case study are presented in this chapter in which the five models representing the same interactive system are illustrated on a laptop platform and on a PDA platform. The five models include the domain model, task model, dialog model, presentation model, and layout model of POMA architecture. Table 9.1 lists the patterns that will be used by the interactive system.

A prototype of a multiplatform interactive system for POMA architecture is implemented. A prototype is implemented in Java language using the Eclipse tool. There is a screenshot of the final layout of the "Environmental Management

Table 9.1 Pattern summary

Pattern name	Model type	Problem
Login	Domain	The user's identity needs to be authenticated in order to be allowed access to protected data and/or to perform authorized operations
Multivalue input form (Seffah and Gaffar 2006)	Domain	The user needs to enter a number of related values. These values can be of different data types, such as "date," "string," or "real"
Submit	Domain	The user needs to submit coordinates to the authentication process to access the system
Feedback	Domain	The user needs help concerning the use of the Login Form
Close	Domain	The need to close the system from the Login form
Find (search, browse, executive summary) (Seffah and Gaffar 2006)	Task	The need to find indicators related to the task concerned, to find environmental patterns related to the indicators, and to find a presentation tool to display the results of the indicators and the environmental patterns
Breadcrumb (Path)	Task	The need to construct and display the path that combines the data source, task, and/or subtask
Index browsing	Task	The need to display all indicators listed as index browsing to navigate and select the desired ones
Adapter	Task	The need to convert the interface of a class into another interface that clients expect; an adapter lets classes work together which could not otherwise be done because of interface incompatibility
Builder	Task	The need to separate the construction of a complex object from its representation, so that the same construction process can create different representations
List	Task	The need to display the information using forms
Table	Task	The need to display the information in tables
Map	Task	The need to display the information in geographic maps
Graph	Task	The need to display the information in graphs
Home page	Task	The need to define the layout of an interactive system home page, which is important because the home page is the interactive system interface with the world and the starting point for most user visits
Wizard (Welie 2004) and (Sinnig 2004)	Dialog	The user wants to achieve a single goal, but several decisions and actions need to be taken consecutively before the goal can be achieved
Recursive activation (Seffah and Gaffar 2006)	Dialog	The user wants to activate and manipulate several instances of a dialog view
Unambiguous format (Seffah and Gaffar 2006)	Presentation	The user needs to enter data, but may be unfamiliar with the structure of the information and/or its syntax
Form (Seffah and Gaffar 2006)	Presentation	The user must provide structural textual information to the system. The data to be provided are logically related
House (Seffah and Gaffar 2006)	Layout	Usually, the system consists of several pages/windows. The user should have the impression that it all "hangs together" and looks like one entity

Fig. 9.1 Graphical representation of the pattern

Interactive System" illustrated in Fig. 9.24. The key features of the current version
of this interactive system prototype are the following:

- Support for well-arranged graphical specifications of hierarchy of POMA networks. This is achieved by the notion of a so-called tree explorer, in which the
  hierarchy of networks can be easily viewed and managed;
- Support for checking the correctness of network dependencies at the syntactic
  level. The editor contains a list of inputs and an output port for each network in
  the hierarchy and helps the user bind the right subsystem ports to the higher ports
  in the network hierarchy;
- Together with architectural compatibility checking, the prototype will allow one
  to easily define new POMA models by composing and mapping patterns which
  have already been defined and formalized.

Figure 9.1 shows the graphical representation of the pattern, which is used to exem-
plify the pattern in this case study.

9.4.2   Defining the Domain Model

Acting in the horizontal line of the POMA architecture (Fig. 8.2) in Chap. 8, this
model is composed of two types of submodels, [POMA.PIM]-independent domain
submodel and [POMA.PSM]-specific domain submodel.

The [POMA.PIM]-independent domain submodel (Fig. 9.2) is obtained by composing patterns and applying the composition rules.

The following example shows the composition of a "**Close**" pattern in eXtensible Markup Language (XML) language:

```
/* XML
<!xml version="1.0" >
<d-class name="Close"
    ....
Compose-to="xml.Jbutton">
    ....
</d-class>
</xml>
```

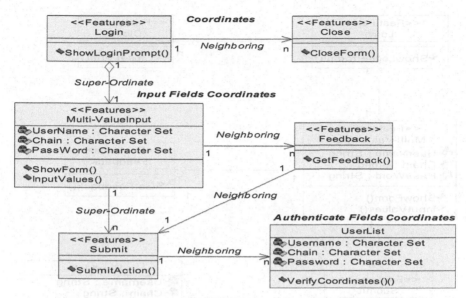

Fig. 9.2 Unified Modeling Language (UML) class diagram of the platform-independent model (PIM) domain model

The [POMA.PSM]-specific domain submodel (Figs. 9.3 and 9.4) is obtained by mapping composed patterns and applying the mapping rules (Table 9.2). This latter model would be used to generate the interactive system's source code by taking into account the generation code rules for a Microsoft platform.

Table 9.2 shows the mapping rules for the domain model patterns for a laptop and PDA platforms.

Therefore, the mapped domain model is obtained. An example of the mapping of a *Close* pattern in Java language follows:

```
/* Java
<d-class name="Close"

    ....

Maps-to="javax.swing.Jbutton">

    ....

</d-class>
```

After the mapping, the PSM domain model is obtained for a laptop platform—Fig. 9.3 and for a PDA platform—Fig. 9.4.

To obtain feedback on the PDA platform, we need to insert *Next* and *Previous* patterns to obtain information in a number of smaller portal displays. The *Next* pattern enables one to access the next feedback information available, and the *Previous* pattern allows a return to the previous feedback information.

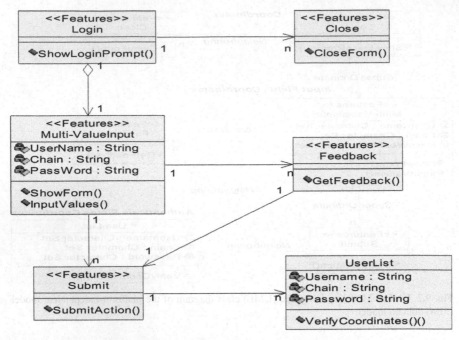

Fig. 9.3 UML class diagram of the platform-specific model (PSM) domain model for a laptop platform

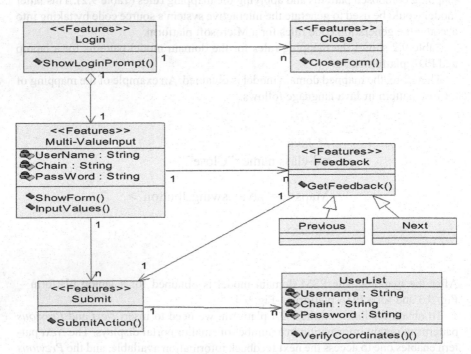

Fig. 9.4 UML class diagram of the PSM domain model for personal digital assistant (PDA) platform

Table 9.2 Example of pattern mapping of the Domain model for laptop and PDA platforms

Patterns of Microsoft platform	Type of mapping	Replacement patterns for laptop platform	Replacement patterns for PDA platform
P1. Login	Identical, scalable, or fundamental	P1. Login	P1.s Login (small interface)
P2. Multivalue input	Identical	P2. Multivalue input	P2. Multivalue input
P3. Submit	Scalable or fundamental	P3. Submit	P3.s Submit (smaller button)
P4. Feedback	Scalable or fundamental	P4. Feedback	P4. Feedback (less items per page) P4.1. Next P4.2. Previous
P5. Close	Identical	P5. Close	P5. Close

PDA personal digital assistant

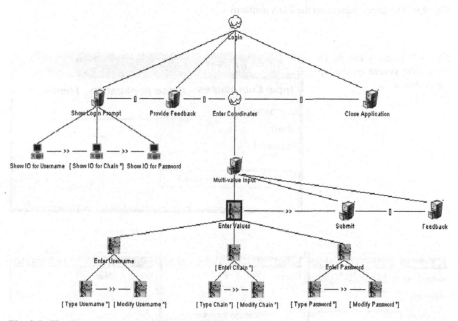

Fig. 9.5 The *Login* pattern on the laptop platform

Figure 9.5 and Fig. 9.6 represent a structure of the *Login* pattern, which enables the user to identify himself or herself in order to access secure or protected data and/ or to perform authorized operations.

Figures 9.7 and 9.8 represent an implementation of the *Login* pattern.

Figure 9.7 is an example of implementation of the *Login* Pattern.

Figure 9.8 is an example of implementation of the *Login* pattern.

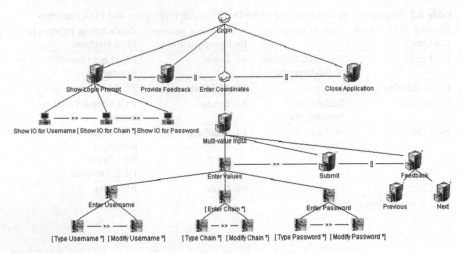

Fig. 9.6 The *Login* pattern on the PDA platform

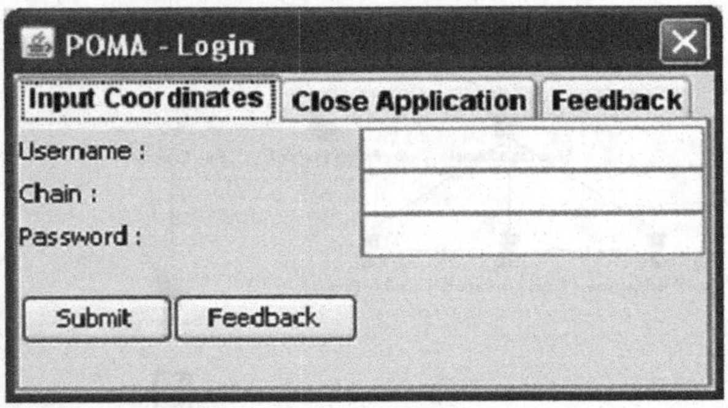

Fig. 9.7 Login view of the interactive system on the laptop platform

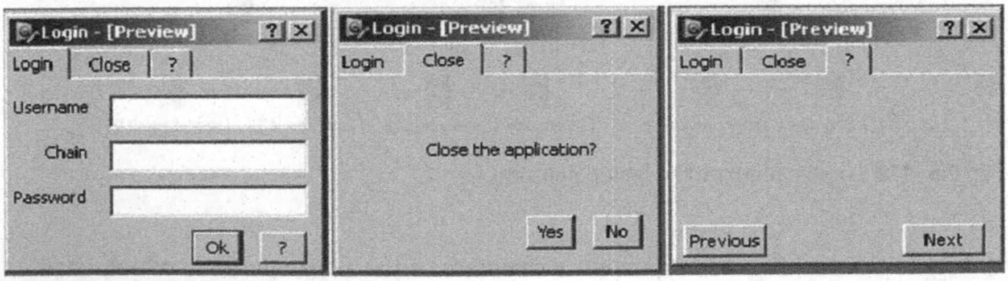

Fig. 9.8 Login view of the interactive system on the PDA platform

The following is an example of the XML source code of the domain model for the laptop platform of an "Environmental Management Interactive System":

```xml
<?xml version="1.0"?>
<xsd:schema xmlns:xsd="http://www.w3.org/2007/XMLSchema">
<xsd:group name="Login">
    <xsd:sequence>
        <xsd:element name="ShowLoginPrompt"/>
        <xsd:sequence>
            <xsd:element name="EnterCoordinates">
                <xsd:complexType>
                    <xsd:all>
                        <xsd:element name="Multi-ValueInput">
                            <xsd:complexType>
                                <xsd:all>
                                    <xsd:element name="ShowForm"/>
                                    <xsd:element name="EnterValues">
                                xsd:complexType>
                                    <xsd:attribute name="Username"/>
                                    <xsd:attribute name="Password"/>
                                </xsd:complexType>
                        </xsd:element>
                        <xsd:element name="Submit"/>
                        <xsd:element name="Feedback"/>
                    </xsd:all>
                </xsd:complexType>
            </xsd:element>
            <xsd:element name="CloseApplication"/>
            <xsd:element name="FeedbackForLoginForm"/>
        </xsd:all>
    </xsd:complexType>
    </xsd:element>
    </xsd:sequence>
    </xsd:sequence>
</xsd:group>
```

9.4.3   Defining the Task Model

After establishing the domain model for the system in this case study, the task model can be interactively defined. Figure 9.9 depicts the task model structure of the "Environmental Management Interactive System." Only high-level tasks and their relationships are portrayed. The overall structure and behavior of the interactive system is given. The structure provided is relatively unique for an environmental management interactive system; the concrete "realization" of high-level tasks has been omitted.

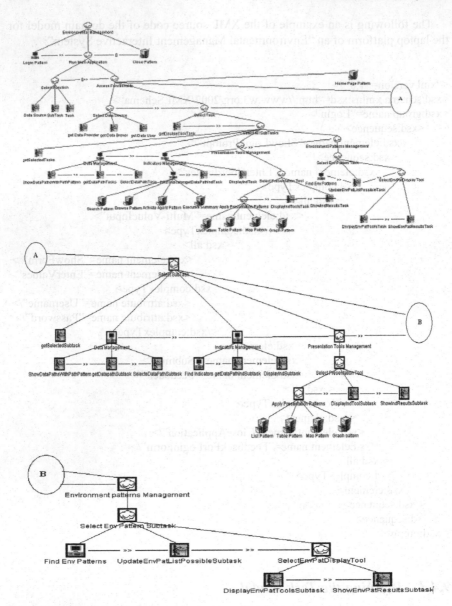

Fig. 9.9 Task model of the environmental management interactive system

A large part of many interactive systems can be developed from a fixed set of reusable components. In the case of the task model, the more those high-level tasks are decomposed, the easier it is to use the reusable task structures that have been gained or captured from other projects or systems. In this case study, these reusable task structures are documented in the form of patterns. This approach ensures an even greater degree of reuse, since each pattern can be adapted to the current use context.

The main characteristics of the environmental management system, modeled by the task structure in Fig. 9.9 can be outlined as follows:

The interactive system's main functionality is accessed by logging into the system (the login task enables the management task). The key features are "adding a guest," which is accomplished by entering the guest's personal information and by "selecting an environment task or subtask" for a specific guest. The two tasks can be performed in any order. The selection process consists of four consecutively performed tasks (related through "enabling with information exchange" operators):

1. Selecting data source to use
2. Selecting task or subtask

   a. Data management
   b. Indicator management
   c. Presentation tool management
   d. Environmental pattern management

Acting in the horizontal direction of the POMA architecture (Fig. 8.2), this model is composed of two types of submodels, which are: [POMA.PIM]-independent task submodels, and [POMA.PSM]-specific Task submodels.

[POMA.PIM]-independent Task submodels (Fig. 9.10) are obtained by composing patterns and applying the composition rules described in the Chap. 8 in Sect. 8.5.2.

[POMA.PSM]-specific task submodels Figs. 9.11 and 9.12 are obtained by mapping composed patterns and applying the mapping rules (Table 9.3). This latter model would be used to generate the system's source code by taking into account the code generation rules.

Figure 9.9 presents a structure of the Task model of the "Environmental Management Interactive System." As shown in Fig. 9.9, the *Login, MultiValue Input Form,* and *Find* patterns can be used in order to complete the task model at lower levels.

Figure 9.10 represents a Unified Modeling Language (UML) class diagram of the platform-independent model (PIM) task model, which is composed of several patterns by applying, manually by the designers, the composition rules described in Sect. 4.1.2. This model underwent mapping by applying the mapping rules (Table 9.3) to obtain another model, which is called a platform-specific model (PSM) task model (Fig. 9.11) for a laptop platform and Fig. 9.12 for a PDA platform.

Table 9.3 shows the mapping rules of the task model patterns for a laptop and PDA platforms.

After the mapping, the PSM Task model is obtained for a laptop platform—Fig. 9.11.

After the mapping, the PSM task model is obtained for a PDA platform—Fig. 9.12.

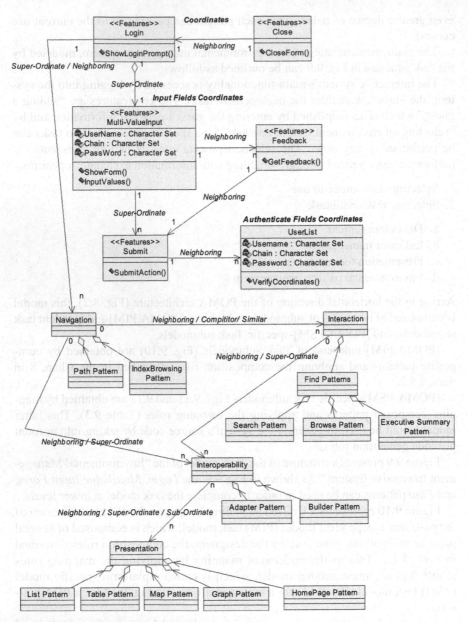

Fig. 9.10 UML class diagram of the PIM Task model

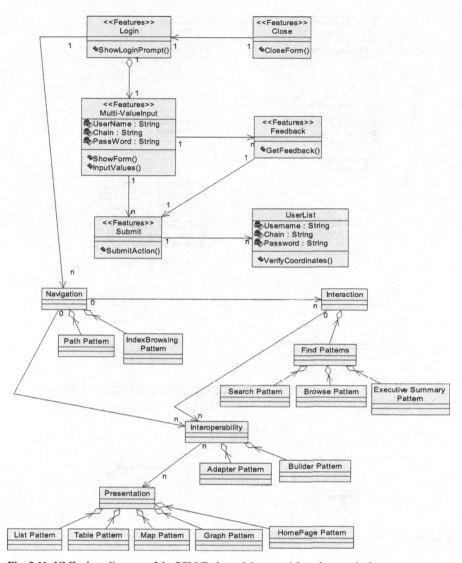

Fig. 9.11 UML class diagram of the PSM Task model mapped for a laptop platform

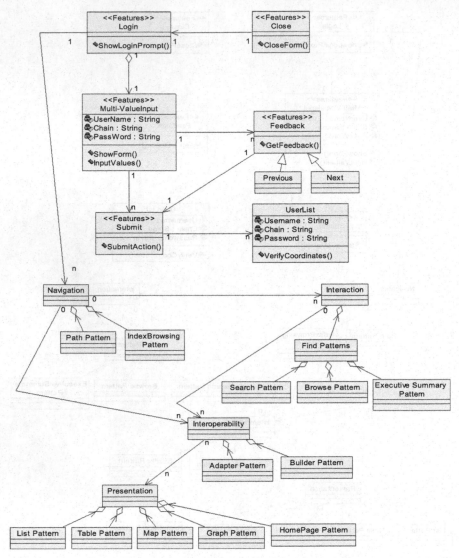

Fig. 9.12 UML class diagram of the PSM Task model mapped for a PDA platform

Table 9.3 Example of pattern mapping of task model for laptop and personal digital assistant (PDA) platforms

Patterns of Microsoft platform	Type of mapping	Replacement patterns for Laptop platform	Replacement patterns for PDA platform
P1. Login	Identical	P1. Login	P1. Login
P2. Multivalue input	Identical, scalable, fundamental	P2. Multivalue input	P2. Multivalue input
P3. Submit	Scalable or fundamental	P3. Submit	P3.s Submit (smaller button)
P4. Feedback	Identical, fundamental	P4. Feedback	P4. Feedback P4.1. Previous P4.2. Next
P5. Close	Identical	P5. Close	P5. Close
P6. Find (search, browse, executive summary)	Identical, scalable	P6. Find (search, browse, executive summary)	P6. Find (search, browse, executive summary)
P7. Path (Breadcrumb)	Identical, scalable (Laptop) Scalable or fundamental (PDA)	P7. Path (Breadcrumb)	P7.1s Shorter breadcrumb trial P7.2 Drop-down "History" menu
P8. Index browsing	Identical	P8. Index browsing	P8. Drop-down menu
P9. Adapter	Identical	P9. Adapter	P9. Adapter
P10. Builder	Identical	P10. Builder	P10. Builder
P11. List	Identical	P11. List	P11. List
P12. Table	Identical	P12. Table	P12. Table
P13. Map	Identical	P13. Map	P13. Map
P14. Graph	Identical	P14. Graph	P14. Graph
P15. Home Page	Identical	P15. Home page	P15. Home page

PDA personal digital assistant

The following is an example of the XML source code portion of the task model for a laptop platform of the "Environmental Management Interactive System":

```
<?xml version= '1.0'?>
<!DOCTYPE TaskModel PUBLIC "http://giove.cnuce.cnr.it/CTTDTD.dtd"
"..\..\..\..\Teresa\CTT\CTTDTD.dtd">
<TaskModel
NameTaskModelID="C:\Momo\PhD\These\Prototype\Environmental_Management_CTT.xml">
<Task Identifier="Environmental Management" Category="abstraction" Iterative="false"
Optional="false" PartOfCooperation="false" Frequency="null">
<Name> null </Name>
<Type> null </Type>
<Description> null </Description>
<Precondition> null </Precondition>
<TimePerformance>
<Max> null </Max>
<Min> null </Min>
```

```
<Average> null </Average>
</TimePerformance>
<Object name="null" class="null" type="null" access_mode="null" cardinality="null">
<Platform> null </Platform>
<InputAction Description="null" From="null"/>
<OutputAction Description="null" To="null"/>
</Object>
<SubTask>
<Task Identifier="Login Pattern" Category="application" Iterative="false" Optional="false"
PartOfCooperation="false" Frequency="null">
<Name> null </Name>
<Type> null </Type>
<Description> null </Description>
<Precondition> null </Precondition>
<TemporalOperator name="SequentialEnabling"/>
<TimePerformance>
<Max> null </Max>
<Min> null </Min>
<Average> null </Average>
</TimePerformance>
<Parent name="Environmental Management"/>
<SiblingRight name="Run Main Application"/>
<Object name="null" class="null" type="null" access_mode="null" cardinality="null">
<Platform> null </Platform>
<InputAction Description="null" From="null"/>
<OutputAction Description="null" To="null"/>
</Object>
</Task>
    ...
  <SubTask>
<Task Identifier="ShowDataPathsWithPathPattern" Category="interaction" Iterative="false"
Optional="false" PartOfCooperation="false" Frequency="null">
<Name> null </Name>
<Type> null </Type>
<Description> null </Description>
<Precondition> null </Precondition>
<TemporalOperator name="SequentialEnabling"/>
<TimePerformance>
<Max> null </Max>
<Min> null </Min>
<Average> null </Average>
</TimePerformance>
<Parent name="Data Management"/>
<SiblingRight name="getDataPathTasks"/>
<Object name="null" class="null" type="null" access_mode="null" cardinality="null">
<Platform> null </Platform>
<InputAction Description="null" From="null"/>
<OutputAction Description="null" To="null"/>
</Object>
</Task>

    ...
</SubTask>
</Task>
</TaskModel>
```

9.4.4 Defining the Dialog Model

Acting in the horizontal line of the POMA architecture (Fig. 8.2), the dialog model is composed of two types of submodels, [POMA.PIM]-independent dialog submodel, and [POMA.PSM]-specific dialog submodel.

[POMA.PIM]-independent dialog submodel (Fig. 9.13) is obtained by composing patterns and applying, manually by the designers, the composition rules described in Sect. 8.5.2.

The Wizard dialog pattern emerges as the best choice for implementation. It suggests a dialog structure where a set of dialog views is arranged sequentially and the "last" task of each dialog view initiates the transition to the subsequent dialog view. Figure 9.14 depicts the Wizard dialog pattern's suggested graph structure.

[POMA.PSM]-specific dialog submodel (Fig. 9.15) is obtained by mapping composed patterns and applying the mapping rules (Table 9.4). This [POMA.PSM]

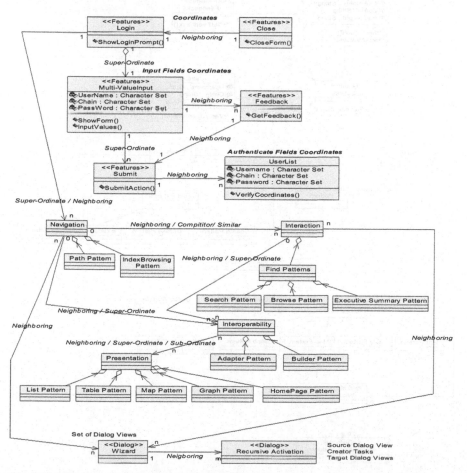

Fig. 9.13 UML class diagram of a PIM dialog model

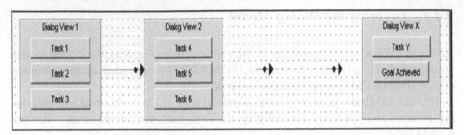

Fig. 9.14 Graph structure suggested by the Wizard pattern

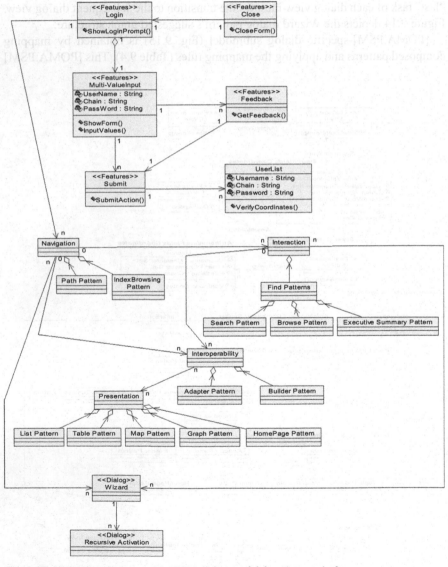

Fig. 9.15 UML class diagram of the PSM dialog model for a laptop platform

Table 9.4 Example of pattern mapping of dialog model for laptop and PDA platforms

Patterns of Microsoft platform	Type of mapping	Replacement patterns for laptop platform	Replacement patterns for PDA platform
P1. Login	Identical	P1. Login	P1. Login
P2. Multivalue input	Identical, scalable, fundamental	P2. Multivalue input	P2. Multivalue input
P3. Submit	Scalable or fundamental	P3. Submit	P3.s Submit (smaller button)
P4. Feedback	Identical, fundamental	P4. Feedback	P4. Feedback P4.1. Previous P4.2. Next
P5. Close	Identical	P5. Close	P5. Close
P6. Find (search, browse, executive summary)	Identical, scalable	P6. Find (search, browse, executive summary)	P6. Find (search, browse, executive summary)
P7. Path (Breadcrumb)	Identical, scalable (Laptop) Scalable or funda-mental (PDA)	P7. Path (Breadcrumb)	P7.1s Shorter bread crumb trial P7.2 Drop-down "His-tory" menu
P8. Index browsing	Identical	P8. Index browsing	P8. Drop-down menu
P9. Adapter	Identical	P9. Adapter	P9. Adapter
P10. Builder	Identical	P10. Builder	P10. Builder
P11. List	Identical	P11. List	P11. List
P12. Table	Identical	P12. Table	P12. Table
P13. Map	Identical	P13. Map	P13. Map
P14. Graph	Identical	P14. Graph	P14. Graph
P15. Home page	Identical	P15. Home page	P15. Home page
P16. Wizard	Identical	Wizard	P16. Wizard
P17. Recursive activation	Identical	Recursive activation	P17. Recursive activation

model is used to generate the interactive system's source code by taking into account the code generation rules.

Figure 9.13 represents a UML class diagram of the PIM dialog model, which is composed of several patterns. This model underwent mapping by applying the mapping rules (Table 9.4) to obtain another model, which is called PSM dialog model (Fig. 9.15 for a laptop platform and Fig. 9.16 for a PDA platform).

However, the sequential structure of the subtask process must be slightly modified in order to enable the user to view the details of multiple subtasks at the same time. Specifically, this behavior should be modeled using the recursive activation dialog pattern. This pattern is used when the user wishes to activate and manipulate several instances of a dialog view.

Table 9.4 shows the mapping rules of the dialog model patterns for laptop and PDA platforms.

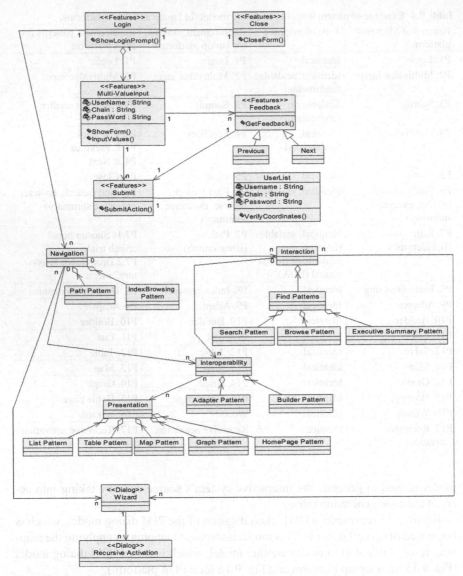

Fig. 9.16 UML class diagram of the PSM dialog model for a PDA platform

After the mapping, the PSM dialog model is obtained for a laptop platform—Fig. 9.15.

After the mapping, the PSM dialog model is obtained for a PDA platform—Fig. 9.16.

Figure 9.17 depicts the various dialog view interactions of the "Environmental Management Interactive System's" suggested dialog graph structure for laptop and PDA platforms.

9.4.5   *Defining the Presentation and Layout Models*

In order to define the presentation model for this case study, the grouped tasks of each dialog view are associated with a set of interaction elements including forms, buttons, and lists. Style attributes, such as size, font, and color, remain unset and will be defined by the layout model.

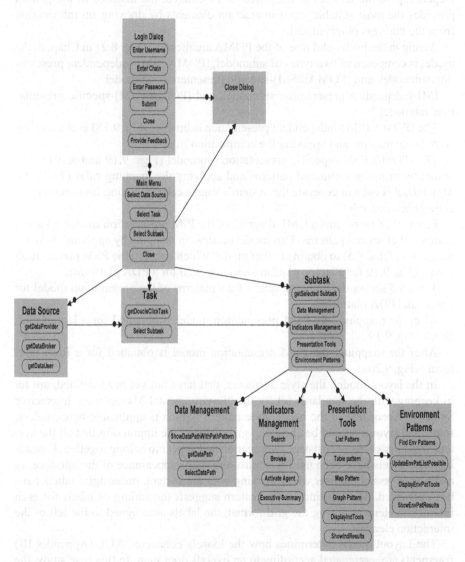

Fig. 9.17 Dialog graph of the environmental management interactive system for laptop and PDA platforms

A significant part of the user tasks of the system revolves around providing structured textual information. This information can usually be split into logically related data chunks.

At this point, the form presentation pattern, which handles this precise issue, can be applied using a form for each related data chunk, populated with the elements needed to enter the data. Moreover, the pattern refers to the unambiguous format pattern which can be employed. The purpose of this pattern is to prevent the user from entering syntactically incorrect data, and is achieved in the following way: Depending on the domain of the object to be entered, the instance of the pattern provides the most suitable input interaction elements by drawing on information from the business object model.

Acting in the horizontal line of the POMA architecture (Fig. 8.2) in Chap. 8, the model is composed of two types of submodel, [POMA.PIM]-independent presentation submodel, and [POMA.PSM]-specific presentation submodel.

IM]-independent presentation submodel, and [POMA.PSM]-specific presentation submodel.

The [POMA.PIM]-independent presentation submodel (Fig. 9.18) is obtained by composing patterns and applying the composition rules.

The [POMA.PSM]-specific presentation submodel (Figs. 9.19 and 9.20) is obtained by mapping composed patterns and applying the mapping rules (Table 9.). This model is used to generate the system's source code by taking into account the code generation rules.

Figure 9.18 represents a UML diagram of the PIM presentation model, which is composed of several patterns. This model underwent mapping by applying the mapping rules (Table 9.5) to obtain another model, which is called the PSM presentation model (Fig. 9.19 for a laptop platform and Fig. 9.20 for a PDA platform).

Table 9.5 shows the mapping rules of the patterns of the presentation model for laptop and PDA platforms.

After the mapping, the PSM presentation model is obtained for a laptop platform—Fig. 9.19.

After the mapping, the PSM presentation model is obtained for a PDA platform—Fig. 9.20.

In the layout model, the style attributes, that have not yet been defined, are set in keeping with the standards set for the "Environmental Management Interactive System." According to the house style pattern (which is applicable here), colors, fonts, and layouts should be chosen to give the user the impression that all the system windows share a consistent presentation and appear to belong together. Cascading style sheets have been used to control the visual appearance of the interface. In addition, to assist the user when working with the system, meaningful labels have been provided. The labeling layout pattern suggests the adding of labels for each interaction element. Using the grid format, the labels are aligned to the left of the interaction element.

The Layout model determines how the loosely connected XUL (Appendix III) fragments are aggregated according to an overall floor plan. In this case study, the task is fairly straightforward since the UI is not nested and consists of a single

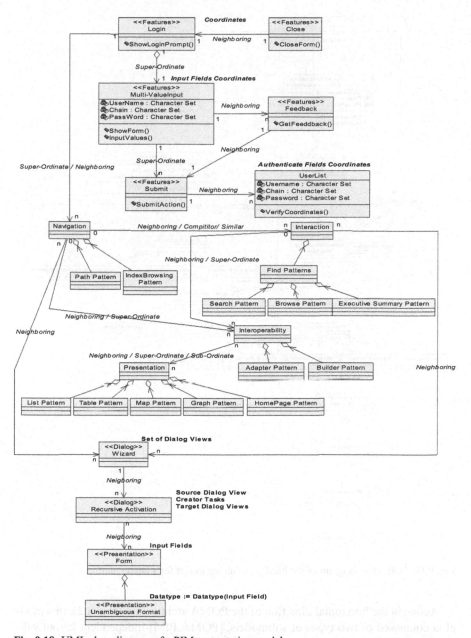

Fig. 9.18 UML class diagram of a PIM presentation model

container. After establishing the layout model, the aggregated XUL code can be rendered, along with the corresponding XUL skins, as the final UI. All interfaces are shown in the final UI rendered on the Windows XP platform.

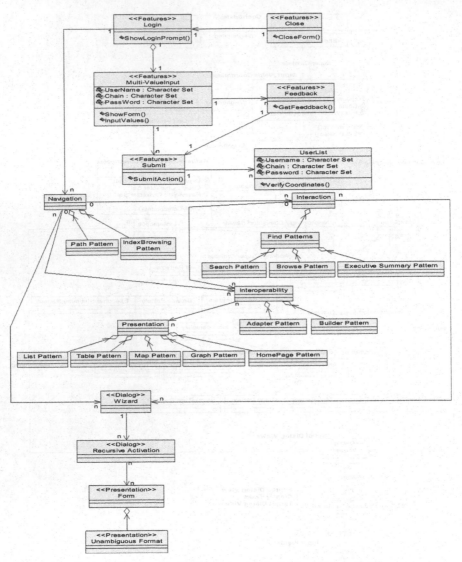

Fig. 9.19 UML class diagram of the PSM presentation model for a laptop platform

Acting in the horizontal direction of the POMA architecture (Fig. 8.2), this model is composed of two types of submodels, [POMA.PIM]-independent layout submodel, and [POMA.PSM]-specific layout submodel.

[POMA.PIM]-independent layout submodel (Fig. 9.21) is obtained by composing patterns and applying the composition rules.

[POMA.PSM]-specific layout submodel (Figs. 9.22 and 9.23) is obtained by mapping composed patterns and applying the mapping rules (Table 9.6). This

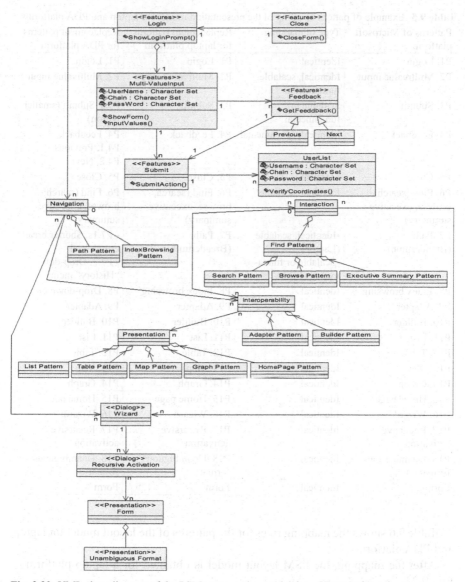

Fig. 9.20 UML class diagram of the PSM presentation model for a PDA platform

[POMA.PSM] model is used to generate the system's source code by taking into account the code generation rules (not included in this research).

Figure 9.21 represents a UML class diagram of the PIM layout model which is composed of several patterns. This model underwent mapping by applying the mapping rules (Table 9.6) to obtain another model, which is called the PSM layout model (Fig. 9.22 for a laptop platform and Fig. 9.23 for a PDA platform).

Table 9.5 Example of pattern mapping of the presentation model for laptop and PDA platforms

Patterns of Microsoft platform	Type of mapping	Replacement patterns for laptop platform	Replacement patterns for PDA platform
P1. Login	Identical	P1. Login	P1. Login
P2. Multivalue input	Identical, scalable, fundamental	P2. Multivalue input	P2. Multivalue input
P3. Submit	Scalable or fundamental	P3. Submit	P3.s. Submit (smaller button)
P4. Feedback	Identical, fundamental	P4. Feedback	P4. Feedback P4.1. Previous P4.2. Next
P5. Close	Identical	P5. Close	P5. Close
P6. Find (search, browse, executive summary)	Identical, scalable	P6. Find (search, browse, executive summary)	P6. Find (search, browse, executive summary)
P7. Path (Breadcrumb)	-Identical, scalable (Laptop) -Scalable or fundamental (PDA)	P7. Path (Breadcrumb)	- P7.1s. Shorter bread crumb trial - P7.2. Drop-down "History" menu
P8. Index browsing	Identical	P8. Index browsing	P8. Drop-down menu
P9. Adapter	Identical	P9. Adapter	P9. Adapter
P10. Builder	Identical	P10. Builder	P10. Builder
P11. List	Identical	P11. List	P11. List
P12. Table	Identical	P12. Table	P12. Table
P13. Map	Identical	P13. Map	P13. Map
P14. Graph	Identical	P14. Graph	P14. Graph
P15. Home page	Identical	P15. Home page	P15. Home page
P16. Wizard	Identical	P16. Wizard	P16. Wizard
P17. Recursive activation	Identical	P17. Recursive activation	P17. Recursive activation
P18. Unambiguous format	Identical	P18. Unambiguous format	P18. Unambiguous format
Form	Identical	Form	Form

Table 9.6 shows the mapping rules for the patterns of the layout model for laptop and PDA platforms.

After the mapping, the PSM layout model is obtained for a laptop platform—Fig. 9.22.

After the mapping, the PSM Layout model is obtained for a PDA platform—Fig. 9.23.

Figure 9.24 is the final layout of the "Environmental Management Interactive System."

The results of this experimentation of POMA architecture are as follows:

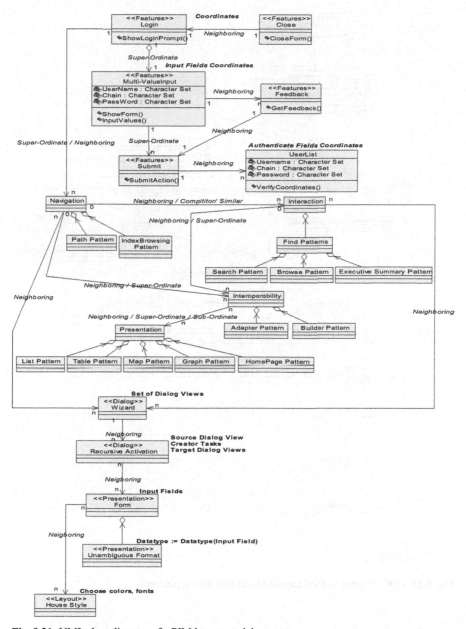

Fig. 9.21 UML class diagram of a PIM layout model

- POMA integrates easily patterns and models together to design interactive systems for different platforms;
- POMA uses easily the pattern composition, pattern mapping and model transformation rules to implement interactive systems for different platforms.

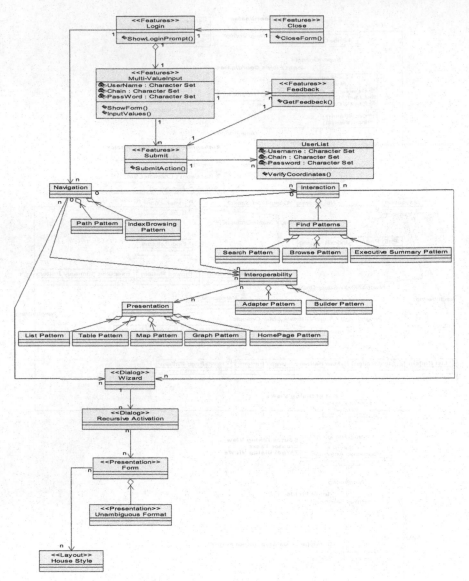

Fig. 9.22 UML diagram of PSM Layout Model for a laptop platform

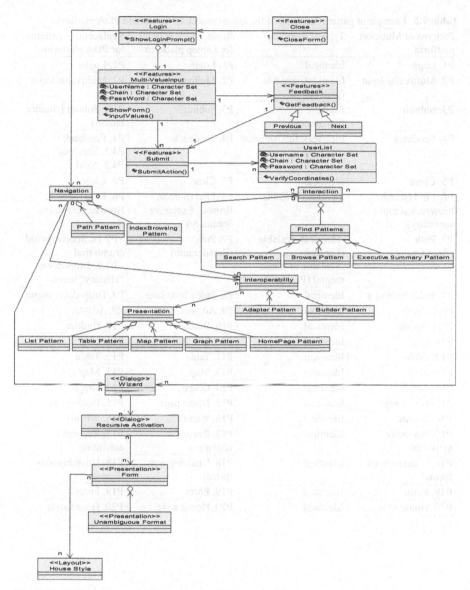

Fig. 9.23 UML diagram of PSM layout model for a PDA platform

Table 9.6 Example of pattern mapping of the layout model for laptop and PDA platforms

Patterns of Microsoft platform	Type of mapping	Replacement patterns for Laptop platform	Replacement patterns for PDA platform
P1. Login	Identical	P1. Login	P1. Login
P2. Multivalue input	Identical, scalable, fundamental	P2. Multivalue input	P2. Multivalue input
P3. Submit	Scalable or fundamental	P3. Submit	P3.s. Submit (smaller button)
P4. Feedback	Identical, fundamental	P4. Feedback	P4. Feedback P4.1. Previous P4.2. Next
P5. Close	Identical	P5. Close	P5. Close
P6. Find (search, browse, executive summary)	Identical, scalable	P6. Find (Search, Browse, Executive Summary)	P6. Find (Search, Browse, Executive Summary)
P7. Path (Breadcrumb)	-Identical, scalable (Laptop) -Scalable or fundamental (PDA)	P7. Path (Breadcrumb)	- P7.1s. Shorter bread crumb trial - P7.2. Drop-down "History" menu
P8. Index browsing	Identical	P8. Index browsing	P8. Drop-down menu
P9. Adapter	Identical	P9. Adapter	P9. Adapter
P10. Builder	Identical	P10. Builder	P10. Builder
P11. List	Identical	P11. List	P11. List
P12. Table	Identical	P12. Table	P12. Table
P13. Map	Identical	P13. Map	P13. Map
P14. Graph	Identical	P14. Graph	P14. Graph
P15. Home page	Identical	P15. Home page	P15. Home page
P16. Wizard	Identical	P16. Wizard	P16. Wizard
P17. Recursive activation	Identical	P17. Recursive activation	P17. Recursive activation
P18. Unambiguous format	Identical	P18. Unambiguous format	P18. Unambiguous format
P19. Form	Identical	P19. Form	P19. Form
P20. House style	Identical	P20. House style	P20. House style

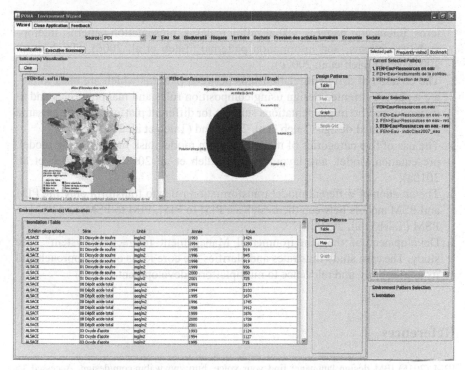

Fig. 9.24 Screenshot of the Environmental Management Interactive System for a Laptop platform

9.5   Key Issues and Contributions

A prototype of this case study was developed for an environmental management interactive system. This prototype was developed in Java Eclipse tool. In this case study, patterns were identified and applied for each of the models that were used during development.

The main purpose of the prototype of this case study is to show that model-driven architecture development consists of model transformation and that mapping rules from the abstract to the concrete models are specified and—more importantly—automatically supported by tools.

In the case study, UML notation was used to design the five models (domain, task, dialog, presentation, and layout). XML notation was also used to describe the five models and the different types of patterns proposed by the POMA architecture. UML and XML allow one to communicate the modeling semantics between the different models, helping tailor the application and corresponding models to different platform and user roles.

This chapter created a practical multiplatform architecture for interactive systems engineering. The main contributions are:

1. The creation of six architectural levels and categories of patterns (navigation patterns, interaction patterns, visualization patterns, presentation patterns, interoperability patterns, and information patterns) (Taleb et al. 2006), (Taleb et al. 2007a) and (Taleb et al. 2007c);
2. The creation of different relationships between patterns which are used to create a pattern–oriented design using composition rules and mapping rules and to generate specific implementations suitable for different platforms from the same pattern-oriented design (Taleb et al. 2006) and (Taleb et al. 2007c);
3. The use of five categories of models: domain model, task model, dialog model, presentation model, and layout model (Taleb et al. 2007b) and (Taleb et al. 2010a);
4. The creation of different model transformation rules to transform only the PIM and PSM models between them such as: PIM to PIM, PIM to PSM, and PSM to PSM (Taleb et al. 2010b);
5. Development of the "Environmental Management Interactive System" case study. The case study illustrates and clarifies the core ideas of this approach and its applicability and relevance to multiplatform development.

References

IBM (2015) IBM design language: find your voice. http://www.ibm.com/design. Accessed 15 April 2015
Lynch PJ, Horton S (1999) Web style guide: basic design principles for creating web sites. Yale University Press, New Haven
Macintosh (1992) Human interface guidelines. Apple computer company. Addison Wesley, Cupertino. http://interface.free.fr/Archives/Apple_HIGuidelines.pdf†
Microsoft (1995) The windows interface guidelines for software design. Microsoft Press, Redmond.   http://www.ics.uci.edu/~kobsa/courses/ICS104/course-notes/Microsoft_Windows-Guidelines.pdf†
Seffah A, Gaffar A (2006) Model-based user interface engineering with design patterns. J Syst Soft 80(8):1408–1422. doi:10.1016/j.jss.2006.10.037. (15 pages)
Shneiderman B (2000) Universal usability. Commun ACM 43(5):84–91
Sinnig D (2004) The complicity of patterns and model-based UI development. Master of computer Science. Concordia University Press, Montreal, p 148
Sun Microsystems (2001) Java look and feel design guidelines. Addison Wesley Professional http://java.sun.com/products/jlf/ed2/book/†
Taleb M, Javahery H, Seffah A (2006) Pattern-oriented design composition and mapping for cross-platform web applications. The XIII International Workshop. DSVIS 2006. July 26–28 2006. Trinity College Dublin Ireland. doi:10.1007/978-3-540-69554-7. ISBN 978-3-540-69553-0. Vol. 4323/2007. Publisher Springer-Verlag Berlin Heidelberg. Germany
Taleb M, Seffah A, Abran A (2007a) Pattern-oriented architecture for web applications. 3rd International Conference on Web Information Systems and Technologies (WEBIST). March 3–6, 2007. ISBN 978-972-8865-78-8. pp 117–121. Barcelona. Spain
Taleb M, Seffah A, Abran A (2007b) Model-driven design architecture for web applications. The 12th International Conference on Human Centered Interaction International (FIC-HCII). July 22–27, 2007. Beijing International Convention Center. Beijing. P. R. China. Vol 4550/2007, pp 1198–1205. Publisher Springer-Verlag Berlin Heidelberg. Germany

Taleb M, Seffah A, Abran A (2007c) Patterns-oriented design for cross-platform web-based information systems. The 2007 IEEE International Conference on Information Reuse and Integration (IEEE IRI-07). August 13–15, 2007. Pages 122–127. Las Vegas. USA

Taleb M, Seffah A, Abran A (2010a) 'Investigating model-driven architecture for web-based interactive systems'. eMinds: Int J Hum Comput Interact II(6):1697–9613

Taleb M., Seffah A, Abran A (2010b) 'Transformation rules in POMA architecture'. The 2010 International Conference on Software Engineering Research and Practice (SERP'10), July 12–15, 2010, CSREA Press, pp. 161–166. ISBN: 1–60132–160–0, Las Vegas, Nevada, USA

Welie VM (2004) Patterns in interaction design. http://www.welie.com/

Chapter 10
HCI Pattern Capture and Dissemination: Practices, Lifecycle, and Tools

Abstract Despite the huge number of human–computer interaction (HCI) design patterns available, it has been recently identified that patterns are still difficult to find and apply, especially by patterns users, mainly software developers. In this chapter, we argue and demonstrate that the lack of an effective pattern representation is one of the main reasons for this problem. We discussed the idea of pattern lifecycle how it can lead to an environment for not only capturing and delivering patterns, but that also can automate the pattern lifecycle including the generation of applications from a pattern-oriented design. At the core of such environment, concept of generative pattern has been introduced in other chapters.

In this chapter, we again discussedthis concept from the perspective to generating a user interface using an extended pattern markup language, UIPML (User Interface Pattern Markup Language).

10.1 Capture and Reuse of HCI (Human–Computer Interaction) Patterns

As discussed in the previous chapters, patterns can be seen as a vehicle—a medium or an infrastructure—to bridge the gap between the two main activities: delivery and discovery. This representation is essentially about how to format the solution in a way that allows it to mature from its solution format into a pattern. In essence, a pattern is a solution alongside other information that supports it. The reason is that in order for a solution to be used by others, they have to be convinced that this is a good solution. Part of this comes by annotating pattern solution with expert analysis and comments, listing of some cases where the solution has been applied and the "success indicators," and possibly some code examples. Bearing in mind that no two systems are exactly the same, and that every new software is a new adventure, patterns are typically annotated with important guidance on how to apply them in different contexts and situations. Some details are left out to allow the end user to rematerialize an abstract pattern back into a concrete solution that is

© Springer International Publishing Switzerland 2015   219
A. Seffah, *Patterns of HCI Design and HCI Design of Patterns,*
Human-Computer Interaction Series, DOI 10.1007/978-3-319-15687-3_10

adapted to the new design. Having decided on what to write, the sibling question would be how to best represent this information: through UML (Unified Modeling Language) diagrams, simple diagrams, images, text, source code, or a combination of all of them.

The success of pattern approach depends on all those three milestones. As we discuss the potential benefits of applying patterns in design reuse, we cannot claim that patterns are "silver bullets." Due to the inherently creative nature of design activities, the direct reusability of designs represents only a small portion of the total effort (Yacoub and Ammar 1999). It requires a considerable amount of experience and work to modify existing designs for reuse. Many design ideas can only be reused when abstracted and encapsulated in suitable formats. Despite the creative nature of their work, software designers still need to follow some structured process to help control their design activities and keep them within the available resources. Partial automation of this process, combined with sound experience and good common sense can significantly facilitate the analysis and design phase of software development (Arutla 2000). Within this process, tools can help glue patterns together at higher design levels the same way we do with code idioms and programming language structures (Chambers et al. 2000). For example, the Smalltalk Refactoring Browser, a tool for working with patterns at the source code level, assists developers using patterns in three ways (Florijin et al. 1997):

From a pattern user perspective meaning any user interface (UI) designer, we can look at patterns in general as artifacts that have three main milestones, organized from a user perspective (Fig. 10.1).

On the pattern user side, we can say that patterns are harvested and represented with the main goal of being delivered to other users who implement them as solutions. A delivery paradigm is essential in the pattern approach because it indicates that patterns arrived effectively to potential users; a knowledge dissemination view. This means that patterns should be represented in a way that software developers can learn, master, and apply easily and effectively in their context. This

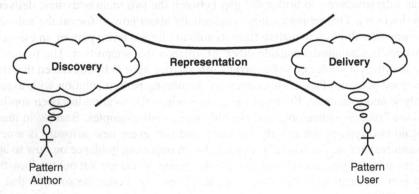

Fig. 10.1 Major milestones and users of patterns

implementation highlights the main role of patterns, promoting effective reuse. If patterns were harvested and written down just for the sake of archiving them, then we have missed on the great benefits of patterns.

On the pattern author side, the discovery of a pattern is only the beginning. Harvesting is a carefully selected metaphor that indicates the hard work associated with patterns. By observing existing artifacts and problems that have been solved successfully, we can detect a repeated structure or behavior that is worth recording. By asserting its importance, we can write down the essential components and—if possible—analyze them. An expert can provide insight as to why this combination is good or why it works well and in what context. Finally, guidance on how to reuse this solution can be added to assist in modifying and reapplying the solution.

10.2   A Survey on Patterns Usages

This section reports the results of a survey on the popularity of patterns among mainstream developers in industrial settings. Our focus is on design patterns for interactive systems as identified early in the design community (Ling 1980; Rouse 1981). They include the design and implementation of UI for highly interactive software systems. The last few years have seen a growing number of new UI-related patterns. Numerous research projects and articles focus on how patterns "should" be generated and used (Alexander et al. 1977) and (Tidwell 1997). We focus on the other end of the journey, namely, how patterns are "actually" being used. The primary contribution of this survey is to investigate how patterns are perceived and applied in practical industrial settings by software developers. Our goal is to identify the current state of affairs and measure the effectiveness of existing pattern approaches and tools. Preliminary results of the survey showed that patterns are less popular among designers than commonly anticipated by research community, even after valuable theoretical analysis and rich pattern literature are produced. The results reflect the strong belief that patterns can indeed be helpful; however, it shows a major gap between this belief and the fact that only few pattern collections are popular, generally the older ones. New patterns are still less popular regardless of their quality. The survey also shows that the number of developers who are actually applying patterns in their work is much less than the number of developers who are just familiar with them.

While pattern authors remained focused on discussing how patterns can be used, we did not find significant studies on how these patterns are actually perceived and applied in practice or how much they contributed to improving the quality and usability of interfaces. Some surveys and studies were done on interface design methods, on users (Colleen and Pitkow 1996; Pitkow and Colleen 1996) as well as interface usability, and how to improve it (Brinck and Hand 1999). Other surveys have focused on existing pattern collections in research community (Mahemoff and

Lorraine 2001) and (Portland 2003). We also found empirical studies on how design patterns are perceived and promoted in the academia as a pedagogic tool (Porter and Calder 2004) and (Clancy and Linn 1999). However, we found only one survey made in 1996 on design patterns usage in practice (Beck et al. 1996). The need for more surveys is necessary to assess the large body of research that has been done on patterns since then, and to examine the different directions in which it is evolving.

The research-specific goal behind this survey was to identify the current state of affairs of patterns, and to measure how effective they are delivered and used in software industry. The study enables us to reveal the strengths and weaknesses of pattern practices and to measure the success or failure of current role of patterns in supporting the UI design process. This allows us to shed light on some grey areas in patterns and pattern tools and to have a better understanding of the needs of UI designers from a pragmatic point of view.

10.2.1   The Survey Structure and Population

The survey came in the form of a questionnaire divided in eight sections totaling 20 questions. The first three sections were devoted to get some information about responders and their work environment as well as sources of their professional knowledge. Section 4 and 5 were designed to evaluate their general perceptions and usage of guidelines and pattern. Section 6 and 7 enabled us to get more detailed information about the practices of using patterns and tools in UI design. The last section collected feedback about existing and future research trends and proposals. The survey was distributed during 6 months and sent as a broadcast to selected professional mailing lists as well as personalized emails. We focused on software professionals in industrial settings who are practically involved in the development of software systems and especially in user interfaces. We targeted large companies as well as medium size companies and consultants. The qualified number of replies was 121.

10.2.2   Analysis Method and Key Findings

The survey analysis is organized under three categories. First, we ran a frequency analysis on users' profile as well as their work environment and knowledge sources. We also evaluated the popularity of pattern collections and tools. Next, we cross-tabulated some questions to report the opinions and practices of patterns among different respondents. All the data collection and statistical analysis were done using SPSS (www.spss.com). Finally, we collected all open-ended questions and analyzed them manually.

Figure 10.2 portrays the distribution of the respondents (Fig. 10.2). The majority of replies (41.3%) came from developers with involvement in user interfaces. Out of all, 12.4% respondents were dedicated UI developers, 19% were system developers with no involvement in UI, and 5% were web developers. While we

Fig. 10.2 The distribution of respondents

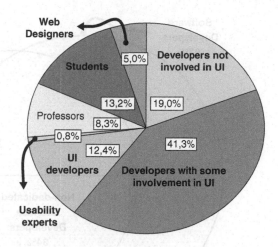

only targeted industrial settings, we had 8.3 % professors and 13.2 % students in the replies, which reflect the fact that some people from the academia are indeed working in the industry as well.

10.2.2.1 Who Develops the User Interface? Who are the Users of Patterns?

The analysis of work environment and responsibilities delegated to development teams (Fig. 10.3) revealed that while a high percentage of respondents worked in UI-related teams (50 %), only a minority (16 %) worked exclusively in interface development teams. The rest (34 %) worked simultaneously in software and interface development. It is clear that the promoted idea of separate and dedicated teams for interface development and the underlying software development did not make its way completely in the industry. However, we did not correlate this to the size of the companies.

When asked about some sources of professional knowledge, the Web was the most commonly used source (86 %), academic training was next (76 %), books (63 %), reuse of similar work (59 %), professional training (46 %), and working with mentors was the least popular at 27 %.

10.2.2.2 The Current Practices of Guidelines and Patterns

Though guidelines are generally considered an important support for designers, only 2.5 % take time to read them carefully and apply them. Out of them, 23 % browse them occasionally, and 66 % do not use them at all in their work. As for the popularity of patterns, 77 % were familiar with design patterns (Gamma 1995), and 40 % with some UI patterns. However, familiarity did not match the actual use of these patterns; only 15 % used UI patterns in industrial projects, showing that most developers know about UI patterns, but do not use them.

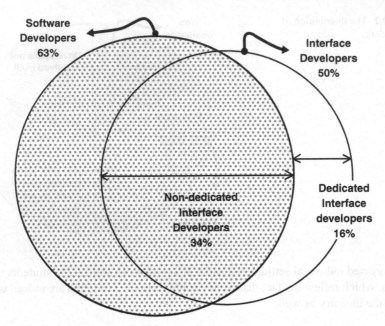

Fig. 10.3 The responsibilities delegated to development teams

The number of popular UI pattern collections was also low. Only seven collections were known to the respondents. Despite the popularity of the Web as a source of professional knowledge, many new UI pattern collections on the Web were not known at all in the survey, regardless of their quality as known in the research community. This certainly requires further study.

10.2.2.3   The Status of Pattern Tools

We identified similar gap regarding existing tools for patterns. Despite the extensive research and rich publications of tool prototypes, only 10% of respondents used tools. These were mostly general design (CASE) tools like Rational Rose, Eclipse, and Sun Java Studio, rather than specialized pattern tools. Only ten tools were reported in the survey, six of them were mentioned only once.

10.2.2.4   The Mainstream Perception About Patterns

We also asked participants how they thought about patterns. The majority (59%) saw them as an effective concept while 35% were not sure. Only 5% did not like the concept of patterns altogether.

Conversely, when asked about the effectiveness of patterns in practice today, only 29% found them useful in their design whereas 44% found them not useful.

Nonetheless, developers showed that they still have faith on pattern; only 7% were on the pessimist side about the future, saying that patterns will never be a real help to developers. Out of all developers, 36% were optimistic and believed that patterns will help future developers while 56% were not sure. This shows that patterns are underutilized in daily practices in the industry, but people still believe that they are a good concept. The difference between the high acceptability of patterns as an idea (59%) and between finding them useful in design (29%) may indicate that we need to support pattern reuse more actively. It points to the need to improve our techniques to facilitate pattern reuse among industrial developers.

The survey pointed at the problem of patterns underutilization in the industry, contrary to what is expected by most pattern authors. We conclude that besides discovering new patterns, we need to develop more techniques to improve existing pattern reuse and integration into the daily activities of mainstream programmers. We also need more pattern tool support to facilitate this reuse. The next sections summarize some of our research investigations to address these concerns.

10.3   An Extended Schema for Representing Patterns

The concept of a schema is used in many domains to present a high level, common view of different artifacts, or low-level details of them. In this section, we present a high-level schema of patterns based on our investigations in the thesis so far.

10.3.1   Why a Schema?

To conveniently handle the entirety of available patterns within a pattern system, it is helpful to define and separate different parts of each pattern according to the interest of the reader. A pattern classification schema that supports the development of software systems using patterns should have the following properties:

- *Simplicity:* It should be simple and easy to understand, learn, and use. A complex schema would be hard to validate and will deter many users from using it.
- *Objectivity:* Each classification criterion should reflect functional properties of patterns, for example the kinds of problems the patterns address, the related design phase, and the context of applicability rather than nonfunctional criteria such as pattern author or whether patterns belong to a pattern language or not.
- *Guidance:* It should provide a "roadmap" that leads users to a set of potentially applicable patterns, rather than a rigid "drawer-like" schema that tries to support finding the one "correct" pattern.
- *Generality:* Like programming languages, the schema should be independent of specific domain, platform, or technology.
- *Extensibility:* The schema should be open to the integration of new patterns without the need for refactoring the existing classification.

10.3.2   A Schema for a Generalized Pattern Model

As highlighted in other chapters especially Chap. 2 and 7, the existing pattern language format that has been often used to document patterns looks as follows (Table 10.1).

However, this narrative format (and its variations) has several limitations. It makes broad use of natural language-based prose and has little context. Hence, the patterns based on this format are strongly "document-oriented," and can seem vague and open to interpretation. This limits their use in automated processing environments and interchange.

Furthermore, the notation is paper-printing oriented and does not provide any means of using the potential and benefits offered by the electronic medium of communication which in turns has several implications:

- There is no standard way in which nontext objects related to pattern (say, solution or scenario of use) can be included.
- There is no standard way in which instances of pattern expressed in the notation can be interchanged across a broad range of devices.
- There is no explicit support for presenting patterns expressed in the traditional notation on Internet-based information systems, such as the Web. (The patterns could be written using some word processing package that can associate presentation and linking semantics, and the result can be converted to, for example, HTML. However, such process is not automatic and resulting documents are highly inefficient.).

Table 10.1 Pattern of design and the underlying representation of a design

If   You find yourself in CONTEXT
         For EXAMPLES,
         With PROBLEM,
         Entailing FORCES
Then   For some REASONS,
         Apply DESIGN PRINCIPLES and/or PRACTICES
         To construct DESIGN SOLUTION
         Leading to NEW CONTEXT and OTHER PATTERNS
 	
A DESIGN SOLUTION (a set of design artifacts)
         Is a representation of an OBJECT (A SYSTEM, A SERVICE)
         That an AGENT (USER OR ANOTHER SYSTEM) can interact with
         To accomplish GOALS (TASKS)
         In a particular CONTEXT
         Using a set of PRIMITIVE COMPONENTS (FEATURES)
         That satisfy a set of USER REQUIREMENTS, QUALITIES,
         CONSTRAINTS;

- There is no standard way to verify whether a pattern is compliant with the notation.
- There is no standard way in which pattern solution implementations can be included.
- There is no explicit support for Internationalization, in particular, for non-English language characters or other special symbols.

These limitations have motivated us to take an alternative approach to devise a pattern notation that can resolve these issues as well as to provide other features that can adequately represent patterns documentation. Representing and documenting patterns using an effective notation enable us to bypass above issues and provides various advantages.

One of our goals is to address the inconsistent properties, elements, and attributes of patterns while findings the commonalities among the variant pattern formats in order to generalize it into a simple, understandable, and flexible format in order to make it easier to document patterns and also to disseminate the essence of patterns to all of its users

Therefore, we use the Alexander's Format as the fundamental basis of our proposed generalized format, but we also incorporated some of the issues from Gang of Four format in order to reduce the communication gap between patterns writers and software developers and overall to provide the object-oriented outlook of patterns.

We suggest a schema as shown in Fig. 10.4. This schema can be seen as relevant to the end-user experiences, the HCI/usability expert, and the software and UI engineers:

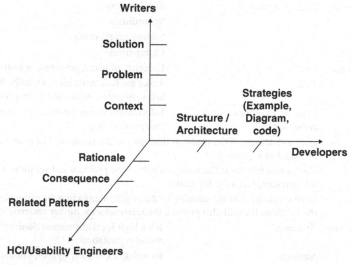

Fig. 10.4 Pattern properties

1. A pattern is a solution provided by an HCI/usability expert to a user problem, which can occur in different contexts of use.
2. The forces, the consequences of the problems as well as the rationale for the solution has to be detailed qualitatively.
3. Usability/HCI engineers have to ground the patterns in the HCI theory and principles. UI developers should also provide an implementation or strategies for implementing the patterns. Consequences should be linked to usability measures that provide a more objective way to assess the pattern's applicability.

This abstract schema shows the major issues related to patterns from the perspective of different users. In this, each professional group is aware of their own concerns as well as the others'. Therefore, each group may be able to address the needs of other groups while contributing toward patterns and pattern languages. In this view, we are incorporating some concepts from different pattern collections in order to reduce the communication gap between pattern writers and software developers and to provide the object-oriented outlook of patterns.

This 3D abstraction highlights the major *ingredients* for documenting a pattern. Table 10.2 provides a summary of the key components that can be used in different

Table 10.2 The proposed format of pattern documentation

Element	Sub-elements	Requirements
Identification	Name	
	Alias	
	Author(s)	
	Date	
	Category	Patterns classification
	Keyword	For search
	Related pattern(s)	Super-ordinate
		Subordinate
		Sibling/neighboring
		Competitors
Context of use	User	Category of users, personas, or profile, etc.
	Task	Tasks are structured hierarchically. All subtasks should be originated from a root
	Platform capabilities and constraints	Information should be organized in device-independent way
Problem	Give a statement of the problem that this pattern resolves. The problem may be stated as a question	
Forces	Forces describe the influencing aspects of the problem and solution. This can be represented as a list for clarity	
Solution	Give a statement of the solution to the problem including the rationale behind the solution. It could also provide the references for further understanding	
Implementation	Structure	It's a high level abstraction done by visual modeling notation
	Strategy	Including examples, figures, sample code etc.
Consequences	Trade-off and results of using the pattern. It could be described by a list of usability factors/criteria/metrics	

pattern templates. This template could serve as a basis for future expansions to serve different needs.

In Gaffar et al. (2003), we called for an approach to generalizing the format of patterns to facilitate the creation of a pattern database. As the idea was discussed and accepted, we implemented the first attempt of this task together with the major HCI pattern authors. The resulting format, the Pattern Language Markup Language (PLML) was created in the workshop to mark the first step toward a common pattern format (Fincher and Finlay 2003). Since then, we went much further into improving the presentation from a common but static presentation (The PLML is a static format) into a dynamic runtime module. We then upgraded PLML into the Generic Pattern Model (GPM) (Gaffar 2005) that offers the flexibility of changing its components as needed. GPM is then used in the tools that are discussed later in this chapter.

10.4 Modeling the Pattern Discovery and Dissemination Life Cycle

In the previous section, we proposed a schema and discussed its usefulness from delivery perspective. Here, we emphasize this idea and argue that a key factor to increasing the usability and usefulness of patterns is the adoption of a model for a complete pattern lifecycle. This would underwrite the activities that should be taken when identifying a pattern, documenting, delivering, applying, and maintaining it. Creating mechanisms to manage the overall pattern lifecycle has received little attention in the HCI patterns community so far. Our investigations and work as presented in the previous chapters provide a basis for better understanding of the process of discovery, representation delivery, and applications of HCI patterns.

Also as highlighted in the introduction of this chapter, the currently prevalent pattern approaches can be divided into two major activities only: pattern discovery and pattern reuse.

- *Pattern Discovery* refers to the activity of writing patterns by domain experts.
- *Pattern Reuse* refers to the activity of applying patterns in a useful design as recommended by pattern author.

We could not find significant work on guiding the user through the activity of finding suitable patterns for reuse. This can have negative impact on promoting pattern reuse (as shown in our empirical study (Gaffar 2004)). In this regard we introduce an intermediate logical layer between pattern discovery and reuse, namely, the dissemination process. *Pattern Dissemination* refers to guiding pattern users through the activities of locating all useful patterns, selecting some of them using different criteria and then applying them correctly in all phases of design and implementation process.

Based on the empirical study and the proposal of dissemination process, we can now redefine the lack of ineffective pattern reuse as a symptom and not a problem. The problem in this chapter is better identified as

- The lack of a dissemination process
- The lack of a common and programmable pattern representation to help in combining and reusing patterns and pattern tools in practical design environments. In the previous section, we explain how the generalized pattern model can solve this problem.

Having attributed the problem to the current narrative format for documenting patterns, we propose an approach to represent patterns as software components by identifying and rewriting their semantics as a model for designers as well as design tools. This model transforms text patterns into programmable objects with well-defined interfaces that reflect the knowledge underlying them. This makes them accessible in any object-oriented programming language as well as in XML for tool interoperability. We also provide a framework that supports a comprehensive dissemination process.

10.4.1 The Challenges of Dissemination

Dissemination refers to "*the activities associated with delivering knowledge and experience from pattern authors to pattern users—or designers.*" For efficient dissemination, we need to reduce the time spent by users in looking up patterns, and the ability to locate all patterns that can be useful according to some search criteria that a user can apply. So far, these activities have been left to the user. Pattern authors simply publish their patterns, generally in books or on the Internet and the dissemination process stops there. Some pattern authors recognized the problem and added links within their collections to other collections. This, however, adds to the confusion of the users as they see similarities between collections. They get distracted or lost in the available maze of patterns. In this context, we have defined the *visibility problem* that new patterns suffer as "*new patterns become diluted in huge pattern offerings and hence get no significant chance of making their way to users.*" This has been confirmed by the results of our empirical study. Consequently, many designers limit their pattern repository to few patterns that they already know and rarely look for new patterns.

10.4.2 The 7C's Lifecycle for Collection and Dissemination of Patterns

We define the 7C's as "a structured process with the main objective to replace the huge cognitive load of manipulating HCI patterns by both authors and users." The 7C's process identifies both logical and physical aspects of the system. The logical aspects detail what actions and activities need to be done. The physical aspects complement the logical ones by specifying the roles associated with each action and activity, and details who is going to do what (Hoffer et al. 2002), (Whitten et al. 2001). As part of the pattern reuse problem is associated with missing roles in the dissemination activities (all left to the user), the 7C's process addresses both how these activities need to be done, and who should be doing each of them. In short, the 7C's process moves gradually from current unplanned discovery and use of patterns into building an automated pattern collection. The process comprises seven steps.

10.4.2.1 Combine—Place Different Pattern Languages in One Central Place

Despite the proliferation of research into HCI design patterns since the 1990s, there has been no successful attempt yet to unify these efforts or collections. Numerous works on patterns have been developed in the HCI community; however, they are scattered in many different places. A central repository of patterns will allow users to concentrate on knowledge retrieval rather than spending time on search for patterns.

10.4.2.2 Clear Out—Add on the Top the Different Formats, One Unifying Description

Ideally, different works on patterns deal with different problems. However, as we went through step 1, we were able to identify that some patterns are dealing with different sides of the same problem (correlated patterns), some patterns are offering different solutions to the same problem (peer patterns/competitors), and some are even presenting the same solution to the same problem (similar patterns), only in different collections with different presentation formats. Since a large number of patterns have different presentation formats, it is difficult to detect these redundancies or useful relations with other patterns until the user has spent some unnecessary time with several of them. Putting patterns in a unified format helps discover these relationships, put related patterns closer together, and possibly remove the redundancies and inconsistencies.

10.4.2.3 Certify—Define a Domain and Clear Terminology

This activity is necessarily human-driven. While it can be easy to find useful relationships among the patterns, the validation of good patterns is largely a matter of people assessing them against experiences and through use to decide if they were "really good patterns." We use a process similar to that of Answer Garden (Ackerman and Thomas 1990) where new pattern proposals are routed to a distributed set of experts in different usability areas. These experts can then provide feedback to pattern writers, pointing them to similar patterns, and otherwise facilitating the process of creating a useful set of patterns.

10.4.2.4   Contribute—Receive Input from Pattern Community

New patterns emerge all the time in many areas of the scientific community, including HCI. It is very difficult to keep track of these emerging patterns. Typically, it would take years before an expert can come up with a thorough collection of patterns (Alexander et al. 1977); (Gamma et al. 1995), or have time to update an existing collection (Tidwell 1997); (Welie 2000). Having a central repository for patterns help unify pattern knowledge captured by different individuals in the future. Furthermore, putting such a repository to use in actual design situations will help to spot areas of design activities where there is a shortage of patterns so that they are made available to the community. The "central" concept refers to either a community wide web-based repository or a local repository within a smaller group of people. In both cases, a repository will help unify the effort of collecting and contributing to patterns.

10.4.2.5   Connect—Establishing Semantic Relationships Between Patterns

A significant part of knowledge associated with patterns lies in the relationships between them. After the Clear Out step removes redundancies, the Connect step is meant to build new connections between patterns. Finding and documenting these relationships will allow developers to easily use patterns as an integral part to develop applications instead of relying on their common sense and instinct to pick up patterns that seem to be suitable. A proven model for the pattern collection helps define ontology for the pattern research area with all proper relationships such as inference and equivalence between them.

10.4.2.6   Categorize—Mapping Patterns into the Assimilation Channels

Within the collection, we need to create pattern classifications or categories to make them more manageable. The first goal of categorization is to reduce the complexity of searching for, or understanding the relationship between patterns. For example, some patterns are just abstractions of other patterns. The second and more important goal is to build categories that can be mapped to different design approaches and methodologies, and then put patterns under their appropriate categories. This is the enabling technique to integrating patterns into different phases of several design approaches. As explained earlier, decoupling the dissemination and the assimilation processes allows same pattern to belong to different categories and be used in different assimilation processes.

10.4.2.7   Control—Machine Readable Format for Future Tools

Defining pattern models that accurately represent pattern semantics through their interfaces and rewriting patterns according to these models enhances the process of automating UI design using different assimilation processes. The ultimate goal of the 7C's process is to allow user to interact with the machine as a viable partner that can read and understand patterns, and then process them in an intelligent way. Having machine-readable patterns is the last step in the process of pattern dissemination and the first step toward assimilating them.

10.4.3 Qualities of Design Patterns

The idea behind the 7C's lifecycle is not to collect all patterns, but only good one. There are several factors that can define the quality of patterns. They are what make the pattern usable and easy to apply.

10.4.3.1 Formality

There have been several efforts (Gamma 1995; Appleton 2000) that provide strategies and suggest guidelines for patterns documentation. However, one of the limitations of these guidelines is that they make broad use of natural language for description, and hence are less formal and vague. Frequently asked questions (FAQs) also help answer user questions but they are usually focused on a single topic, often specific to a technology, and rarely provide reasoning for their answers. Patterns are more formal in their approach and exist at a higher level of abstraction than the strategies or guidelines. Patterns offer various advantages over guidelines and are anticipated to play an essential role in information technology. Still, patterns do not attempt to necessarily replace the FAQs, strategies, or guidelines in every manner. Rather, they should be considered as a key complement to overall initiative of a business application realization.

10.4.3.2 Practicality

Patterns provide practical "ready-to-go" solutions. A pattern describes "good" practical solutions to a common problem within a certain context, by describing the invariant aspects of all those solutions. Given a problem, patterns include a compact, focused, complete, and straightforward way of describing a solution. Since they provide the consequences of applying that solution, the user can decide and act upon in a timely manner if the solution is applicable to his/her situation.

10.4.3.3 Experience

Patterns form an "expert" system in practice. Patterns, when well-defined and coordinated, are more than a mere static disjoint "collections" of recipes. Patterns are tried-and-tested ways to deal with problems that recur. It is expected that those who have experience in a particular field of knowledge will have internalized certain solutions to these problems. As a result, they recognize a problem to be solved and know which solution need to apply in the particular situation. A pattern describes this internalized expert knowledge and states the problem, context, and solution, so that others with less experience can benefit from this knowledge. In this sense, patterns themselves can be considered as a "smart FAQ" or an "expert system" that encapsulates the knowledge and experience of the author. This enables them to be used as a *knowledge base*.

10.4.3.4   Reusability

A pattern presents a higher-level view of the same problem inflicting often multiple industries and provides a solution for it. It can also connect to other patterns in existence (in the same or other catalogs) for whole or in part of its solution (inheritance). Patterns thus encourage reuse.

10.4.3.5   Abstract, Modular Framework

Complex problems are often composed of several steps that need to be dealt with independently and then combined to arrive at a solution. Patterns represent these steps at a high level via "intelligent" distribution and allocation of responsibilities. They provide a framework that works in unison to fulfill a given task.

10.4.3.6   Community

Patterns help a broad community. Patterns communicate solutions to a community of architects, designers, and engineers, who make use of them at different levels and for different purposes. The goal of the pattern community is to build a reusable body of knowledge to support design and development in general.

10.5   Tools Support for Pattern Reuse and Dissemination

Beside the pattern lifecycle and representation, one of the key elements that explains the misuse of patterns also is the lack of tool support, which makes it difficult to capture, disseminate, and apply patterns effectively and efficiently. Tools need to be developed with three major objectives in mind. First, tools are needed to support UI designers and software engineers involved in UI development. Second, as a research forum for understanding how patterns are really discovered, validated, used, and perceived, tools are also required. Third, automation tools are needed to support the usage of patterns as prototyping artifacts and building blocks.

The following are some of the required features that should be provided a tool supporting the pattern approach:

- Tools have to be designed to accept proposed or potential patterns in many different formats or notations. Therefore patterns in versatile formats can be submitted for reviewing.
- A common editorial board for reviewing and validating patterns is also required. Before publishing, collecting and contributing, patterns must be accessed and acknowledged by the editorial committee. We are inviting the HCI patterns practitioners and researchers to set up and join this committee.
- A pattern ontology editor to capture our understanding of pattern concepts and to put them into relation with each other (Taxonomy) will be an important step toward a systematic usage of patterns as well as the emergence of a pattern-assisted design tool.
- Tools are needed to allow us to attach semantic information to the patterns. Based on this information and our ontology, patterns will be placed in relationships, grouped, categorized, and displayed.
- A pattern navigator can also provide different ways to navigate through patterns or to locate a specific pattern. The pattern catalogue can be browsed by pattern groups or searched by keywords. Moreover, a pattern wizard will find particular patterns by questioning the user.
- A pattern viewer will help in providing different views of the pattern, adjusted to the preferences of the specific pattern user's need.
- In what follow, we presented two different types of tools. First, the use of online databases accessible as a vehicle to document and share patterns on the Internet. Second, we introduced an integrated pattern environment that supports the dissemination process as well as the pattern-assisted design and automated code generation.

10.5.1   An Online Database for Patterns Documentation and Sharing

Too often, good patterns are hidden in Web pages that become severely underused in the daily activities of interface designers. This is because, the web page approach alone fails to provide the means to access appropriate patterns as needed and does little on the way of reusing them as an integral part of the development processes. Even if pattern authors are actively discovering and writing new patterns, it is difficult for users to keep pace with changes in the HCI community at large just by searching the Internet. Designers and developers often work under tight constraints and limited resources. Eventually, if software developers have to manually read, analyze, and understand every pattern in details to select the ones they need, the pattern system becomes unmanageable, even when it included useful patterns.

A better approach is to put patterns in a central database and make it accessible online through the Web or other Intranet facilities. A database of patterns can

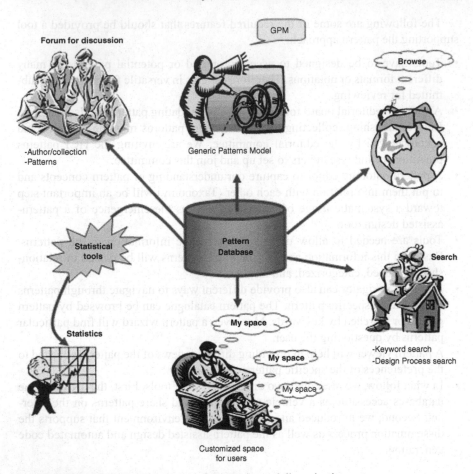

Fig. 10.5 The online database approach for capturing and disseminating patterns

become a valuable resource that software developers and project managers depend on for efficient information retrieval and reuse (Fig. 10.5).

Compared to Web pages and document-based approach for capturing and delivering patterns, an online database has some advantages:

- *Scalability:* A separate database can store and manage larger data volume than files attached to a specific application.
- *Facilitate efficient updates:* Unlike flat text files, a database categorize its contents into tables or objects which helps improve the lookup and editing of contents.
- *Connectivity:* Several applications can connect to the same database, reducing the need for extra copies of data files and multiple updates (see integrity).
- *Promote interaction with other software:* A database can provide application-independent information that can be called and used by several software tools and applications.

- *Reliability:* A database usually has advanced capability to enforce reliability against mishaps like programmer errors and power outages.
- *Integrity:* If properly designed, database can ensure integrity by having a single copy of each data object, so changes can be centralized to one place. This can greatly reduce redundancy and inconsistency.

10.5.2 Pattern-Based Assisted Dissemination and Design Environment

The central aspect of automating pattern-oriented design is its dependence on a predefined process. An established design process instigates quality design by allowing designers to follow structured methods in their activities. In our approach, we established the need for both dissemination and assimilation processes. We implement the dissemination process completely decoupled from any specific assimilation process. This allows it to offer patterns that can be integrated simultaneously in several assimilation processes. "Free patterns" that do not belong to any process are hard to integrate in design. Similarly, "proprietary patterns" that are specifically tailored to manually fit one design process using one specific example defeat the main purpose of pattern generality and abstraction. We see that a pattern can be integrated in several assimilation processes by properly encapsulating its knowledge and presenting its behavior through a well-defined interface.

Furthermore, there is usually more than one way to implement a specific pattern in different software systems. Furthermore, given the wide variety of user interface styles and development platforms, each pattern implementation can exist in various formats. For example, the Web *Convenient Toolbar* pattern that provides direct access to frequently used pages such as *What's New, Search, Contact Us, Home Page,* and *Site Map,* can be implemented differently for a Web browser, and a Personal Digital Assistant (PDA). For a Web browser, it can be implemented as a toolbar using embedded scripts or a Java applet in HTML. For a PDA, this pattern is better implemented as a combo box using the Wireless Markup Language (WML). It becomes more convenient due to the PDA-related limitations like screen area, bandwidth, memory, and processor speed.

10.5.2.1 Usability Pattern-Assisted Design Environment (UPADE) Architecture

UPADE provides a unified interface to support the development of UI designs and improve software production. It is a prototype written in Java that aims to support HCI pattern writers and UI developers. By leveraging the portability and flexibility of Java, UPADE enables developers to easily and effectively describe, search, exchange, and extend their own patterns as well as those created by others. UPADE offers features to combine patterns while supporting their integration at high design level and automate their composition.

As a tool for automating the development of UI designs, UPADE embodies several functionalities. It helps both pattern writers and developers to use existing relationship between patterns to define new patterns or create a design by combining existing patterns. Moreover, in order to facilitate pattern combinations, the tool supports different hierarchical, traceable design levels. In our case study associated with UPADE, three levels are possible: pattern level, design level, and code level. At the pattern level, developer can see description of patterns, search a specific pattern, create a new pattern, and save it into the database. At the design level, developers can combine patterns, support the integration of patterns at different design stages, replace one pattern occurrence by another, and validate the selected pattern compositions. Finally at code level, developers can see the structure of the design in terms of classes, methods, associations, and inheritance relationships in a particular programming language. Additionally, UPADE provides a mechanism to check and control how patterns are created or modified. By using the database information, UPADE automatically examines the patterns and offers a related feedback to the designer.

10.5.2.2   Key Features Offered to Both Pattern Authors and Users

The main UI includes the following components (Fig. 10.6):

- "Browse" provides a description of existing patterns, some illustrated diagrams, and several practical examples. In this mode, UPADE produces and delivers patterns information. The information is presented using the incorporated format showing related design processes, pattern category, name, description, and examples. Categories are presented as a browse tree for navigation as shown in Fig. 10.5. By default, UPADE allows browsing patterns with their associated process name. However, software developers can switch to browse by category.

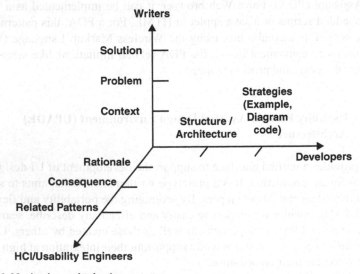

Fig. 10.6 Navigating and selecting patterns

- "Search" improves efficiency of using UPADE by accelerating the searching of patterns. The search window presented to developer offers two kinds of searches. Users can have a simple search for patterns by keywords. They can also select from several advanced search criteria in the 'Criteria Combo Box' and apply it.
- "Edit" helps developers create their own patterns or modify existing ones. Since patterns are reusable components, a well-developed pattern should be saved for reuse in other designs (Florijin et al. 1997). UPADE allow developers to create new patterns and associate new implementation rules, or constraints with them. The use of constraints allows developer to decide how certain patterns can be combined with each other in the design mode.
- "Design" develops structured steps to combine patterns, support integrating them at several phases of design, and validate their composition. As shown before, besides describing a solution, a pattern also describes several possibilities of how it can relate to other patterns and how it can be composed of other patterns. In this way, the generic nature of patterns is preserved. The creativity of design is also preserved by allowing designers the freedom to mix different patterns together. The process of freely mixing patterns together can be hard to validate in a complex network of patterns. Relationship constraints guide users into avoiding "invalid" or "less preferable" combinations and warn about unforeseen consequences. By offering validation of pattern relationships, UPADE helps designers in selecting more appropriate combinations during their design.

In "Design" mode, UPADE can support combination and organization of existing patterns from more general to more specific details. For example, the software developer can embed "Page Managers" patterns into "Information Architectural" patterns, and both "Navigation Support" patterns and "Information Containers" patterns into "Information Architectural" patterns. Moreover, the designer has the freedom to organize "Navigation Support" patterns and "Information Containers" patterns inside the layout; they can move, combine, or delete them altogether. These activities aim to explore how to organize and combine existing patterns to customize and format the new ones. "Design" editor provides a mechanism to check the validity of combined patterns using the set of constraints associated with them. It examines the compatibility of certain patterns and gives the related instruction to the designer.

Once the "Design" tab is selected (Fig. 10.7), UPADE can help start a new pattern-oriented design as follows:

- Pattern developers need to browse the tree in the "Browse Tree Pane" to view available patterns.
- Then they can select a pattern and drag and drop it into the "Drawing Pane" area.
- They repeat these two steps until all desired patterns are collected into the drawing area.
- Next, by selecting "Link Mode" button, developers are guided to connect each pattern to others by choosing from different relationship types that are available in the combo box of the control menu. While developers can choose the way they want to connect patterns to generate their own design, and the type of relationships, UPADE will check the validity of all connections selected by

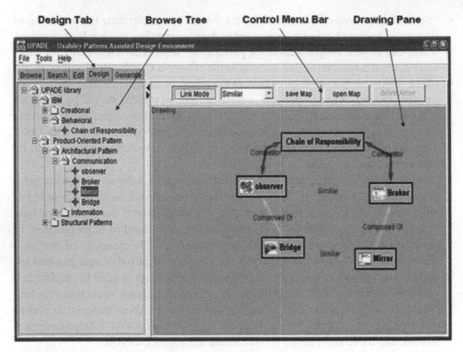

Fig. 10.7   Combining patterns in a new design

users and allow only valid ones. Users can override this mechanism, but they are provided with the consequences of their selections to help them make informed decisions. At the end, the developer can save the new pattern composition map into XML format for use by other XML-compatible tools.

UPADE is designed to be customized and extended, with the realization in mind that some designers have achieved a local set of patterns and conventions for style and structure, and only need a tool to assist them in creating new design more quickly that honors those conventions.

10.6   Key Contributions

Despite the wide acceptance of HCI design patterns within HCI and software engineering community, the current process of pattern reuse is a simple process of publishing numerous patterns using different media, and leaving it up to the users to do their best in figuring out how to trace and use them.

We suggested an addition to this concept to help define and standardize the process of pattern dissemination and assimilation. This process leads to an effective reuse of the knowledge contents within patterns. We proposed and developed UPADAE, first as an online digital library to share patterns, and then an environment to patterns-assisted design approach. In both categories, we prototyped several options at the database level (persistent layer), the processing level (tools), and the UI for both pattern writers and users.

The generalized pattern model and the associated notation to represent pattern have been discussed to facilitate interaction between patterns authors and users, and to pave the road for code generation from patterns descriptions.

References

Ackerman MS, Thomas WM (1990) Answer garden: a tool for growing organizational memory. Proceedings of the ACM conference on office information systems. ACM Press publishing, New York, pp 31–39. (Cambridge, Massachusetts, USA)

Alexander C., Ishikawa S., Silverstein M., Jacobson M., Fiskdahl-King I, Angel S (1977) A pattern language. Oxford University Press, New York

Alur D, Malks D, Crupi J (2003) Core J2EE patterns: best practices and design strategies. Sun microsystems core design series. Prentice Hall PTR, Upper Saddle River

Appleton B (2000) Patterns and software: essential concepts and Terminology. http://www.sci. brooklyn.cuny.edu/~sklar/teaching/s08/cis20.2/papers/appleton-patterns-intro.pdf. Accessed April 15, 2015

Arutla K (2000) Tool support for pattern oriented analysis and design. Master thesis, Department of Computer Science and Electrical Engineering. University of West Virginia, Morgantown

Beck K, Coplien JO, Crocker R, Dominick L, Meszaros G, Paulisch F (1996) Industrial experience with design patterns. Proceedings of the 18th International Conference on Software Engineering, IEEE Computer Society Press Publishing

Borchers JO, Sally F, Richard NG, Lyn P, Elke S (2001) Usability pattern language: creating a community. AI Soc (AIS) 15(4):377–385

Brinck T, Hand A (1999) What do users want in an HCI Website. EACE quarterly (European Association of Cognitive Ergonomics), vol 3. (issue no. 2, August)

Clancy MJ, Linn MC (1999) Patterns and pedagogy. Proceedings of the thirtieth SIGCSE technical symposium on computer science education. ACM Press publishing, New York, pp 37–42. (New Orleans, Louisiana, United States)

Colleen MK, Pitkow JE (1996) Surveying the territory: GVU's five WWW user surveys. World W Web J 1(3):77–84. (CA, USA)

Chambers C, Harrison B, Vlissides JM (2000) A debate on language and tool support for design patterns. Proceedings of the 27th ACM SIGPLAN-SIGACT symposium on principles of programming languages, Boston, Massachusetts, USA, January 19–21. ACM. 277–289

Fincher S, Finlay J (2003) CHI 2003 report: perspectives on HCI patterns: concepts and tools; introducing PLML. Interfaces, the international journal of human computer interaction 56:26–28. (British HCI Group publishing, Winchester)

Florijin G, Meijers M, van Winsen P (1997) Tool support in design patterns. Proceedings of ECOOP '97, 11th European Conference on Object-Oriented Programming, Utrecht University, Jyväskylä, Finland, June 9–13 1997. In: Askit M, Matsuoka S (eds) Lecture notes in Computer Science no. 1241. Springer, Berlin

Gaffar A (2004) The other side of patterns: a user-centered analysis. Preliminary results of Pattern Usability Study, presented at UPA: Usability Professionals' Association, Bloomingdale, Illinois, USA in conjunction with CRIM (Computer Research Institute of Montreal)

Gaffar A (2005) Studies on pattern dissemination and reuse to support interaction design. Concordia University, Montreal

Gaffar A, Sinnig D, Javahery H, Seffah A (2003) MOUDIL: a comprehensive framework for disseminating and sharing HCI patterns, position paper in CHI workshop entitled: perspectives on HCI patterns: concepts and Tools. 3 pages

Gamma E, Helm R, Johnson R, Vlissides J (1995) Design patterns: elements of reusable object-oriented software. Addison Wesley

Hoffer JA, George JF, Valacich JS (2002) Modern system analysis and design, 3rd edn. Prentice Hall PTR, Upper Saddle River

Mahemoff M, Lorraine JJ (2001) Usability pattern language: the language aspect. In Hirose M (ed), Human computer interaction: interact '01, proceedings of IFIP TC.13 international conference on human-computer interaction, July 9–13, 2001, Tokyo, Japan. Ohmsha Publishing, Tokyo, pp 350–358

Ling RF (1980) General considerations on the design of an interactive system for data analysis, vol 23. ACM Press Publishing, New York, pp 147–154. (Communications of the ACM, Issue 3)

Mahemoff M, Lorraine JJ (2001) Usability pattern language: the language aspect. In Hirose M (ed), Human computer interaction: interact '01, proceedings of IFIP TC.13 international conference on human-computer interaction, July 9-13, 2001, Tokyo, Japan. Ohmsha Publishing, Tokyo, pp 350–358

Porter R, Calder P (2004) Patterns in learning to program: an experiment. ACM International Conference Proceeding Series. Proceedings of the sixth conference on Australian computing education—Dunedin, New Zealand, vol 30. Australian Computer Society publishing Inc., Darlinghurst, pp 241–246

Portland pattern repository, survey results (2003). http://c2.com/cgi-bin/survey

Rouse WB (1981) Human–computer interaction in the control of dynamic systems, vol 13. ACM computing surveys (CSUR) ACM Press Publishing, New York, pp 71–99. (Issue 1)

Tidwell J (1997) Common Ground. A Pattern Language for Human-Computer Interface Design. http://www.mit.edu/~jtidwell/common_ground.html

Van Welie M, Van der Veer GC (2000) Patterns as tools for user interface design. International workshop on tools for working with guidelines, October 7–8. Biarritz

Whitten JL, Bentley LD, Dittman KC (2001) System analysis and design methods, 5th edn, McGraw Hill Irwin, New York

Yacoub S, Ammar H (1999) Tool support for developing pattern-oriented architectures, Proceedings of the 1st symposium on reusable architectures and components for developing distributed information systems, RACDIS'99, August 2–3, 1999, Orlando, pp 6658–6670

Chapter 11
PatternCity: A Gamification Approach to Collaborative Discovery and Delivery of HCI Design Pattern

Abstract Huge frustration is observed among the pattern users—the developers and novice designers using patterns to develop software products—as they usually spend a significant amount of time just to find the right pattern for their use from a very large and heterogeneous collection of patterns that are available via different websites and databases. Since software developers are used to working under a tight schedule in various environments with different needs, they should find patterns in a clear and understandable format or ready-to-go state along with a proper organization.

This chapter is an effort to overcome such drawback while closing the communication gap between different professional groups, who are interested in patterns and pattern languages. The goal is to introduce a methodical approach, in general, and a generalized format, in particular for pattern discovery, representation, and delivery. We first overview the current drawbacks of HCI design patterns which motivate the search for a new tool to document and deliver patterns. Then, we detail the ideas that lead the concept of *PatternCity, a serious game in which* HCI design patterns are represented as a building in a virtual world, and where the players can collaboratively build and improve these buildings.

11.1 Introduction

As discussed in the previous chapters, patterns have been documented and made accessible via web pages. Information about patterns and the patterns collections was stored in a database in some collections. A web-based approach to access a central database of patterns may have the following advantages:

- A consistent set of attributes is used to describe patterns; the differences between two patterns are evident so that one pattern can be chosen over another in an informed manner.
- The collection can make interrelations between patterns explicit by categorizing and interlinking them.
- A digital database may also produce data about the access frequency of specific patterns, which can be used to estimate its popularity among the user base of this

© Springer International Publishing Switzerland 2015   243
A. Seffah, *Patterns of HCI Design and HCI Design of Patterns*,
Human-Computer Interaction Series, DOI 10.1007/978-3-319-15687-3_11

database (as patterns are only patterns if they are reused in similar context) this may reveal the need of reformulation or dismissal of a pattern.

The fundamental question addressed in this chapter is that how can a designer access the content of this database while finding the right pattern at the right time? As, by definition, one does not know the name of the pattern searched for the first time; a pure text search may not be enough. Categorizing the patterns and adding keywords to them could help to alleviate this problem. But the discovery of previously unknown concepts remains a difficult task due to their textual form.

When building a platform for these different stakeholders, various problems arise. To begin with, they may come with different expectations, styles of communication, and goals. To give a quick overview over the broad range of possibilities, we defined three personas (User eXperience UX Researcher, UI Designer, and Front-end Developer). The user of the platform may also have different roles: a pattern author, seeking to spread knowledge about his insights, may try to publish and promote on this platform; while others simply enjoy the social and fun aspect of this community.

A related work that needs to be mentioned is the Pattern Almanac (Rising 2000). It is an attempt to make accessible (via a unifying user interface) a very large collection of all existing patterns and patterns languages. Several databases accessible via the Internet have also been proposed. However, these attempts fail in increasing the "ease to use and learning patterns" while making the pattern user experience a pleasant and enjoyable activity. As discussed further, the PatternCity project aims to overcome such goal while bridging the gap between patterns discovery and dissemination.

11.2   The Problem of Representing and Delivering HCI Design Patterns

HCI design pattern writers, who are usability expert with background in psychology, focus on usability, and human aspects of the user interface design. They generally prefer to use narrative formats to convey solutions to common user problems with supporting theories and concepts of interaction design and human factors. On the other hand, user interface designers are typically software developers who need concise and pragmatic guidance through their design and coding activities. They often find it hard to translate text pattern knowledge into concrete design (Lin et al. 2000). Moreover, with the plethora of patterns available today, mainstream developers get inundated with huge number of pattern literature and links in many books and on the Internet. They have to manually read and sift through piles of texts looking for some useful patterns to apply (Gaffar 2005).

In this regard, besides focusing on *what* should be presented in terms of information contents within patterns, a fundamental challenge is *how* it should be packaged and offered to developers in an appropriate way to help understand and apply them

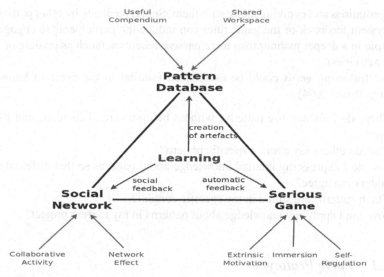

Fig. 11.1 Components of proposed platform

correctly and efficiently. As will be discussed in this chapter, more flexible notations and views are required to represent different types of pattern information.

The founding ideas of the PatternCity concept.

Built around a central database that includes all information about patterns and their usage, PatternCity combines a serious game and a social network combined into a 3D virtual world (Fig. 11.1).

The *database* containing information about HCI patterns is first of all meant to be a shared workspace: the information is not only consumed, but actively produced by the participants. Unlike a book, many authors need to contribute their respective perspective on a specific topic in order to find a representation of knowledge that is universally accepted. Ultimately, this may lead to a state of maturity where the organically grown content gets an authoritative character (similar to a Body of Knowledge).

In order to support this collaborative activity, we added aspects of a *social network*, emphasizing the possibilities to communicate freely, to build up a circle of friends, and to stay aware of the activity of friends or related events. We also use the process of group identification as an attractive element to invite new participants: being invited by preexisting acquaintances may help new participants to familiarize and engage with this system.

These features are embedded within the context of a *serious game*: active participants can earn credits and other awards, increasing their motivation. This playful approach to a serious topic also encourages immersion, potentially leading to a more effective learning. Finally, this context allows us to establish rules, allowing this socio-technological system to regulate itself.

Ultimately, we can frame our solution as artifact-based, *constructionist learning*. The core of learning here is not memorizing details, but rather creating knowledge representations and evolving along with them. Social feedback by other participants and system feedback of the game rules can induce the participants to engage with the topic in a deeper manner than mere passive reception (such as reading or classroom activities).

The following *goals* could be established (similar to the cycle of knowledge building (Stahl 2004):

- Where do I already use patterns, without being aware of its name and its concept?
- What do others say about a specific pattern?
- How do I express my internal knowledge about patterns so that different stakeholders can agree?
- Which patterns are suited in my specific context?
- How can I apply my knowledge about patterns in my current project?

11.2.1   Early Prototype

The most recent result of works done in this topic was a clickable prototype (Fig. 11.2). It contains all essential elements: it refers to the concept of social network (user has profiles, friends, and can communicate with them), establishes a database of patterns (each user can create patterns), and brings in components of a serious game (it is possible to buy patterns, see the high score of designers and patterns, and other statistics).

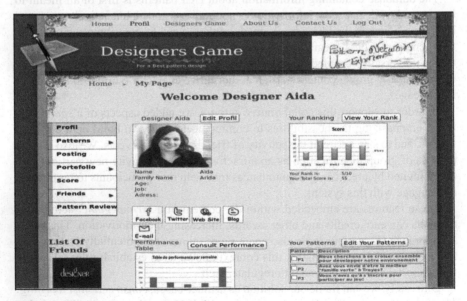

Fig. 11.2 Early prototype: user dashboard

However, the interface does not clearly state how this game is functioning, and thus, why it would be enjoyable to join. Even if there was a page explaining the rules of the game, it would be quite difficult to convince a new user to engage with this system: the overall design does not look like a game any more than a blog or promotional website. Additionally, he would have to register before seeing any content.

There are big improvements to be made in the areas of storytelling (what does the site do? what is my role? which advantage does it give me? how can I be a part of this community?), wording (what is the concept behind this term?), consistent use of terms and motivation (why should I participate?).

In addition, some important aspects of the problem stated above were not addressed.

First of all, it does not take into account the diversity of the audience: as it proposes only one way of describing patterns (narrative, text-based form), it does not encourage discussions where different actors can contribute their respective perspectives.

Second, the list-based browsing, even if combined with a keyword search, does not help the user find the applicable pattern if they do not know its terminology beforehand. The interface should invite the discovery of new or previously unknown patterns. Most importantly, the site does not fulfill the characteristics of a (serious) game (Ang and Zaphiris 2005): neither does it frame the action by a narrative, nor does it suggest explicit or implicit goals and rules.

It is for these reasons that we have decided to explore new approaches and ideas for this project, instead of iteratively evaluating and refining this prototype.

11.2.2 Exploration Phase

The exploration that followed was led by the question: *how can we design a user interface that is playful, expressive, and suited to our needs?* Our main approach here was to try different metaphors and narratives, applying them to patterns and online communities, with the goal that the purpose of the interface should be clear at first glance.

11.2.2.1 Pattern of Minesweeping

The pattern of *Minesweeping* (Welie 2008) inspired us to try out a playful discovery of patterns (Fig. 11.3). The size of the square carries meaning, such as representing its popularity; positioning and color can show related patterns. Additionally, filters allow the usage of this interface for different tasks: giving an overview of patterns, patterns of other friends or a specific category. This interface would motivate mainly through its aesthetics: animations and colors encourage the use to "do something" with it, for the pleasure of manipulating it.

Fig. 11.3 Playful discovery
of patterns

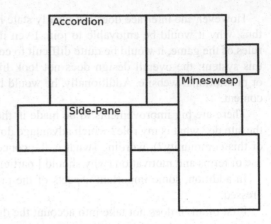

11.2.2.2 Metaphors for Learning Patterns

Another method of motivating would be a system of *reputation*: points and badges
reward positive behavior, as seen at Stack Exchange(http://ux.stackexchange.com)
and other sites following the philosophy of gamification (Deterding et al. 2011).
This would be very direct and behavioristic feedback, and would not suffice in itself
to keep the user on site. However, it may be used to reinforce originally intrinsic
motivation ("I want to learn about patterns" or "I want to document patterns") or
narratively induced goals.

As an example of such a narrative, the metaphor *Formula One* was
studied (Fig. 11.4). This game is divided in three phases: To become a member of
a team, the participant needs to show an example where he used the corresponding
pattern at least once. Then every team tries to improve their pattern ("tuning"). Finally, all patterns are published and voted by the community; the racing car moves
forward as the popularity of the pattern increases. These phases are repeated in fixed
time intervals; existing patterns may be improved further, or new patterns can be
created. This relatively simple game would combine "serious" work with fun, leveraging the spirit of competition as a motivator, and fostering collaborative activity
around the topic of interface patterns.

Fig. 11.4 Native context

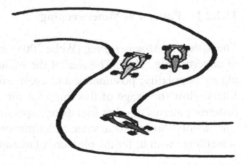

11.2.2.3 Metaphors for Recognizing Patterns

Another metaphor would be that of the card game *Pairs*: the participant needs to find "two of the same kind", either two different examples of the same pattern, or alternatively an example and the name of the pattern. By this, we could recognize patterns in their real-life context, and induce curiosity about patterns the participant did not know before. Here, we transfer the common knowledge of how to play Pairs to a different context of application, a method commonly used at language learning software.

11.2.3 The PatternCity Concept

Based on these initial conceptual ideas, the concept of *PatternCity* evolved. Its core idea consists of two parts: every pattern is represented as a building in a virtual world, and the players (represented by their avatars) can collaboratively build and improve these buildings. The PatternCity also includes the following buildings:

- Forum, a place for meetings where designers and developers can discuss and share experiences regarding the use of patterns;
- City Hall, the place to register a pattern and get the approval to add it to the PatternCity.
- Trade Centre, the place to buy and sell patterns.
- Pattern Academy, the museum where the most innovative patterns and patterns authors are featured.
- Tourist Information Centre, a place where to go to get information, advise, and directions to visit and explore the PatternCity.
- The designer house is the place where all patterns proposed by a distinguished designer are featured.

The two main characteristics of the PatternCity components are pattern buildings and players.

11.2.3.1 Pattern Buildings

A building can be viewed from the inside as well as from the outside. When viewed from the outside, only the most important aspects of it are shown inside of the windows. It is only when he entered the building that the user can explore the details of the pattern.

Each of these details is hidden behind an object metaphor (e.g., a guest book to read and write comments, a vitrine to show the examples). In this way, we represent concepts as objects (an approach similar to the learning environment *Pattern Park* (Franke et al. 2007), where (software) patterns are represented by different rides in an amusement park.

These buildings are grouped into streets and townships, forming a digital city that can be shown on a map. In this city, some buildings have a special function: the Academy nominates and awards prizes to the best patterns, pattern collections can be shown in a *Gallery*, and the *Stock Market* displays the current popularity of each pattern. There is also a Town hall for signing up, filing bug reports, giving feedback, and reading the archives of the city newspaper. In the Information Center, the player can view the current statistics about the city, and he may also find a Forum specific to a topic for news, blog entries and chat sessions.

There are different ways of navigation proposed: a map displays patterns by author, category, or personal bookmarks. Once he has chosen his destination, a navigation system leads him the way through the different streets. The navigation bar also shows his current position (on the map, as well as textual) and its surroundings. When navigating to a place he was before, the player can go there quicker.

11.2.3.2   Players

The described environment serves as a shared space where all players can work together: the common goal is to "build up" the city. This happens not only by creating new buildings, but also by improving existing ones: the size of a building reflects its popularity. To break down this goal into smaller, individual goals, the game automatically gives feedback by giving reputation points for positive behavior. This encourages the player to try out the actions he can do, and continues to reinforce his motivation.

The players in the city also form a virtual community: direct communication between players is possible through a chat (synchronous medium) and messages (asynchronous medium). These tools are integrated into this game to foster social connections as well as collaborative work between real players.

To stay aware of modifications, prizes, and new buildings, the player can consult the recent activities or events concerning the player or one of his friends. Additionally, the game leader, represented by "the Architect," sends messages to inform about status information when trying to build a new pattern, or when participating in an Academy contest. For citywide information, the architect can publish a newspaper, containing statistics, new features, or upcoming community events.

Most importantly, players do not only actively contribute by adding text and images to the pattern database, but have many design choices while doing so. As an example, the interior decoration of a building can be rearranged and modified, giving each building a particular flair. The position of the building is also a matter of choice: in this way, the structure of the city grows organically. Even the names of streets and townships may change, if a poll shows that many players agree on it. It is also possible to include elements of *End-User-Programming*: in this way, the player could even customize the interactive behavior of objects or add completely new objects.

In the same spirit, access to moderator functions is not limited to the administrator, but can be delegated to motivated and experienced users. A reputation system may keep track of the overall activity of a player. The amount of reputation of a player also helps other players to distinguish between beginners and experienced users (similar to Forums where the number of posts of a user is shown).

Players can also buy pattern shares at the *Stock Market*. Unlike the real stock market, the total number of shares is unlimited; the value/"popularity" of a pattern is calculated as a function of its number of visitors during a certain time period, its average ratings, and its current completeness. Buying a pattern means speculating that it will increase in popularity, and as it will be shown on the user profile as well, it also means endorsing and recommending this pattern to others.

Unregistered users can watch the city and its contents, but cannot interact with other players, modify buildings or buy at the *Stock Market*. If they want to participate in this game, then they will need to register at the Town hall.

In case of inappropriate behavior, that is, behavior that violates the "Charter of PatternCity" posted at the Town hall, users with the role of police officers may warn and, if needed, restrict the possibilities of a player (no communication, no edits) or even block his account temporarily.

The player can enter and leave the city by taking a bus; that is the reason why players do not have their own houses in the city. In fact, *PatternCity* is a city where patterns habitants and where designers and developers are the creators and users of the city.

11.2.4 Implementation

In order to realize this concept and define a *visual language*, a chapter prototype (Appendix A) has been developed then transformed into a Balsamiq (http://www.balsamiq.com) wire-frame. The environment resembles *Second Life* and *Visimmo3d V3D events*.

The interface resembles adventure games in many ways: characters move in a (pseudo)-3D-Space, within a predefined area of the screen, by following the mouse clicks. Doors or streets indicate the possibility to go to another scene (interior of a building or street view).

Objects, as they represent concepts and data, allow interaction with them: they show their name (or function) when the mouse hovers over them, and reveal their details in a pop-up window when clicked. The setting is dominated by architectural design: the special buildings each have a unique expressive architectural style differentiating them from normal patterns.

In the following paragraphs, we will add some comments to the wire-frame prototype. There are two versions of it, with and without the label names. As the last sketch explains, these label names are only visible when the user hovers over the corresponding object. These "tool-tips" help new users to playfully discover their action possibilities, but without cluttering the interface with too much text.

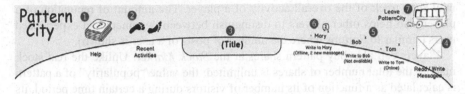

Fig. 11.5 Top bar

11.2.4.1   The Top Bar

The *top bar* (Fig. 11.5) allows user communication and general game functionality. At the top left (1) a lexicon offers help. The user can type a question, and the system tries to find a similar "frequently-asked question." These questions are logged, so that questions that *are* frequently asked can be added to the help. The window that opens when clicking on the footsteps (2) gives an overview of recent activity during the user's absence or while he was doing something else. A title (3) indicates the current location of the showed scene. On the right side, communication tools are offered for the envelope (4) which allows initiating a new conversation with a person in the current scene, related to the content of the current scene or to the user's friends. For every user, its current status is shown (online/not available/offline). Recent conversations (5) and incoming messages (6) are shown on a per user basis. (To communicate within a bigger group, the group can meet in a Forum.) Finally, a click on the bus (7) quits the game.

11.2.4.2   The Bottom Bar

The *bottom bar* (Fig. 11.6) assists navigation, on the left, a map of the city (1) along with a detail view, (2) shows the current position of the player (Note that this map is updated as the city grows.) The map icons show the buildings on the city map filtered by different aspects: depending on the navigational strategy of the user, he may search for a pattern with a certain name or within a certain category (3), for patterns by a specific user or author (4), highly rated and popular patterns (5) or patterns that the player already viewed or has the intention to view (6). He also can go back to the buildings he was before (a history of visits similar to web browsers) (5),

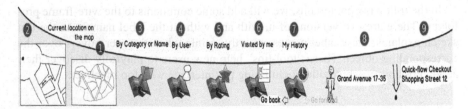

Fig. 11.6 Bottom Bar

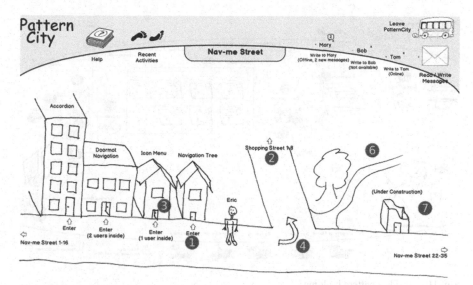

Fig. 11.7 Street view

or see the chronological order of his visits (7). On the right, the current location is displayed in a text form (8), as well as the current destination (9).

11.2.4.3 The Street View

The following sketch shows the *street view* (Fig. 11.7). Arrows indicate the possibility to go to other scenes: the player may enter a pattern (1) or advance to the next street segment (2). Some doors are open, indicating the presence of other players (3). A big arrow (4) indicates the navigational direction, in this case, how to get to Quick-flow Checkout (5). The city may also contain green spaces (6) or unfinished buildings (7) which have not been published yet.

11.2.4.4 The Accordion Pattern

As an example how pattern buildings can look like from the inside, the *accordion pattern* (Fig. 11.8) has been depicted. Information that explains the pattern itself is posted on the back wall: A pattern description must contain a textual description (1) and at least one example (2) (screen-shots, possibly annotated). Additionally, a schema that reduces the pattern to its core (3), implementation tips as well as links to existing libraries (4) and scientific background information (5) can be added. The player can also view this information as one document (e.g., for printing) (6). Meta-information can be found on the right wall: a list of recent changes by editors (7), a diagram shows the relations of this pattern to other patterns (can be used instead

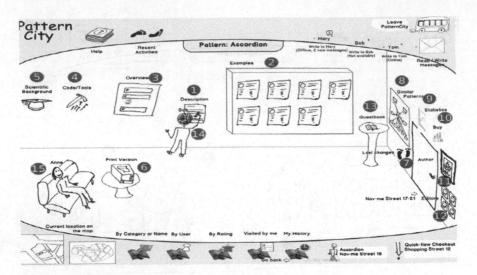

Fig. 11.8 Inside a pattern building

of, is not compatible with, is a part of, contains subpatterns) (8). Statistics about the number of visitors over time (9), the possibility to buy a share of this pattern (10) and icons representing the author (11) and participating editors (12) are also provided. Finally, the player can leave his comments in the guest book of this pattern (13).

All of these objects open a pop-up when being clicked that reveals the complete information. Other players and their actions are visible in real-time: here, Bob is currently editing the description (14), while Anne is studying the print version of the pattern (15).

In which respects this concept is a game? Although there is no clear goal in order to "win the game," it describes a system of rules in which some states are more desirable than others. This open-endedness allows the player to fix himself the goal that the wants to reach. To own many patterns, to be an editor of many patterns, to receive many awards, or to have many friends are all equally valid, intrinsically anchored goals. The aesthetic environment and the open question about the role of The Architect also contribute to make "work" "pleasurable", a serious game.

Note that the descriptions from the above paragraphs are not completely identical with the scenario (which was written first). Also, the terminology needs to be more consistent: the name of the special buildings, the distinction between authors, editors and users, and other concept need refinement and a clearer definition. For now, these inconsistencies remain to remind that this is not the final concept yet, but rather a prototype of it.

11.3 Conclusion

The use of patterns in Interaction Design, or related fields such as web design and GUI design, is gaining momentum in practice. Many patterns collections are now publicly available in books or online. With the huge number of patterns, organization and classification is becoming a practical issue. No definitive pattern collection is available, terminology and formats are different for each pattern collection. This makes comparisons difficult.

In this chapter, our goal is to increase the overall awareness of user interface patterns for the different stakeholders. We suggested a platform of three components: Pattern Database includes helpful information about user interface that is produced by the participants. Their collaborative activities are supported by the social network component that emphasizes the communication. The last component is serious game, a context in which the earlier features are embedded.

Based on these components, the concept of PatternCity evolved. It consists of two parts: building in a virtual world that represents a pattern and avatars. They represent players who can collaboratively build and improve the buildings. Even if we do believe that the proposed PatternCity concept is applicable to all types of design patterns (Appendix A), we have focussed on HCI/UI design patterns, mainly for two reasons. First, because of our expertise in the field of HCI as designers, researchers and educators, we have developed a very large catalogue of patterns. Second, HCI patterns are most often documented by designers who have a background in psychology. This makes it challenging to describe patterns in way that they are easily transferable and understandable by software developers, the end users of these patterns.

Appendix A

New Prototype of PatternCity

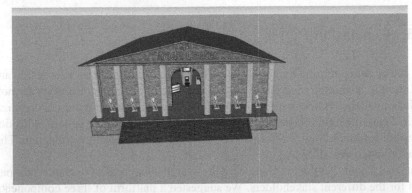

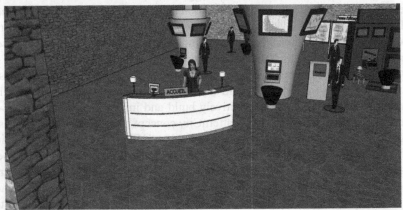

References

Ang CS, Zaphiris P (2005) Developing enjoyable second language learning software tools. A computer game paradigm. Idea Group, New York

Deterding S, Sicart M, Nacke L, O'Hara K, Dixon D (2011) Gamification: using game-design elements in non-gaming contexts. In Human Factors in Computing Systems (CHI) Extended Abstracts. 2425–2428. ACM New York, NY, USA

Franke D, Freischlad S, Friedrich L, Haug F, Klein B, Koslowski R, Stechert P, Ufer J (2007) Final report of the project design patterns. Department of Electrical Engineering and Computer Science, University of Siegen

Gaffar A (2005) Studies on pattern dissemination and reuse to support interaction design. Concordia University, Montreal

Lin J, Newman MW, Hong JI, Landay JA (2000) DENIM: finding a tighter fit between tools and practice for web site design. CHI Lett Human Factors Comput Syst 2(1):510–517

Rising L (2000) The pattern almanac 2000. Addison Wesley Publishing Inc, Boston

Stahl (2004) Building collaborative knowing. In: Strijbos J-W, Kirschner PA, Martens RL (Eds) What we know about CSCL: and implementing it in higher education, pp 53–86, Kluwer Academic Publishers, Boston

Welie (2008) Patterns in interaction design. http://welie.com/patterns/showPattern.php?patternID =minesweeping. Accessed on April 15, 2015

Chapter 12
A Pedagogic Pattern Model for Upskilling Software Engineering Students in HCI Design Practice

Abstract In this chapter, we describe a pedagogical pattern process that structures and transcribes salient points of simulation-based learning applied to Human–Computer Interface (HCI) design. First, we outline Christopher Alexander's pattern language design theory. Second, we examine Jean Houssaye's trialectic Pedagogic Triangle. Then, we combine key aspects of Alexander's and Houssaye's theories in order to document instructional practices in the teaching of engineering design. The practical and theoretical relevance of our unique approach is summarized in our Pedagogic Pattern Model (PPM). The model examines the instructional practices of experienced university instructors involved in HCI design courses. Through collective analysis, PPM focuses on capturing reflective classroom experiences via structured case studies of teaching HCI design practice.

12.1 Introduction

Design is a fundamental issue in software engineering, computer science as well as the management of information systems programs. This can be explained by the growing pressure on engineers and other design-oriented professionals to ground their design concepts and decisions on a systematic body of knowledge and empirical evidence of successful design practice (cf. Van Aken and Romme 2009). Hevner and Chatterjee (2010) refer to Design Science Research in Information Systems. They include a selection of papers from the Design Science Research in Information Systems and Technologies conferences (DESRIST) that look at key principles of Design Science Research and the integration of research on design sciences linked to design practices. In this context, this chapter addresses the increased demand for more clearly relevant design-oriented research and training based on real-world problems.

However, few publications exist in formalizing the way in which engineers can be trained in design with regard to existing good practice and to issues, topics, and paradigms that the field covers and those grounded in related domains. These domains include the study of the psychological and social aspects of users, their

© Springer International Publishing Switzerland 2015   259
A. Seffah, *Patterns of HCI Design and HCI Design of Patterns*,
Human-Computer Interaction Series, DOI 10.1007/978-3-319-15687-3_12

behavioral styles and patterns, user experience modeling, design and prototyping tools, user-oriented and usability evaluation, traditional and future design paradigms, as well as the role of theory in decision-making during design and design conception (e.g., Bergin 2012; Pedagogical Patterns Project 2001; Gamma et al. 1995). One manifest challenge of these domains is the way in which good practice can be formally captured, documented, and disseminated. More often than not, practices embedded in a specific project are difficult to reapply in other projects and organizational contexts. In effect, little work and tools exist to guide practitioners in capturing their successful, and unsuccessful, design practices. A Finnish study confirms this when it points out that: "…Most of the teachers aimed at promoting purposeful inquiry in their pedagogical designs did not necessarily know good methods and practices for structuring and scaffolding students' inquiry efforts" (Lakkala et al. 2005 p. 351).

This observation is equally true in the teaching of design to software engineering students. These students are often not familiar with the underlying theories and models of design. For example, many software engineering teaching programs include, invariably, a course on software design with UML (Unified Modeling Language), software design patterns as well as a series of user-interface design lectures. Such instructional programs are not enough to train software developers in critical design skills. In addition, the large majority of software and HCI design textbooks do not address instructional design good practice and how instructors need to, or should, present such good practice to students. Moreover, it is not uncommon for cognitive psychology-based user-interface design to be seen as a nuisance that gets in the way of "real and traditional" software design. This results in the tendency of many software engineering students and instructors to consider user interface design practices and knowledge as haphazard, and thus unimportant. This explains, for a large part, why students find it difficult to fully understand and master user-interface design methods. Clearly, then, the knowledge and training given is not sufficiently appropriate. If we accept the fact that user-interface design is indeed a key component in modern software development, the question is then how to teach such a challenging topic?

We argue that students and teachers need to go beyond ad hoc descriptions of design practices by examining how design patterns can be scripted, justified, and used via current design tools and techniques. What is needed is a robust instructional approach for design education. In this sense, the essential features of pattern-based good design practice need to be logically and explicitly coherent from an instructional point of view. It is in knowing the logical underpinning of how an instructional practice can be captured and documented in order to empower instructors to share good design practice from one context to another in terms of needs of the learners and other stakeholders. In this case, it is in adopting a theory-driven logic to teaching/learning (pedagogics) that instructors can be empowered not to blindly reproduce someone else's practice at the expense of the unique possibilities of their own context. We argue that it is through the understanding of the theoretical (epistemological) dynamics of a teaching/learning process that can lead to improving instructional practice (Labour and Kolski 2010, pp. 130–132).

With this in mind, we propose a Pedagogic Pattern Model (PPM) as a framework to communicate the salient points of simulation-based learning when designing HCI concepts and practices. PPM is related to the emerging notion of "pedagogical patterns," which has been introduced in different domains notably in computer science through the *Pedagogical Patterns Project* (Bergin 2012). The aim of the pedagogical patterns approach is to capture the essence of practice that can be communicated to those who need the knowledge, such as new instructors needing to learn "what is known by senior faculty by easy transference of knowledge of teaching within the community" (Bergin 2012). This is in line with Wade (2002) for whom "pedagogical design patterns" seeks to capture expert teaching practice, communicate expertise, solve common recurring problems, provide a vocabulary of solutions, and work with other patterns. Such as this approach is presented, it appears that these documented "patterns" are portrayed as inherently "pedagogical" in themselves (reminiscent of a type of Platonic essentialism).

In order to avoid epistemological, if not semantic confusion, the specificity of the Pedagogic Pattern Model is that the knowledge creation process resides in underlying sociocultural practice mediated by computer-based interaction, and is not intrinsically in what can be identified post hoc as discernible "patterns." In this sense, the encapsulation of a given socio-cultural HCI practice—emerging as a designated "pattern"—and represents one key epistemological element, among others, that needs to be taken into account in a knowledge creation process. In short, patterns act as a *starting point* to be adapted to the local socio-cultural HCI context, based on an explicit "model," i.e., a synthetic portrayal of the generic features of a pattern-building process (Labour and Kolski 2010: 115–116). A set of documented patterns is thus not a manual of one-size-fits-all, ready-made recipe to be applied blindly. It is vital to emphasise this point in order to avoid confusion about the role and limits of such the PPM approach.

In operational terms, PPM uses a unique type of "alphabet" to transcribe key instructional events. In doing this, the alphabet allows a coherent transposition of events from one given context to another. This transposition implies keeping the essential features of a sequence of events, while altering its more secondary features to the possibilities of a given context.

The originality of PPM is that it provides a guideline for structuring instructional frameworks in a logical manner based on good practice. First and foremost, we contend that the inner driving force of such an approach depends on the inventiveness that a teaching/learning framework affords the instructor. In this sense, French philosopher, Chartier (1932/1967) espouses this point of view in highlighting a paradox of inventiveness. For Chartier (1932/1967 p. 106), the ingenuity of tomorrow comes from the study of tried and tested practices of the past. How then to identify and render coherent these past practices? One recognized authority in the world of science and engineering, who has adopted such a view of good practice, is design architect Christopher Alexander.

Alexander developed his approach after observing that users understand more about designing the building they need than a qualified expert-architect. The role of such an expert is to capture and harness users' lived knowledge. Based on this observation, Alexander et al. (1977) produced an approach called "pattern language" in designing and building different objects. This approach gave rise to the design pattern movement that has crossed over to other domains ranging from software design to the social sciences (e.g., Labour and Kolski 2010, pp. 126–129).

12.2   A Five-Step Approach to Using a Pedagogic Pattern Model

The five basic phases of the "Model" (in the sense of portraying essential elements and their relationships within a given structure, see Table 12.1 below) can be summarized in the following way:

Table 12.1. Pedagogic Pattern Model of Case study #1: Simulation of adaptable, adaptive and/or personalized HCI design

A.1. Knowledge domain pole of the Pedagogic Triangle		
–	Classroom context	Discourse community context
Aims	Without object	To improve the identification of design errors of potential future designers
"Initial" state	(at TØ) Copy of the slides used and explanations given to the students	(at TØ) Existing knowledge including resources (e.g. books) and explanations given to the students
"Final" state	(at T1) The same as TØ plus learners' solutions and instructor's comments	(at T2) The same as TØ

A.2. Instructor pole of the Pedagogic Triangle:		
–	Classroom context	Discourse community context
Aims	To teach HCI design	To learn about design errors in HCI design
"Initial" state	(at TØ) Intention to encourage students to learn, viz. through simulation	(at TØ) Intention to acquire data concerning students as potential HCI designers
"Final" state	(at T1) Satisfaction that the students can design a HCI system	(at T1) Intention to analyze available data (i.e. the dossiers)

A.3. Learner pole of the Pedagogic Triangle:		
–	Classroom context	Discourse community context
Aims	To pass the exam	To obtain the degree and get a job with skills required for the job market
"Initial" state	(at TØ) Acquiring skills to pass the exams	(at TØ) Hope to acquire knowledge about HCI design
"Final" state	(at T1) Satisfaction of developing skills via the production of a quality HCI specification dossier	(at T1) Confidence to be able to produce real HCI specification dossiers in companies (knowledge transfer)

a. General description and context
b. Spatiotemporal boundary markers
c. Overall action plan of pedagogical techniques/tools
d. Group interactions at each pole of Housaye's Pedagogic Triangle
e. Feedback

12.2.1 General Description and Context

It is in this initial phase that the overall teaching/learning (pedagogic) situation is set. The aim is to describe what Alexander (1979, p. 253) calls a "systems of forces" that bonds a series of opportunities and limits of a given situation. This description is visually represented by French educationalist, Houssaye (1992, p. 235, 1994) as an all-encompassing circle (Fig. 12.1, see below).

12.2.2 Spatiotemporal Boundary Markers

Temporal markers act as markers of when a sequence formally starts and ends. In this case, the *TØ* marker designates the *Initial state* of the instructional sequence for the learner, the instructor, and the researchers. The *T1* marker indicates the *Final state* of the instructional session for the learner and the instructor. The *T2* marker

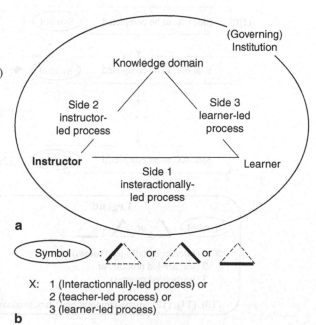

Fig. 12.1 a The Pedagogic Triangle adapted from Houssaye (1992). **b** Symbols indicating the three learning processes of Houssaye (1992)

identifies the *End state* of the researcher's analysis of what was done and what could have been done in the instructional session.

Spatial markers pinpoint two basic levels of analysis regarding instructional sequences. First, there is the "Classroom context" associated with instructor–student interactions in a given space–time. Second, the markers also indicate the "Discourse community context." In this way, PPM takes into account, in the design of instructional sequences, that the curriculum of future engineers is bound by norms (e.g., of what is considered as legitimate knowledge) and values (e.g., deontological) of a scientific and professional community. Ideally, there should be a reciprocal relationship between the two levels through the description and analysis of the changing needs, preferences, and expectations of "Classroom context."

12.2.3   Overall Action Plan of Pedagogical Techniques/Tools

In order to render the action plan operational, a diagrammatic system was developed based on Houssaye's Pedagogical Triangle (1992). In essence, the Pedagogical Triangle consists of three apexes—Knowledge domain, Instructor and Learner—circumscribed by a circle indicating the limits and the opportunities of a given instructional context (see above "General description and context"). Each apex interacts with another and this leads to formally distinct learning processes, see Fig. 12.1 (below). Each process is visually represented by three triangles with different shaded sides, see Fig. 12.2 below.

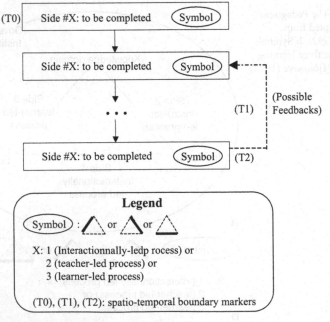

Fig. 12.2 Guide to the process of the overall action plan

In using the Pedagogic Triangle, a series of task boxes are proposed indicating which learning process predominates in a given sequence (Labour and Kolski 2010: 118, 120). Houssaye argues that if more than one instructional process is "activated" simultaneously, it is likely to be cognitive overloading, if not conflict between processes that are intrinsically different. Each symbol is then put in a "Task box" with a description of the predominating learning process, according to the "action plan" and a succinct description of the task objective. The appropriate spatiotemporal boundary markers (TØ, T1, or T2) are found on the left hand side of the Task box, see Fig. 12.2 below. There are no limits as to the number of boxes that can be put in the model. Task boxes are linked by arrows. Downward arrows show the initial flow of the sequences and upward arrows indicate feedback dynamics.

12.2.4   Group Interactions Between Poles of the Pedagogic Triangle

The phase describes the selected presence of an interaction linked to an anticipated learning process. These interactions involve intra- and inter-group processes between the Learner-led, Instructor-led, and knowledge domain poles of Houssaye's Pedagogic Triangle (see Fig. 12.1 above). The interactions need to be regulated in order to avoid cognitive overloading or conflict between the processes. Such interactions represent what the ancient Greeks called *pharmakon*, i.e., certain phenomena are neither good nor bad, they can cure or kill, it all depends on their dosage.

12.2.5   Feedback

Systematic feedback is indispensable in order to adapt to the changing needs of learners and instructional contexts. The feedback reexamines the sequences and their effects on learners.

In the section that follows, a specific instructional context is formalized according to the principles of the Pedagogic Pattern Model. To do this, we present a simulation-based learning context in an HCI design case study.

12.3   Case Study in HCI Design

12.3.1   Protocol

Since the beginning of the 1990s, we have conducted various studies in several HCI design courses. We asked engineering students to play the role of HCI designers of interactive systems in rival "companies." The studies were conducted with classes of 20–25 students in their fourth year of a Bachelor's degree in Electrical

Engineering and Industrial Computer Science (average age of students is 23 years), and with students doing a Master's degree in Information Technology (average age is 24 years).

The protocol used in our studies is made up of three phases. The first phase includes a preliminary preparation phase of a 12 h instructor-directed class in HCI design. The application domain is focused on the design of adaptable, adaptive, and personalized HCI as used by different types of users. The pedagogic content is grounded on several works, such as those of Rasmussen (1986), Schneider-Hufschmidt et al. (1993), Hoc and Amalberti (1995), Calvary et al. (2003), Brossard et al. (2011), as well as the instructor's personal professional experience gained in several industrial projects.

During the second phase of 6 h (90 min a week over 4 weeks), the students were organized in teams of four or five. All the teams were seated in the same room, with each team being only several meters from each other. Each team represented a company. The companies (teams) competed against each other in submitting a tender for the design of an adaptable, adaptive, and/or personalized HCI system to be used by several types of users in a complex industrial organization. The projected users were to perform tasks in normal and abnormal situations.

One of the rules of the simulation is that the teams should avoid revealing information to their "competitors." During the sessions, the teams were able to question the instructor who acted both as the game master and an "employee" made available to competing companies by the organization that had launched the invitation for tender. At the end of the week, each team had to submit a specification dossier (in PDF format by email) presenting their analysis of the problem and a model-based description of an adaptable, adaptive, and/or personalized HCI. Three extracts of specification dossiers are shown in the following figures: (a) a UML use case of different types of users (see Fig. 12.3 below), 12.3b two screen pages extracted from a mockup (see Fig. 12.4a below), and 12.4c an UML sequence model describing the dynamics of a proposed interactive application (see Fig. 12.4b below).

In the third phase, we collected feedback from the instructor about each student's dossier. We used 35 evaluation criteria deemed crucial in the HCI field (usability problems, relevance of the solution, methodological weaknesses, quality of the models used...). A panel of instructors studied and graded the dossier of the teams and the oral presentation of their work.

12.3.2   Spatiotemporal Boundary Markers

At the heart of our model is section B. To characterize the experience found in the case study, we drew up Table 12.1 below. The table portrays a double-entry format juxtaposing the "classroom" (local) and "discourse community" (global) contexts in terms of temporal markers. This description is followed by a diagrammatic expression of the Pedagogic Pattern Model (Fig. 12.5, see below).

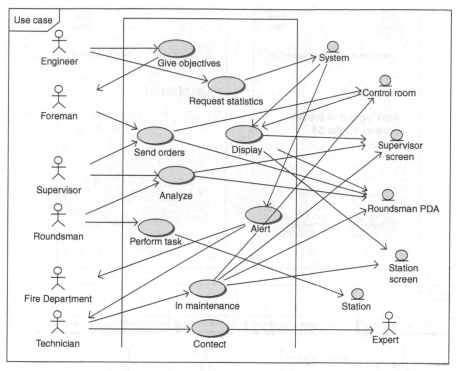

Fig. 12.3. Example of an UML use case, showing seven types of users (given in a specification dossier)

12.3.3   Action Plan of Pedagogical Techniques or Tools Used

Taking account of the three-part rule of the design pattern approach, a diagrammatic representation of the action plan is presented in Fig. 12.5 below. The figure portrays the overall process in a more schematic way, followed by a step-by-step commentary of the structure that our Pedagogic Pattern Model affords its user. In this way, Table 12.1 and Fig. 12.5 present the data in a way that they can be compared and contrasted with other similar pedagogic contexts. These elements suggest that our approach is able to identify common instructional features in different contexts.

Table 12.1 shows an overall process that goes from TØ to T1 based on the three different phases of the Pedagogic Triangle. The first phase is an instructor-led process (side #2 of the Pedagogic Triangle). The second phase is a learned-led process (side #3 of the Triangle). The third is an interactionally led process (side #1 of the Triangle). All three sides are concerned in the teaching/learning process, but at different given moments in order to avoid conflict between teaching/learning processes. This is followed by an instructor-led process (side #2 of the Triangle) during which the instructor undertakes a self-evaluation about the module. It is at this juncture that a loop back of information operates to improve future instruction sequences (see Fig. 12.5 below). Finally, the instructor-led process (side #2) moves

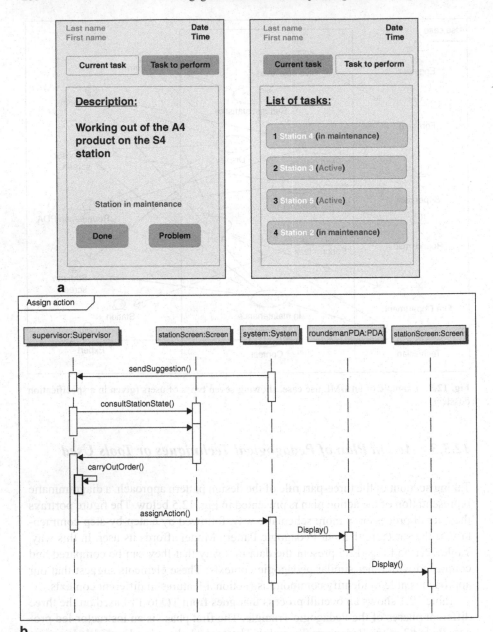

Fig. 12.4. a Example of two screen pages, as part of a mockup of an interactive system available on a PDA (given in a specification dossier). **b** Example of an UML sequence diagram (given in a specification dossier) based on an order sent from one actor to another via the interactive system

on to a broader analysis as a HCI researcher, within a given discourse community, to finish at T2. The consequences of the Pedagogic Pattern Model portrayed in Table 12.1 and in Fig. 12.5 are made explicit under the concepts of "group interaction" (see Sect. 12.3.4 below) and "feedback" (see Sect. 12.3.5 below).

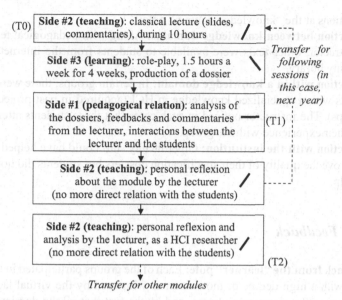

Fig. 12.5. Overall action plan of an HCI design simulation

12.3.4   Group Interactions at Each Pole of the Pedagogic Triangle

Interactions at the "learner" pole:

- **Interaction between groups of learners:** The sub-groups (teams) were in competition as rival "companies." It was therefore important for each group to avoid transmitting important data to the other groups.
- **Interaction within groups of learners:** As the work was difficult and long, members of each group had to cooperate to finish their task. The instructor noted down the exchanges of ideas and points of view of each group.
- **Interaction with the institution:** There was a small possibility that the students had discussed with students from previous years or with other instructors (though few of them were specialized in HCI) about the on-going project. This was a calculated risk taken by the instructor, but such intrusive influence has never been identified.

Interactions at the "instructor" pole:

- **Interaction between groups of instructors:** not applicable as the instructor worked alone.
- **Interaction within groups of instructors:** The instructor had discussed with colleagues about innovations in pedagogy, but there was no discernible consequence on the module in question as its action plan had been predefined based on previous experiences of other modules.
- **Interaction with the institution:** The instructor took into account the fact that other classes had also conducted similar simulations involving HCI design and evaluation in the previous year and software engineering in the two previous years.

Interactions at the "knowledge domain" pole:
- **Interaction between knowledge domains:** Along with pedagogical texts from the instructor, other texts were available to students from the internet and the university library.
- **Interaction within a knowledge domain:** In certain groups, there were several students with a specialized knowledge in HCI (acquired in past projects or internships). The instructor noticed in such cases that these students attempted to share their experience with the group.
- **Interaction with the institution:** Other faculty staff could have helped students to improve the quality of their specification dossiers but students did not avail of this help.

12.3.5   Feedback

- **Feedback from the "learner" pole:** Each of the groups participated in the simulation with a high degree of motivation as witnessed by the virtual lack of absenteeism in the simulation classes, and by the fact that all the dossiers handed in included many positive aspects in accordance to the instructor's evaluation criteria. Thanks to the simulation, the potential designers felt they had worked on a project that was close to industrial reality. The students also appreciated the competitiveness between the groups. In short, there was no visible presence of learner boredom or the intrusion of the all-knowing instructor interfering with learners' work.
- **Feedback from the "instructor" pole:** Learners appreciated the simulation as a valuable asset to their formal university instruction. The professional nature of student dossiers and their active participation satisfied the expectations of the instructor. During the oral examination, a panel of instructors questioned the learners. This provided valuable input to the instructor in how to better explain the general description and context of the simulation module in the following years. This feedback leads to the conclusion that the danger of learners falling back on prefabricated knowledge was not a dominant feature of the simulation.
- **Feedback from the "knowledge domain" pole:** An analysis of the dossiers will be followed by the submission of a scientific publication as a way to get feedback from the HCI community.

12.4   Conclusions

This chapter investigates the underlying pedagogy of teaching design practices for software developers. The design practices are, or can be, captured in the format of HCI design patterns as defined in the other chapters of this book. We propose a model to capture good instructional practice seeking to develop knowledge creating process in students. Our Pedagogic Pattern Model (PPM) is based on patterns that have been recognized in many areas of education involving group work, software design, and HCI. The approach can be seen as both an extension of HCI design patterns, and of pattern languages in general aimed at fostering the teaching of design via good practices.

More specifically, the chapter examines the experiences of instructors whose goal are to capture pedagogic patterns in teaching design. To do this, PPM marries key aspects of Christopher Alexander's pattern language approach to Jean Houssaye's trialectic theory. This led to a Pedagogic Pattern Model, which consists of five phases: (1) General description and context, (2) Spatiotemporal boundary markers, (3) Overall action plan of pedagogical techniques or tools used, (4) Group interactions at each pole of the Pedagogic Triangle, and (4) Feedback.

The strength of the model is that it presents different instructional constructs in an educationally coherent manner. This is achieved through a specially developed transcription mode, which describes events concerning the learner, instructor, and knowledge domains. In this chapter, the transcription of instructional practice focuses on simulations in Human–Computer Interface design (HCI) by effectively incorporating the cognitive, emotional and socio-cultural aspects of users' experiences and behavior patterns.

It is hoped that the capacity of PPM to transcribe and document good practice contributes to a more hands-on interdisciplinary approach in the dissemination of design practice when preparing our students for the professional world. From this perspective, the Pedagogic Pattern Model contributes to an overall vision of HCI design as a domain at the intersection of computer sciences, design sciences, and social sciences, including the fields of education and psychology.

References

Alexander C (1979) The timeless way of building. Oxford University Press, New York
Alexander C, Ishikawa S, Silverstein M, Jacobson M, Fiksdahl-King, Angel S (1977) A pattern language. Oxford University Press, New York
Bergin J (2012) Pedagogical patterns: advice for educators. createspace independent publishing platform. joseph bergin software tools. http://www.pedagogicalpatterns.org/. Accessed 11 Nov 2014
Brossard A, Abed M, Kolski C (2011) Taking context into account in conceptual models using a model driven engineering approach. Inf Softw Technol 53(12):1349–1369
Calvary G, Coutaz J, Thevenin D, Limbourg Q, Bouillon L, Vanderdonckt J (2003) A unifying reference framework for multi-target user interfaces. Interact Comput 15(3):289–308
Chartier EA (aka Alain) (1932/1967) *Propos sur l'éducation*. Digital version of *Propos sur l'éducation*. Paris: Presses Universités de France, 13th edition. http://classiques.uqac.ca/classiques/Alain/propos_sur_education/propos_sur_education.pdf. Accessed 1 Nov 2014
Gamma E, Helm R, Johnson R, Vlissides J (1995) Design patterns: elements of reusable object-oriented software. Addison-Wesley, Boston
Hevner A, Chatterjee S (2010) Design research in information systems: theory and practices. Springer, Germany

Hoc J-M, Amalberti R (1995) Diagnosis: some theoretical questions raised by applied research. Curr Psychol Cogn 14(1):73–101

Houssaye J (1992) Théorie et pratiques de l'éducation scolaire I: Le triangle pédagogique. Peter Lang, Switzerland

Houssaye J (1994) "The relevance of the pedagogical triangle: understanding operating principles of the pedagogical situation". Paper presented at the annual meeting of the American Educational Research Association (AERA). New Orleans, USA

Labour M, Kolski C (2010) A pedagogics pattern model of blended e-learning: a step towards designing sustainable simulation-based learning. In: Tzanavari A, Tsapatsoulis N (eds) Affective, interactive and cognitive methods for e-learning design: creating an optimal education experience, IGI Global, Hershey, pp. 114–137

Lakkala M, Lallimo J, Hakkarainen K (2005) Teachers' pedagogical designs for technology-supported collective inquiry: a national case study. Comput Educ 45(3):337–356

Pedagogical Patterns Project (2001) http://www.pedagogicalpatterns.org. Accessed 27 Oct 2014

Rasmussen J (1986) Information processing and human-machine interaction, an approach to cognitive engineering. Elsevier Science, Amsterdam

Schneider-Hufschmidt M, Kuhme T, Malinowski U (eds) (1993) Adaptive user interfaces. Elsevier Science, Amsterdam

Van Aken JE Romme G (2009) Reinventing the future: adding design science to the repertoire of organization and management studies. Organ Manag J 6:5–12

Wade SJ (2002) The application of pedagogical design patterns to the development of distance learning materials. distance learning colloquium. Organised by LTSN-ICS University of York, UK